THE LOUD HOUSE

BY

DR. ALHASAN SISAWO CEESAY, MD

© 2017 by Dr. Alhasan Sisawo Ceesay, MD

All rights reserved. No part from this book may be reproduced in any form without written permission from the publisher, except by a reviewer who may quote passages in a review to be printed in a newspaper or magazine.

FIRST PRINTING

PUBLISH KUNSA.COM

ISBN 978-1-910117-86-6

INSCRIBED TO

My Parents, Wife and Children, Teachers, Friends, Colchester Friends of Manding Charitable Trust UK and Friends of Manding Alpena, Michigan, USA; and the downtrodden

Nothing is more endearing than a peaceful home. Some even alleges it to be home fit for angels.

Dr. Alhasan S. Ceesay, MD

PREFACE AND ACKNOWLEDGMENTS

Ebenezer Balford in Kidnap said of the house of Shaw that "Blood built it and blood shall bring it down." One can freely use similitude to the loud house as being homed by madness that would be brought to an end by ineptitude. The loud house respects no time when its tantrums chose to well out. A neighbours' child once referred to this antisocial abode as; "Home of a confused quires." Locals call this house 'Jali Kunda' meaning home of noisy Griots in contention for attention.

Kunsa Mori, Fatong Seyabalo, the Bongokos, and Tonyila Komong are sole residents of the loud house but one can hear their arguments miles away from the mad house. The duo competes on baseless trivial things such as positioning of shoes, endless telephone conversations making the other devoid of quality family relationship or just mare outlook of the other.

One can hardly make tail out of head as to what normally cause such hideous row of loud argument between two said to be committed for life to each other in health, wealth or otherwise. Be the better judge as you browse pages in this work which determine to seek solutions to such despicable nuisance of a life.

Ladies and gentlemen; noise built this God forsaken house and lightening and thunder shall bring it down. Let me emphasise that a few of us foreigners when in

America and Europe not only become poison chalets but worst turn into incarnated acultural bitting Chameleons. I would like to thank readers and joint effort of many who encouraged me to write. I am grateful and appreciated contributions of each and every one and million thanks to all of your kindness which touched me deeply.

Profound gratitude to all who gave me support and helped me put this work into print. In the mean time allow me express profound gratitude to my wife Mrs. Fatou Koma Ceesay and our children: Famatanding Ceesay, Binta Ceesay and Roheyata Ceesay for bearing and persevering patiently through with me in thick and thin during my drive to bring medical aid and service to villagers.

Also I am immensely thankful to illustrious Gambian Lawyer Ousainu Darbo, Lorna V. Robinson, Henry V. Valli, Cloyed Ramsey, Rev. Mark D. Meyer, Bishop McGhee, Prof. Eunice Khan, Prof. Betzabie Alison, Noreta & Cloyd Ramsey, Dr. Charles T. Egli, Dr. Nelson Herron, Dr. Peter Wilson, Dr. Laura Spooner, Dr. Barbara Murray, Dr. Phil Murray, Dr. Richard Spooner, Dr. Linda Mahon-Daly, Dr. Avery Aten, Mrs. Marcia Aten, Dr. Richard Bates, Mrs. Patricia Koblyski, Penny West, Ahmed Nizami, Mohamad Sheriff Azan, Asfaque Mohamad, Abdullah Shahim, Asiya Qadri, Malkaight Singh, Ganem Hadied, Sulayman Bojang, Mahmud Adam and Lois R. Leonard for standing by my dreams.

I write to raise funds for building of a hospital at NGO: Manding Medical Centre, Njaewara village the Gambia.

I am author and book Publisher in the UK since 2013:Publish Kunsa Ltd; www.publishkunsa.com Purchasing or donating cash or in kind will help us deliver needed healthcare service to villagers and especially children who die prematurely from childhood diseases and malaria for lack of medical facilities or trained personnel. Sale from this work will support the operations of Manding Medical Centre at Njawara, North Bank Region, the Gambia. Also check www.friendsofmadinggambimed.btck.co.uk to learn more.

In addition, it will in due course provide scholarship to indigent rural students needing financial support to pursue medical or agricultural degrees.

Dr. Alhasan S. Ceesay, MD

Dr Ceesay displays first book 2002

Chapter One: Life in a tide

In the annals of romance Kunsa and Fatong epitomised envied romance in its highest quality. These were the talk of town and young girls seek to be just like them. They were abundantly popular and pleasant people to be one's friend. Their nimble feet amazed onlookers in dance venues. All this enamour happened while in separate abode with their parents. What on earth went wrong to cause observed madness at Jali Kunda hoiuse on the duos coming together as husband and wife?

Armchair Psychiatrists alluded that the phenomenon may have emanated from sheer disappointment or high expectation of the Fatong of Kunsa. That Kunsa being perceived as low class or the poor of the poorest lead to Fatong Seyabalo's regretting having married to Kunsa. Fatong must now reconcile with herself and accept the relationship emanating as love at first sight and that life is full of hillocks, one of which is poverty among many other challenges in its tapestry.

A saying by Mandinkas goes thus: "Ceaseless daily quarrels blindfolds and degrades love as it kills its soul."

It goes without doubt that bitter ranchos dull connubial romances and prevents exploitation of uncharted love tapestry. Mediation by well meaning interjectors only made matters worse.

The devil seems to have upper hand in this unexpected fiasco. Others surmised that the duo is neither symbiotic nor compatible for one is academically oriented while the later is just business oriented and cared very little in reading or writing books. There was no bridge linking the two and as time went on motions of the other easily disturbs the equilibrium of the later.

This gave birth to loudness heard during incessant temperamental arguments. Lovers normally operate as creative teams on the contrary couples at odds become disgruntle and experiences backward thrust of their relationships; most of which are sadly doom to fail. The relation crashes down like a tidal wave from a midnight tsunami. When asked about his boisterous wife; Kunsa Mori had nothing but praises for her.

He characterized her as a wingless angel of special creation. She is queen amongst beauties and does embrace as well as heals broken hearts. Being typical woman she is soft at heart but strong in will to endure all life doles onto her.

He said, "Fatong Seyabalo is brilliant and an adept negotiator but like most women she sheds tears to express doubt, love, solitude, suffering and her pride.

She is the jewel of my heart and I cannot do without her being by my side as consol that handles trouble times while carrying heavy burden. She is my bundle of joy, love and happiness sculptured in one tender frame. Her love for me is unconditional and unique."

He added further, "However do not ever challenge her for she fights for her rights at the same time breaks to pieces on being told about other people's tragedies. In short her worth is immeasurable and I feel lucky to be her mate and husband in life. For me she special and priceless princess whose being and strength of heart I not only adore dearly but respects fully."

With all the above expressed endearments a puzzling state emanated. An unfolded chaos buffered by persistent argument never stopped Badibous' former admired romantic magnets managing to stay together in thick and thin of their marriage and were blessed by it with three beautiful daughters; who are now married and studying in Europe.

Chapter Two: The Bongko Family

This is tale of a cursed family. From the onset the inlaws of both sides never blessed the marrying of Foroding Bongko and Musu Fisirr Waleh. The two however felt intertwine from first day they met in the streets of Monrovia, Liberia, West Africa in 1989.

The bongkos married three months upon meeting. These love birds leaved adorably until the birth of the first born child. It was then hell broke loose as DNA test revealed that the baby girl was not fathered by Foroding but by former friend of Mr. Foroding Bongko.

Well tradition requires that the couple raise the child as theirs but trust never remain between them. Foroding decided instead of devocing Musu Fisirr Waleh he married another woman not out as much pure love as he had for Musu but in exercise of his polygamus rights.

The baby girl in question grew up to be a very beautiful lady attracting fancy of none other than the son of the President of the Republic. The wedding was the most celebrated and talked about in the region. She was showered with money, boxes upon boxes of gold, dressings and jewellery princesses would vie to own.

Sinderella has become a princess and did something most unexpected. She was disowned by her biological father until rumour brought it to attention that his first born girl is to marry the son of the president. The ungrateful beast was shameless enough to show up at home of his inlaws to claim a traditional father's dowry.

The girl not only had him sent away but told him in clear language that her father is one who adopted, rared her and took care of her mother all these years of her life. She refused to recognise him or allow a penny of the dowry land in his hands.

Here is fulfilment of the saying one rips the seed he plants. It took pleadinmg of elders and the father inlaw of the newly wedded to allow some remonaration to serve as parental libation to the ungrateful and greedy biological father.

On leaving the father thanked her daughter and President for recognizing him as biological father of the bride. On the way he turned and said to his duagther, "I will never wish you bad but have from today hence forth put the 'Dunia Shoe' onto your nibble feet."

The attendents laughed at the poor man but only his daughter knew what he meant and hidden future impact of it to her childrend and their children yet to be born. However, pride stopped her from seeking pardon or apologising to the oldman. Soon the old man disaapear into an alley and was never heard or seen around the county.

Mansa Ding and his bride Musu Nyima remained very happy together for well more than thirty years and were blessed with three gorgeous daughters; before hell broke lose in the most hurific vengeful manner.

First the President lost his post to the opposition, who ceased all his illbegotten wealth and property through use of anti corruption laws. He even had to served a fives years sentence for having stolen state coffers. This event signalled meaning and beginning of the cursed cast upon the newly wed by her biological father some years ago.

Upon being freed from penetary the former president sent emmeseries to help locate the biological father to seek his forgiveness of any transgression towards him either by his son or daughter inlaw. The search went on for more than two years until a herd's man reported sighting of an old farmer of many herds of cattle, goat, sheep and abundant land matching the description given by the search team.

To lead the search team to this farmer; the hesrds man demamded a huge ransome and time to talk to the famer to see if he would like to meet the seach team. He was paid fifty cows and ten bulls upon successfull completion of the mission.

He met the oldman three days later at a secrete location and begged him to receive the search team upon his terms.

He accorded the request upon his daughter being brought along and her apologising for regading and reducing him to a non enentity. Further more he requested the president be present and receive back all gifts he gave onbehalf of his son without first recognising him as biological and only father of the child involved. Lastly he wanted to meet privately with his grandchildren. This agreed then the meeting will be held at an undisclosed private and safe venue.

RIP: Cousin Mamurndar Jobe, CEO Mamurdary Photo Studios, Gambia, West Africa 1979

Cherno Jobe 2017, elder son of Mamurndar Jobe

These requests were relayed to the team and the former president who were more than delighted to have a chat with his humble inlaw now more prosperous than ever dreamt possible for a simple villager. The meeting took place at home of the president's chief opponent amid generous hospitality the president never accorded any during the days of his reigne.

At the end of the traditional greetings and well wishes the former president stood up with head down said; "We are most grateful for chance to clear the air and engender friendship, and peace towards all. I am personally happy to meet my inlaw after learning that power only belongs to God and remains temporal thing for mortals.

Hence onbehalf my entire family, especially my son, we apologises for whatever mistake, misjudgement and error we transgressed towards my inlaw. Hence everyone he requested is here waiting to meet with him at his convenience. I seek God's and your approval to bring this curse to an amicable end."

He sad down with head bowed in shame but happy inside that he was man and honest enough to face his mistakes which he now want to be foirgiven by his true inlaw and not the corcoarch and opportunist inlaw that disowned him moments after losing the presidency and upon going to jail. Soon his son stood up and said: "I take full responsibility of shame that shrouds the family and I sincerely apologise for it from the bottom of heart. We are sorry and hope God will help my wife and I make for lost time and to remove hurt we caused my father inlaw."

Musu Nyima in her most stunning looks and local dress right there and then ran to her father and huged him in joyful welling tears. She knelt and kept saying: "Daddy, I am very, very sorry and please forgive our youthful mistakes. No one is truer dad to me than you.

I spent sleepless night in tears trying atoning for my transgressions towards you. Please have a heart and forgive your only daughter." Her father was so happy and emotional that he asked the grandchildren join them to hear what he was about to say in the open for the first time to his new family.

Upon hugging each of the three children he aske all be seated and took another libation drink. He was a simple and a humble man which now reflected in the short succinct reply he gave. He looked at his daughter and said, "I have forgiven all your transgression and for the love of you today has wiped out all the hurt your childish actions ever caused me.

Deep down I am today the happiest father on earth and feel blessed to meet my beautifu grandchildren. God bless and today we leave this venue as one people and one family."

The children asked if they can join him and help herd or milk the cows. This sounded melodious inhis ears. His own is volunteering to help in the field even after life at the presidential Palace.

This joyous day came to close when the Imam offered prayers for both sides. Off course grandpa invited the kids to spend the rest of the weekend with him at the farm which was applauded by all present. The kids busied themselves at the farm competing on naming the goats, bulls and even the cat that was the least interested in them.

The autheers of cow felt warm and easy to draw milk from. Few risk suckling like goats. They had such great fun in life and promised to spend all their holidays and most of their weekends with grandpa at his animal farm. The moral of this tale is that one should never ever be beligerant because of promising circumstance, towards parents for they too were responsible of the germination and growth at the same time suffered for you to have a chance in this life.

Lengend has it that after many, many decades of joyful reunion with his grand children and daughter the old sage in his deathbed told his family thus: "Remain humble, hard working and kind to self and others. Above all depend on no one but God. At no time should you depend much on anyone in this life because even your own shadow leaves you when you are in darkness.Good bye." It was after this remark that he closed his earthly eyes and proceeded gentlely to his maker in heaven.

Mr. Omar Ceesay, Brother 2017 (RIP)

Welcome: Ibrahim Mbalo and mum Famatanding Mbalo-Ceesay, Sweden 2018

Chapter Three: Secrets of the Heart

The first thing any heart pleads with God is to be given power of endurance, love and tolerance. The heart start beating from time it is formed to the trillionth minute of its life. Nothing is as efficient and enduring as the heart which keeps its secret deep in its four chambers. The heart is where our inner most secrets lurk. In the heart dwells the milk of human kindness.

No wonder it is commonly heard folks challenging others to have a heart. Kind people and philanthropists are said to have a big heart of gold. However, in some this is the home of treachery and darkness as portrayed by inhuman action in battle. The heart is the vehicle of love and emotion. Empathy makes us tolerant and bonds this with a committed heart.

Women become pregnant multiple times because of loving hearts our mothers possess. No heart no love says the romantic pilgrim. Without the heart the rest of the organs are certain to die sooner than later. Poets serenade the heart by comparing it with angels on our side. Here are few salient tenants or acts that can keep the romance or marriage pulsating. Virile relationship keeps the marriage intact. Let us face it by calling a spade for what it is.

All or most relationships viers' towards procreation and a virile male and normal female are prerequisite to a successful end reward. The primary quest of pleasure is acheived by reward acrewed from the act.

LOVE with its taproot, branches and leaves need to be nourished through affectionate understanding, compassion, affection and above all constant communication between couples. Failure to adhere to this simple tenant leads to the type of noisy relationship often heard coming out of the loud house aka 'Jali kunda luoo' meaning grounds of the Griots.

PRESENTS; no matter how trivial, small or odd, be it monetary or just a bouquet of red roses can make the lady of the house smile from brim to brim while planting the most affectionate kiss on the lip or where ever desired. The surprise gift is worth the reward.

TRUST most be established and kept alive by both in a relationship. Do not allow others such as girl friends and neighbours steal your affection from your spouse. Do not misuse or abuse your spouses trust for you may end up loosing one that thought kindly of you.

You owe honesty to your spouse and yourself. It is very painful and disgraceful if not belittling cheating anyone especially one committed to you for life. It is a dispecable and self degradating act indeed.

TEAM WORK elevates ramantic secretes of the heart. Even stone hearts have core armour waiting to be ignited in their dark chests. It is winning together that spark the embers of a relationship spackle bringter. Togeherness makes relation fit for purpose and intriguing. No score keeping as in the case of those at the mad house known as the loud house aka 'Jali Kunda Luoo' nicknamed by Gambian locals.

Also note that CHILDREN copy ways their parents relate. Hence be civil and loving to allow their future secret hearts accept reality of life. They will normally form lasting opinions on romance, commitment and marriage emulating you the parents.

Bad examples will not allow them look forwards to marriage for fear of having to relive same horrible life as seen during their childhood days all over again if in relationship.These children will hate their parents for failing to love them by setting good examples to them. Bad behaviour or example destroy and most of the time dinys children right to better future relationships.

CARE for each other; for grass being greener at the other side is due to constant watering and adding nutrients to make it fit and lush green. So you should relish it by nurturing your unique relationship.

Work on making the relationship admirable and loving to make others to like yours. Always put God and each other first to maintain a true sense of security. Give deaf ears to detractors.

HONESTY is necessary ingredient in relationships. It must be couched with commitment along selfless love to have a successful marriage. No wealth, big artificial acquisitions, homes, and cars keep relationship alive for long. These wordly artifacts can dicipate into thin air with the slightest change of circumstances. Hence shield yourself with faith and honesty in dealing with others.

FRIENDS can destroy or help build relations. Be careful not to tempt the secret heart. Take no advantage of each other and never mistake loyalty for desperation or weakness of your mate. Finally this state of Romeo and Juliet romance can grow dull leading to crushing your marriage.

It can also miraculously build it higher to levels pending both works towards such endings. Never be rude or insulting to your partner. It pays to be always kind, respectful and understanding of each other. Be with God and stand by each other in this life's short sorjoun.

Chapter Four: An ode to Love

Love, an instinct of adoration innate to man is a unique phenomenon that almost sacrifices one heart to another. It is an adoration that touches the heart beyond any yearning. Love is the force that melts hearts into one and yet leaves the individuals intact.

Love causes a mother who cannot swim to plunge head long into a raging river to safe her drowning child knowing she could drown with him. The embers of love keep us fired and restless about another. Love remains the most mystical relationship that can develop between two strangers. For the love of you I would give my heart as token of friendship one suitor told his future bride.

Love is blind but the lover can never lose sight of the one that caught his or her fancy. Love and instinct is what cause ladies to go through pregnancy and risk of labor over and over till menopause. Love makes us affectionate, attractive and beautiful at heart.

It is the most pleasant and devotional feeling one can have for another human being. It is a chemistry of the heart and mystery, which alchemists could not explain. Love is what makes the voice of one's lover sound like melodious music that none utters other than our lovers. Love has fueled our partnerships since recorded times. Love is our passions' slave.

In biblical resonance Corinthian chapter 13, verses 4 – 8 it speaks of love thus: "Love is patients. Love is kind. It does not envy, it does not boast, it is not proud, it is not rude and it is not self-seeking. Love is not easily angered and it keeps no record of wrongs. Love dose not delight in evil but rejoices with truth. It always protects, always trusts, always hopes and always preserves. Love never fails."

William Shakespeare in Romeo and Juliet said of love as "My bounty is as boundless as the sea. My love as deep, the more I give to thee the more I have, for both are infinite." Love is indeed the romantic spring that never dries for another, as it is greater than a feeling. It is a process that recognizes two hearts in continual desire for each other in laughter, trust, and sharing.

Loving is sharing the world of life with another. It's a people unifier and is never empty or wasted as it opens the gates of happiness. George Eliot asked "What great thing is there for two souls to feel they are joined to strengthen each other, to be one with each other in silent unspeakable memories?"

I say love is the ultimate test of one's commitment to another. It is an unexplainable passion for another human. A solder commits his or her life for love of country and ideology like freedom and democracy. William Wordsworth said, "The best of a good man's life are his little, nameless, unremembered acts of kindness and love." This reminds us that love is shared self-giving which end in self-remuneration. Mother Teresa admonished us: "To spread love everywhere we go, to all children, families and next-door neighbors."

Man falls in love partly to avoid solitude and withering away. It is said that love works wonders and in miracles as it weakens the strong and empowers the weak. A good example can be clearly adduced form story of the case of Delilah and Samson the giant.

Love made the great brut Sampson to allow her cut a tuff of his hair, which rendered him instantly weak and lead to his eventual capture. A fit only love can for armies tried but failed to conquer this monster of a man. Does love not favor the weak one with passion in this case while at the same time destroying reason?

Love dose turn the world going in circles. Victor Hugo told us that the most profound symptom of love is a tenderness, which becomes at times almost insupportable. Ralph Waldo Emerson simply puts love as "A mutual self-giving, which ends in self-recovery."

Germaine De Stail said love is emblem of eternity; it confounds all notions of time. It effaces all memory of a beginning, all fear of an end. In short, dear reader, love for me is a free force, a spirit and part of a being needing to be fed by another's' heart to avoid it burning out.

Love is neither a slave to any king nor servant as it develops and dwells equally in both hearts but follows the laws of nature, which makes the sexes seek love. Again, allow me serenade love by simply saying hurray to priceless love for letting me tick and feel for another heart in this life. All good things come to an end but true love lives on forever.

It is hoped that this invigorating fairy tale of love left you ruminating on yours years gone by and that you enjoyed reading the work of a novice trying his hand at love story telling for the first time. The tapestry of interwoven true love was generously bared to readers. The story makes us mellow.

Alasan Mbalo Sr, Alasan Mbalo Jr and Mrs. FamatandingCeesay-Mbalo visiting Dakar, Senegal in 2016.

Mr. Sisawo Bajoja Ceesay, Father

BK: L-R: Dr. Alhasan Ceesay, Mum Famatanding Tarawaleh, Babuccar Dibba. FT: L-R: Fatou Dibba, Penda Diba, and Isatou Dibba, Banthurst, Gambia 1965

Mrs. Binta Ceesay, (Elder Sister)

Dr. Ceesay and wife Mrs. Fatou Koma-Ceesay, Colchester, UK, 2000

Miss Famatanding Ceesay, (Daughter)

Miss Binta Ceesay, (Daughter)

Roheyata Ceesay (daughter) at Manchester College, Manchester UK 2015

Dr. Alhasan Ceesay: Graduating from the American University of the Caribbean School of Medicine, 1992.

Dr. Alhasan S. Ceesay holding favourite Africa

L – R: Dr. Alhasan Ceesay, Prof. Sul Nyang, Mr. Cloyd Ramsey and Prof. Francis Conti

Auntie Meta Ndow (RIP) with Alasan Mbalo Jr, Brusubi

The Gambia 2014

Gorgeous Mrs. Fatou Koma-Ceesay

The younger Njawara Ceesay Kunda family at meeting

Dr. Alhasan Ceesay and Mr. Sisawo Ceesay, Father

Bathurst, The Gambia, 1960

Dudou Ceesay, brother in green, with family

Dr. Ceesay and wife Mrs. Fatou Koma-Ceesay

Dr. Alhasan Ceesay graduating from the American University of the Caribbean School of Medicine, 1992

In loving memory of Auntie Meta Ndow,

Holding Alasan Mbalo Jr. Brusubi 2015

RIP: Late Mamurndar, aka Kebba Jobe, Gambia's best photographer of the 1960s

Alasan Mbalo Jr, Brusubi, Gambia 2014

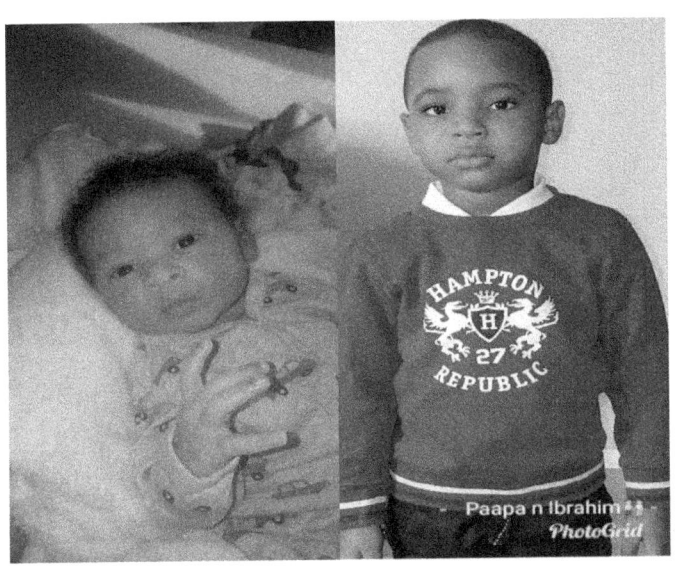

Baby Ibrahim Mbalo with Brother Alasan Mbalo Jr.
Sweden 2018

Mrs Fatou Koma-Ceesay, Gambia 2015

Chapter Five: The Trail

In the beginning there was the Adam's apple link like love once swallowed it becomes hard to regurgitate love. However divergent trails do rare their ugly heads under pressure of time. Let us then commence from day one of foundation of this love made in heaven was laid. The two vowed to be inseparable in life and it all happened when Kunsa Mori met his magical moment in lady suiting all criterions he looks forward on a wife.

Fantong Seyabalo was instant love at first sight and still remains that magnet in kunsa's heart. Hence they had no problem tying the connubial Knot on December 25th, 1997 in Conakry, Guinea, West Africa. There was a short honey moon for Kunsa was to start medical school on January 9th, 1998 at The American University of the Caribbean School of Medicine in Plymouth, Montserrat, West indies.

They were poor and had not had the current free internet and mobile facilities and luxury that most take for granted today. It was very challenging being separated right after tying the knot uniting their lives.

Alhasan Ceesay Leaves Our Sanctuary for Medical School: A word from Bishop Mason and Rev. Hugh C. White. You will be delighted to learn that Alhasan S. Ceesay was accepted yesterday (Tuesday, November 11, 1986) into the medical school of the American University of the Caribbean, Plymouth, Montserrat, West Indies,

Alhasan is hoping to commence his studies at the medical school this coming January 7, 1987. You know that Bishop McGehee and the Diocese have given Alhasan sanctuary for more than three years.

Mariner's Inn has provided him with housing and sustenance. Bishop McGehee in his letter to Dean of the Medical School in the West Indies said, "I know Alhasan personally. He is a person of integrity, intelligence, human sensitivity, and God knows, perseverance against formidable inequalities." For the past several weeks a small group of persons in the Diocese have raised $15,000 towards the $30,000 required for his medical training.

You may wish to join in the support of Alhasan. The purpose of this memo is to give you that opportunity. You do understand that every dollar raised will go directly to his personal support. You may make a monthly or quarterly pledge to be paid over the next eighteen months, beginning December 15, 1986 and going through to July 15, 1988.

All monies received for this purpose are tax deductible. Evelyn Bayer at the Diocese Centre (4800 Woodward Avenue, Detroit, M! 48201) will take your pledges or your money. We are confident that Alhasan Ceesay will serve all people wherever he is. He is personally committed to returning to the Gambia as a doctor to his people.

Signed: Bishop Mason and The Rev. Hugh C. White

A copy of my letter followed for Editor of the Diocesan newspaper to print in The Record.

Dear Editor, I will be most delighted if you would kindly publish this note in the next issue of the Record for me to extend deep appreciation and gratitude to the Diocese of Michigan, my support group, Mariner's Inn, and all who steadfastly stood by me to seek resolution of my intractable INS case. Thank you is awfully inadequate and words cannot aptly convey to you what the help you rendered meant to my villagers and I.

I take this opportune moment to express profound gratitude for your generous and the overwhelming support accorded me. The fruits of your benevolence will be shared with the sick and needy in due course.

To those not aware, I am pleased to report my being accepted at the American University School of Medicine in the West Indies effective January 7, 1987. Most relieving is the fact that I will be able to meet with my family in Guinea Conakry on my way to the school.

All of this would have been impossible had it not been for love, encouragement and support you provided me during these difficult times of my life. Therefore, allow me to convey to you, in advance, sincere appreciation of my family and villagers for the kindness you always touched us with during my exile days or years.

We are very grateful and a million thanks to all of you who one way or the other contributed to make this chapter and day possible for my villagers.

Thanks for being true friends of human rights and for being so kind and helpful to my mission and me. I will certainly return to serve the Gambia as soon as that is possible for me.

Thank you! My gratitude to this country (America and Americans) is immeasurable. It is here that life taught me how to forge ahead for my people and for nothing more I am thankful for the love and friendship of the people from whom I learn the true meaning of sacrifice and good will towards others. The French capsule my feeling best in the saying, "Tout est bien, qui fini bien."
All is best that ends well. God bless all of you. "Au revoir mon ami." Goodbye my good friends. I will see you in the Gambia. We certainly look forward to welcoming you in our villages to thank you for your stand in this unusual case.
Sincerely
Alhasan S. Ceesay

With this newfound relief I braced myself for the task that lay ahead. I got my little possessions, I had, all packed, bought my air ticket to Guinea Conakry via Amsterdam and the London and Antigua to Montserrat, West Indies.

I made my last pilgrimage to the Diocese of Michigan early on December 19, 1986, the day of my flight out of America.

Everyone seemed to want to hug me and wish me well and a safe journey. They were also relieved that life has now signaled progress for me and that the prospect of meeting with my family was super.

The Bishop broke down, at his office, when I shook his hands for the last time.

He and I have grown very close and are now parting for, possibly, for good. I took a last look at him, with tears dripping on my cheeks, and walked out saying thanks, goodbye and God bless you sir. I heard his footsteps behind me up to the end of the corridor and I disappeared into Rev. High C. White's office and found him on the telephone making final arrangements for me at Detroit Metro Airport for a 1.00 pm flight from Detroit to Chicago for both of us.

The scenery of well wishers repeated itself at the corridor where I met a throng of people wanting to see me for the last time. I will never forget (The Rt. Rev) H. Coleman Bishop McGehee, jr, Patricia Koblyski, Hugh White and the Ceesay-Committee, Lois R. Leonard, Evelyn Bayer, Marry Ellen Robertson, and Rev. Walter White, executive director at the Mariner's Inn.

Rev, Hugh C. White and I entered the car amidst tears and cheers from those onlookers and good friends of mine. This was the beginning of the closure of my life in exile and the Mariner's Inn saga.

At the Metro airport and after the formalities, Hugh and I bought few soft drinks but none could finish his because of the Erie feeling that we are now about to separate for long, long time to come, or perhaps forever. We arrived at O'Hare International Airport in Chicago two hours early.

This gave us time to browse around and renew our commitment not to loose contact of each other, especially the Bishop and my friends at the Episcopal Diocese of Michigan.

Time flew rapidly and soon we had the PA announcing boarding time for Amsterdam. The Rev. Hugh C. White and I shook hands for the last time at O'Hare International on December 19, 1986 and I broke down for the first time since I left Diocese of Michigan in Detroit.

I have bid farewell to the last of the true friends I had in America. These were friends who uphold the doctrine of human rights and justice for all. We prayed together and I joined the boarding queues. Hugh too had a tear or two escape him.

He stood watching for a while before he disappeared into America and I headed for Africa and the Caribbean. Very soon elation took over my sadness for leaving behind such good friends I made during the saga of my exile years.

The flight was routine and went smoothly. I landed at Amsterdam, Holland, 5.00 Am, the next day. I could not believe that this time the sun has risen for me and that I am not in the Mariner's Inn but on my way to motherland Africa.

The thought and feeling of relief I had at that December 20, 1986, can never be repeated. I prayed and thanked God for letting me survive the ordeal and for the kind people He brought into my life during those trying moments.

The transit took seven hours instead of the four I was told while booking the ticket for the flight. At the end of the waiting and having gone through the Airport formalities for Conakry we boarded a KLM flight destined for Guinea Conakry at 1.00pm.

I was so eager to leave that beads of sweat ran down my face in wintry Holland. My adrenaline was surge supper high and all I wanted was to be in Conakry with my family. The iron bird finally started to taxi for take off from Amsterdam for Conakry International 5.00 pm and besides a few air turbulent moments the flight was calm and steady and I did manage to sleep most of the nine hours flight.

KLM taxied at Conakry International 5.oo pm, December 21, 1986, nine hours after my first Trans Atlantic flight for five years.The blue skies and warm breeze or climate was a dramatic relieve from the dreary grey wintry weather I just left behind in frigid Amsterdam, Holland.

Once more life was familiar scenery and the people were cheerful as they welcomed us to Guinea Conakry. I took two or there deep breaths cool evening tropical fresh air and praised God for letting me this far and for freeing me from the torturous trial my life had seen in the past six years since Liberia. I then went into the arrival formalities almost dazed for my mind could not accept that such fortune could be mine.

I picked up my luggage after the arrival rituals or formalities and only to find out that my suitcase was missing. It had all the presents I brought for my family and fiancée Fatou Koma. Two hours passed before Fatou Koma and her friend came for me. Evidently, she had been at the Airport on arrival of an earlier KLM flight, which originated from Dakar Senegal.

At that time she was told that I was not onboard the one from Dakar but should check back for the KLM flight from Amsterdam. She returned to Conakry hoping that I will call while I was already at the arrivals. Luckily she returned at 7.00 pm and we hugged and kissed several times before anyone of us could utter a word or two in.

She was just delighted to see me well and back in Africa. It was a momentous ecstasy and indeed exhilarating for us. Every second seemed unbelievable. It shows that I was free and at last with the woman I ever loved in my life. It was to us like a dream and we held onto each other not to be separated again for the rest of our lives.

It all happened on an African soil. We prayed and thank God for being kind to us and for letting us see each other in good health, even if our spirits were broken by the threats that lingered over me in the past six years.

We took a taxi and headed for Conakry, capital of Guinea, West Africa, through which journey we kissed incessantly right to our destination at the

International Hotel at the outskirts of town. I spent the night at the hotel and told my future wife all that happened to me, and the luggage caper, even though KLM promised to try and locate it.
She was just happy and felt lucky and thankful that I was alive and was in Guinea with her. The next day I moved to Alhaj Saikou Omaruff Nimaga's home down town Conakry.
He was my fiancee's uncle and he had insisted I stay there for the rest of my short stay before I head for Montserrat in the West Indies. The reunion with some of my family members from the Gambia and would be in-laws was an unbelievable dream.
My uncle Alhaj Sherif Sey arrived on Wednesday from the Gambia to brief me about the family. He told me father was too frail and could not come but he was there in spirit with us.
The entire family in Gambia was concerned about my state and urged that I keep up the fight to clear my name. They were convinced that God would vindicate me and that I will one day return to serve the Gambia.
Uncle Sey told me that father always prays for my progress and fulfillment of my dreams in life. I was happy to see him and to know of the state of the family back in the Gambia. I did not sleep that night. I was worried about my poor aged parents and impact my case might have had on them. It might be the reason why my parents were afraid of meeting me in Guinea.

However, on Thursday evening a delegation of elders was sent to Fatou Koma's parents asking or seeking the hands of their daughter to marry to me. This delegation of twelve, at the behest of my fiancée, Fato Koma, insisted that we be married before my departure for Montserrat in the Caribbean.

She told her parents that she would a sphincter if they deny her the choice of a husband. The parents acquiesced and I paid the dowry and all that was asked or required for the marriage to be blessed and consummated.

At first, Fatou's father, Alhaj Ousman Koma was hesitant about my marrying his daughter, in view of the prevailing history, and he pretended to block the proceedings hoping to get higher dowry offer. I assured him of the eternal love I have for his daughter and that I will never let her suffer or ever dreamt of divorcing her.

I told him that Fatou Koma is my soul and mine even in death. We will remain one person should he give her hand in marriage to me. Hence, Alhaj Marruf Nimaga, Mohamed Dansugu and a group of elders, between who was my future father-in-laws' best boyhood friend, all assured Alhaj Ousman Koma that the marriage was going to be sanctioned. With this pressure on he finally recapitulated and let what God wanted between Fatou Koma and I materialized.

Fatou Koma-Ceesay is of the Sarahule tribe and Daughter of Alhaj Ousman Koma and Jalian Ture of Kindia village, Republic of Guinea Conakry.

We met in 1979 while I was a student at the A. M. Dogliotti School of Medicine, University of Liberia in Monrovia, West Africa. It was love at first sight that never faded but grew daily for both of us, up to the present day of our lives. She is the beauty of the world in my eyes.

She is stunningly beautiful, sexy, young, intelligent and all I like or wanted in a woman. The romantic fantasies of life become reconciled with reality when one meets that one individual that stands out in our hearts of hearts and emotions. It is much more than a feeling, which removes protective barriers one may have erected.

Fatou Koma-Ceesay was the unquestionable love for me the moment we laid eyes on each other. I finally realized a soothing or comfort and sharing I hardly experienced with others. As time grew we developed and matured into being twins that loved, struggled and shared everything in life.

One look at her will allow you class her as the queen of the palace of beautiful queens. With her beauty goes an exceptionally well-mannered, sociable and intelligent lady. Her father, Alhaj Ousman Koma, always teases me by accusing me of having stolen the jewel of his compound, which is an under-statement when one sees or meets my stunning

Fatou Koma-Ceesay. I am yet to hear anyone utter objectionable remarks about my dream girl.

Her mother said that I must have had very long arms that reached out from the Gambia to Kindia in Guinea Conakry and snatched their princess's heart. In short, this lady is my dream wife turn real and I will never allow her escape me.

Hence, I wrote the following letter to my parents on 2/21/1980, while in Liberia, informing them about Fato Koma and my intention of marrying her in due course.

A.M. Dogliotti College of Medicine
University of Liberia
Monriovia, Liberia
West Africa
2/22/80

Dear Parents,

I have through my life aimed at bringing joy to your hearts. Unfortunately circumstances seem to impede me. However, I am today pleased to report that, despite my bewilderment, I have met a lady in Kindia, Guinea Conakry whom God made our hearts and spirits as one.

She is called Fatou Koma, a Sarahule and Muslim daughter of Alhaj Ousman Koma, the Imam of Kindia. She loves me and has refused to marry anyone since I met her.In view of the unusual determination and love we have for each other I as you to kindly bless our proposed marriage and for you to send letters of appreciation and concordance etc to her parents, especially Alhaj Ousman Koma and Jalian Ture in Kindia.

Fatou and I met in 1979 and she and her family have since remain kind to me. I fully understand your difficulties but I beg for your approval of my eventual marrying of Fatou Koma as soon as possible. This is one woman I love more than any that came to my life.

I have already written to her father about my intentions. A copy of which (the letter) is being enclosed herein for you perusal. I will upon hearing from you finalize the formalities.

I am asking her hand in marriage not only because we love each other but because she has also been an honest, lovely woman to me and had stood her grounds for me. If everything seemed puzzling and untimely then that is what God has planned for Fatou Koma and I. I have reached an age where a good lady partner will be normal and advantageous if not realistically traditional.

Again, I love Fatou Koma and do know what I am about to get into. We await your unquestionable approval of my marrying Fatou Koma. Bare with me I know what I am doing and if all it all ends you will be happy with my Fatou Koma.

I will return with a good wife on my side and a good skill to serve the Gambia when I finish my studies. Regards, God bless and reply soon.

Your Son
Alhasan S. Ceesay

My parents wasted no time in writing to Alhaj Ousmab Koma and all those concen in the above request. But as fate had it Fatou and I had to seat it out until my return to Guinea in December 1986 before we could finally marry.

I had sent the following letter to my future father in-law, Alhaj Ousman Koma during the same period that I contacted my parents requesting their approval of my wedding Fatou Koma. It read:

College of Medicine
University of Liberia
Monrovia, Liberia
West Africa
2/23/80

Dear Alhaj Ousman Koma,

I am Alhasan S. Ceesay, son of Mr. Sisawo Ceesay and Mrs. Famatanding Tarawaleh of Njawara village, Lower Badibou, District, the Gambia. We are Muslims and of the Mandinka tribe. I am currently studying to become a doctor of Medicine when I complete my training.

I met your daughter, Fatou Koma in Monrovia, Liberia in 1979. God made our hearts one and indeed very close at heart and spirit. It is in this light that I write with deep humility and courtesy to ask you, your wife, Jalian Ture, and all relatives of yours to give me the hand of Fatou Koma in marriage. My father is now 90 years old and cannot travel to Guinea as would be required by tradition, so he would be writing to you shortly. Upon hearing from you my uncle Alhaj Sherif Sey will be deligated by the family to travel to your place in Guinea to formalize the consummation.

Fatou Koma and I love each other very much and would like your approval of our marriage. Islam will be the corner stone of my house and all I can assure you is I love your daughter and believe she is good enough to be my wife for life.

Let the record show that I commit myself to doing all I can to maintain her well and give her all the love and protection I will give to myself. In Allah's name, Fatou Koma and I, anxiously await your reply and tacit approval.

Your son-in-law

Alhasan S. Ceesay

If I were to come into this world again, I would prefer the convenience of the two that brought me into earth. They were the most befitting parents and the Gambia is my Garden of Eden in which Fatou Koma is the perfect match for me in my heavenly life.

Hence, after almost eight years of waiting Fatou Koma and I got married at a mosque in Conakry on December 23, 1986. My uncle Alhaj Sherif Sey deputized for my parents since they were too old and for fear of alerting authorities as to my where about in Africa, did not come to witness the low key ceremony we had agreed on.

My uncle left for the Gambia the following day, after consummation of the marriage, to report to my family and reassure them of my being well and committed to return to the Gambia when the proper time comes.

Fatou Koma, now Mrs. Ceesay, relaxed in my arms like a tender baby. How sweet it rings in the ear to hear people call her Madam Koma-Ceesay or Mrs. Koma_ceesay.

Our honeymoon was very short for I had to be in Medical School by January 7, 1987 in the West Indies some twelve thousand miles from Conakry. We agreed that she stays in Guinea until my situation improves or when I finish my clinical rotation.

I wrote the following letter to Bishop McGehee and Hugh White while in Guinea informing them of the new change in my life etc.

Kindia
Guinea Conakry
West Africa
24/12/86

Dear Bishop McGehee & Rev. Hugh White
RE: Surprise permanent union
It gives me great pleasure to inform you that my fiancée Fatou Koma and I were married today in view of the circumstance known to all of you and love being the paramount reason behind the enactment.
Her's and my parents insist that time had it for us to marry come what may as both of us are advancing in age. Hence, I would be most grateful if you bring this low-key wedding to attention of the Diocese, the Ceesay Support Committee and Parishes and well wishers in Detroit.
I will be enrooting to the American University in Plymouth, Montserrat, West Indies in two days time. Will write or call while in Plymouth. Again share the joyful news with friends. Regards
Your friend in Christ
Alhasan S. Ceesay
I later in the saddest fashion, through Rev. Richard Smith, found out that either mails never left Conakry because of poor service or were lost while on international transit to USA. Rev. Richard Smith harped on it to destroy my integrity before the Bishop and company.
It worked but let us follows the Richard saga at a later section of the chapter. So I took my return flight to medical school on the 5/1/87 heading via London, Antigua and my final destination Plymouth, Montserrat in the West Indies.

The flight took 14 hours by the time we flew across the Atlantic from Guinea Conakry via Paris, London and then Antigua into Plymouth, Montserrat. Motserrat is a very small volcanic Island of no less than 6000 people in the West Indies. The Northern sector was occupied white residents while the rest of the island indigenous West Indies.

On arrival to Plymouth, using Lait flight, we were given permits and then we took a taxi ride to the ultra-modern campus of the America University of the Caribbean (AUC) after ten minutes ride of winding and hilly road.

The university was perched atop of a hill offering reflection panoramic view of the beauty of sea and land and also served as the island's main tourist attraction. This scenery and levied students resident permits made AUC a natural source of revenue for the island state.

There were not many attractions to see except the hot springs and lovely flowers mingled with warm and kind residents. 400 American and Canadian students attend the medical school and these created a lively social atmosphere while attending the school.

The people were friendly and I had lots of friends amongst Montserratians. Huge tourist ships dock at the harbour twice weekly. Tourism was full bloom when I arrived in Montserrat. At the university campus I was roomed a fellow classmate, Robert Lowry, an Afro-America from Brooklyn, New

York. Even though I spent only a few days with him before moving out, I found Robert Lowry to understand and a kind person. Came January 7th, 1987, I got up very early, prayed and went to be officially inducted or registered as member of the class of 1987 through 1992 which ceremony took place at 8.30 AM.

Classes started the same day and our class of fifty students was among the largest to enroll at the university. Some who had done Dentistry; others were secretaries and research assistances before deciding to read for a medical degree as career. Most of the entrants had degrees in biology, chemistry and mathematics.

A few were transfer students from other Caribbean medical colleges. Every thing including my classes went on well until med semester when my asthma flared. I reacted severely to the pollen and humidity and was hospitalized on several occasions.

This ill heath of mine made the school officials concern as to whether my health would allow me complete the semester or even continue attending or the program at the university. I insisted to be allowed to continue and made it clear the asthma normally goes away in a week until the next pollen season a year later.

I literally forced myself to attend classes under heavy medication of Salbutamol, and prednisolone. I went into serious asthma attack while taking the final exam of the first semester at AUC.

Hence I had to repeat the semester. I moved from the dormitory believing that I might be allergic to some perfume Lowry uses or pain on the wails. I had a room next door to school and my landlord was none other than the university Gardner, William Ryan.

This kind man checks me at night to see if my asthma did not flare. The attacks abated with falling levels of pollen. Fate had to have it that I will complete medical school but the experience that followed was not one I would even wish for my ardent enemy.

Fatou Koma was sent to be with me nine months after my restarting of medical school. Wife joined me at the middle of the third semester and it helped me relax while continuing the struggles.

She arrived after the infamous surprise visit of Richard Smith on behalf of the Diocese, who had been against my attending AUC from the onset we brought up the idea as an alternative to solving my INS nightmare.

Like most, Richard Smith, fails to know how much willpower God gave me and my determination to get through medical school with or without his involvement. Hence, when Richard insinuated that I failed to let my friends at Diocese know of my marriage. I got angry because I did write to the Bishop and Hugh about it while in Guinea Conakry to let them know God's gift to me in Guinea.

Richard harped on it and made me look the person I was never meant to be as he failed to see the link and possibility of poor mail service in Africa. I was operating on assumption that the Diocese knew through letters I sent them before leaving for the Caribbean.

My wife's joining me finally gave Richard Smith ammunition to detach me from the Diocese and the Ad Hoc Ceesay Committee disregarding the effect my asthma had on me in my first semester at the island.

When Richard was through he persuaded all, except one angel, Mrs. Lois R. Leonard, went along with him and discontinued their sponsorship of my medical education at the American University of the Caribbean School of Medicine.

Fatou's arrival to Montserrat coincided with my having lost all means of support but true love being what it will always be, Fatou refused to return and leave me under such predicaments. Simply, she weathered the storm with me without ever regretting it or demeaning me.

She at one time volunteered to write to the Bishop and send photocopies of her arrival time in Montserrat to clarify the matter for them but I refused on the grounds that some of them have known about it for I wrote to them about our marriage before leaving Guinea.

I assured the Committee that as long as I am on thee right, God would see me through this ordeal, even though it might or was going to be of the greatest uphill battle for me.

God relieves of us of all burdens if we believe in Him and the types of Richard Smith and company. I told her we must be kind to our selves and fellow humans. We must never fail to help the needy, as did our parents, parents' parents for generations of life.

Later that year, by December 6th, 1987, we received the following letter from my father in-law, Alhaj Ousman Koma. He wrote to us while visiting a friend, Alhaj Ebrahima Conteh in Monrovia, Liberia.

Wife and I were very surprised and at the same delighted when we read the letter. We had prayed long for her father to come to terms with our marriage. We needed his blessing for the anything to work out for the future of our family and children. So his reconciling sealed the marriage forever in the African traditional way.

Even though the letter was no monetary source for us it lightened the shock and confusion the Richard Smith Caper brought onto our lives. Please understand that both fatou and I wholeheartedly forgive Richard Smith for being the devil's advocate in my life. Without further ado here is the panacea.

C/O Alhaj Ebrahima conteh
99 Saikou Ture Avenue
P. O. Box 154
Monrovia, Liberia
West Africa
December 6th, 1987

Dear Alhasan,
"Ah salaam aleikum. Wa rahmatullah wa barakatu."
I receieved your letter of September 1, 1987, only a few days ago. I am no longer in Kindia but in Monrovia, Liberia.
The several letters and money you sent I deliberately refused to receive. You know that I was greatly annoyed at Fatou Koma foe leaving the husband I had given her.
However, time, your assurances in the letters just received and the fact the rest of my family agreed to the marriage between you and Fatou Koma have brought me to accept the marriage as one favoured by God.
I, therefore, now give you all my blessings. I shall pray for your well-being and total success. As I say this I want Fatou Koma know that you are the last man I will ever give her to marry. So you must remain together until the time Allah calls you to your final destination.
It means much to me to hear that Islam is at the center of your lives and that you are keeping the salat as prescribed by Allah in the holly quruan and

practiced by the holy prophet Mohamed sallaho alahi wasalam. Once you have both Islam and education you have been greatly favoured by Allah, so never relent in your quest for piety and knowledge.

You must continue to write and by Allah's grace I will reply your letters. With prayers that Allah's peace and blessings be upon you both. I am closing now

Faithful Yours
Alhaj Ousman Koma
Your father in-law

Fatou and I were in cloud nine and more than delighted and relieve knowing that my father in-law had seen the light at the end of the tunnel. Hence we sent him the following reply the next mail day in Montserrat.

School of Medicine
AUC, Plymouth
West Indies
December 18, 1987

Dear Alhaj Ousman Koma,

Fatou and I were delighted and relieved by your recent letter dated December 6, 1987, which reached us today. We are indeed touched by your final acceptance of our holy union in marriage.

It is a profound holy anointment from God and you, our father. We are all in good health and spirit. God has atlas given peace to our marriage and minds for knowing that all of you loved us.

May Almighty God and His prophet, Mohamed grant to all of us good health and longevity. Be rest assured that only death will separate Fatou and I. Also I will do all I can to help the rest of the family where possible.

Our regards and best wishes to all and remember us to others members of the family. Looking forward to hearing from you soon. Please have the people at your mosque pray for us. Wasallam

Your Son-in-law

Alhasan S. Ceesay

This letter and what it meant rejuvenated my wife and me. At last everyone on both sides of the families is now for our marriage. God had finally sealed us forever. We thanked God and slept in each other's arms until morning. I continued to fight to complete my medical education.

My landlord, William Ryan, turned out to be a humane person and indeed a caring landlord. Wife and I at times went without food for days and it was only the landlord who would once on a while bring food to us to feed our dwindling bodies.

The University cared the least whether we went hungry and only catered for its tuition fees believing that money was being sent to me from Diocese of Michigan.

Wife and I collected berries, any edible leaf on the island, fruits, and pears for meals. She would rather starve with me than use the little money we had to fly back to Guinea. She said, "When I married you I did so not only for the good times but also the bad ones. God is only testing us. Let us put our hands up to Him. He does answer prayers." Indeed we prayed and I worked harder on two fronts, the school and meeting the bills.

My experience is that when it rains for me it pours cats and dogs ceaselessly for a very long period at a time. If you think life was bad enough as it is, wait you read about what happened to tiny island of Montserrat on September 16th, 1989. We just could not believe the challenge that followed that treacherous day when Hurricane Hugo hit the Island with vengeance.

Late Mrs. Huja Sarr, (RIP), Banjul, The Gambia

Chapter Six
Hurricane Hugo: September 16, 1989.
Day Hell Broke Loose

For readers who do not know, a hurricane is a tropical cyclone with winds of 74 miles per hour or greater and are usually accompanied by torrential rain, thunder and lightening, never heard or seen, that some times move into temperate latitudes such as the Caribbean zones. A year prior to hurricane Hugo neighbouring Jamaican was devastated by hurricane Gilbert.

Most Montserrantian never expected or experienced winds stronger than 60 miles per hour and only reads or hear about the terrible thing Gilbert did to Jamaica. This was all rudely changed by 11.45 p.m. on Saturday September 16th, 1989. This day gave Montserrat and its neighbouring islands a rude awakening and a taste of her first hurricane in fifty years. The first was in 1660, the second in 1928 and now hurricane Hugo in 1989.

This wild bestial wind of September 16, 1989 blew mad all night with a fury that destroyed all of Monsterrat to pieces. Ninety percent of the homes had their roofs blow away with the high tide that swept the Island. Things were smashed or smithereens while the thunder and lightening blazed with vengeance.

One could at one time hear the cows, sheep and other domesticated animals frenziedly and frantically running to their doom as the wind and rain built up vehemently.

Mine and wife's life became threatened and at serious risk when a flying galvanized sheet left us at the mercy of wind and rain and flying tree trunks with galvanized sheets from nearby buildings.

As matters got out of hand we knelt and fervently prayed for our lives and survival of everyone on the path of this monstrous wind. The hurricane must have poured at least 5 to 15 inches of rain on the island in less than ten minutes on top of the destructive bellows of wind.

It was until Sunday, September 17, 1989, that the wind slowed down to forty miles per hour. And by 1.00 P.M. people were able to or dared to venture out and survey the damage left behind by hurricane Hugo.

Only thirteen elderly people became casualties of the hurricane and the whole nation lay in twisted rubbles. All I saw near my place were metal and concrete inter-twined and blown to some far away location or ditches. Fallen trees, tables, telephone poles, galvanized sheets and all of these in a meshwork of cables and parts of roofs from buildings blocked roads to what were left of the university campus.

Upon daring to venture to the campus I saw a small Hiroshima of Japan. Everything just looked like after the dropping of the Atomic Bomb. Thank God no student died or got injured. The students held on well but were very frightened.

There was no pandemonium. It was as if everyone was partly spellbound or sedated for the scenery was too calm and orderly. Some demanded immediate evacuation while others just wondered about in a daze. The few who were in control of themselves helped gather the remaining food supplies and water.

Everyone stayed in the first floors of the dormitories since the roofs of all second floors were no longer there or safe shelter for anyone as they were inhabitable waterlogged rooms. Monday saw a lot of student meetings and the Dean came in to alley our fears and to let us know that efforts were being made to get in touch with the outside world.

Yes, Montserrat was completely isolated from mankind during the first two days of the aftermath of hurricane Hugo.

By Tuesday, September 18, 1989, most of the students had enough of the encounter to their necks. All they kept asking was when they will be able to leave Montserrat. With this, rumors ran wild on the grounds of the ruined campus.

The once showcase of Montserrat was now reduced to rubbles and twisted galvanized sheets all over the places. It was not until Wednesday September 19,

1989, that we had a glimpse of the outside world in the form of a British Frigate, HMS Alacrity, which docked at Montserrat. One of her helicopters flew over to survey the island and then headed to Antigua perhaps in consultation with the British and American Embrasures and consulates.

Later that day more planes flew over us but none dropped anything or came down. The helicopter landed men from the Frigate and these went to work, setting up communication centers and helping the government and the governor of Montserrat. Everyone tried to recover as much as possible of his or her retrievable belongings.

The British sailors helped to clear the feeder roads and the ship served as lifeline to the rest of the world. At the campus we cleared the tennis court and made a helicopter-landing path. It worked, for in one overpass flight of the helicopter the pilot saw the big cross with a circle around it.

He circled the campus twice and flew back to the ship. After a long half an hour later he came directly and hovered for a while before heading to the temporal landing ground the students had prepared. The huge helicopter landed smoothly and frightened and eager students swamped the pilot.

Being an experience fellow he asked his co-pilot to take off and leave him on the ground with the students. The rush tampered immediately as the metal bird too off and hovered over campus.

All of us wanted to touch the gentleman and thank him for bringing hope to our hearts. He spent roughly twenty minutes with the students discussed with the staff and likewise the student government before being flown back to the ship where he relayed our messages to the American Consulate in Antigua.

That very day, the American vice councilor, Steve Vanhuness, reported to the campus. Yes, and yes again, America does take care of its own in time of crisis like this one. Steve spoke with Dr. Paul Tien, president and owner of the university, and with the student government and then left for his base in Antigua.

The campus settled while diplomatic maneuvers took place between Antigua and Washington, D.C. The general student body was expecting a word or two from the consulate but no matter how uneasy life was for them they must wait for Washington's directives on how to relief or evacuate them from the Island.

Meanwhile several lists of students by name, nationality and home addresses were constantly being compiled and prepared for possible evacuation. The Consular returned the next day with word from the state department that a plane was on the way to take only American and Canadian students to the United States at a cost of $178 per student.

By Friday, September 23, 1989, most of the students were ferried to Antigua by a British Coats Guard ship that brought supplies to Montserrat.
Only the staff, a few students, my wife Fatou Koma and I were left on Campus. The American Consulate refused to evacuate Fatou and I because we were not American or Canadian according to Mr. Steve Vagueness, vice-consular at the U.S. Consulate in Antigua.
I broke down and tried to contact the Gambia High Commission in London on several times but was unable to get through for scarcity of International lines at the time. I tried the next day but could not get anywhere with the telephones, which sapped the little money left in my account.
This left Fatou and I in more financial recariousness. At this time I started worrying about Fatou and wanted help to return her home until life returns to normal. It was just plain risky for her to remain on the island. People believing that the university would never open its doors again came looting at night.
At one time I had to stand my grounds from rouges wanting to break in the makeshift room Fatou and I used while trying to sort things out. It was pathetic and shame how adversity reduces some men to less than animals. At this stage I never cared what the Gambia may or may not do to me all I wanted was and safe place for the lady who gave so much of herself to me.

And now not only mine but her life is at risk from attack by night hooligans. A sympathetic, Mr. K. Cotter and all at the Command Centre need be praised for their hard work and kindness. They were very helpful and sympathetic about my plight.

For the first time and in mall my travels I felt like an orphan stranded and marooned in a tiny island in the middle of the Atlantic Ocean.

It felt scary but as usual, I left my fate in God's hands and at the same time prayed for His forgiveness, mercy and guidance over Fatou Koma and this nightmare.

Fatou Koma-Ceesay turned to be much stronger and steadfaster than I credited her. It was during one these depressed moments that Professor Steve Deschner and his wife Derby came to my help. I had already had a difficult night with looters who thought that the school would not open for years. On hindsight, it was a very tough night that Fatou and I had prepared our minds for death on a desolate Island.

It was difficult trying to remain sane in situations like this and at the same time protect my wife from molestation and fortune hunters of hurricane Hugo. Dr. Deschner spoke to me and offered to talk to one Miss Gayle Baumgardner at the Condominiums with regards to her sheltering my wife and I until a more safe state or place could be found for us. Meanwhile one of the last American students to leave the island, Dean Mcfinning offered his car for me to sell and use the money to buy air ticket for my wife to fly to Gambia or Guinea Conakry. A word or act of encouragement during difficult times or failures is worth more than a dictionary of praises after a success. Miss Gayle Baumgardner, a former Peace Corps volunteer, now resident in Montserrat, turned out to be another of those rare breed of kindness.

Upon being told of our predicament at the campus by Dr. Deschner, she accepted to lodge us at the Shamrock villa and out of her kind-heartedness she loaned me money to buy air ticket for Fatou Koma-Ceesay to fly to the Gambia until the improvement of the situation.

I would reimburse her by working for her and helping her clean the mesh hurricane Hugo left behind at the condominium complexes. We were overwhelmed by her generousness and noble act for a humane cause. My wife and I shall ever be obliged and most grateful to her. I am personally profoundly grateful to Miss Gale Baumgardner.

A friend in need is a friend indeed. Gayle's participation was a touch of an angel's hand from heaven. With this understanding reached. Drs Deschner and Ronda Cooper helped me transport my books, and little belongings left with us to the condominium.

Drs. Deschner and Cooper continued to show great interest in us and we are indebted to both for time and help they gave us. On hindsight, everyone on the Island agreed that it was wicked to leave us stranded on the island while other students were taken out to America. Gayle and I went to town and bought Fatou her ticket to freedom.

Fatou Koma, who lightens my spirit, had to leave for the Gambia after two weeks of stay at the condominiums with me. So we flew to Barbados to the British High Commission for her to secure a transit visa via London on her way to the Gambia. This done we headed for Barbados International Airport.

There, Fatou began to shed tears uncontrollably. I tried to square up my shoulders, stepped back a little and in a voice choked with love and emotion said, I wished I were going with you to Africa.

My eyes were full of mist and deep down I was crying and yet praising God for saving our lives and for relieving my wife from the difficulties that lay ahead in the coming days at Montserrat.

Very soon the PA announced the boarding for BA flight to Heathrow, London. Fatou Koma was jus able to hug me and say, "Good luck and good bye Dr. Ceesay." And she disappeared into the boarding queues for British Airways flight 259 heading for Heathrow, London.

My studied composure cracked as I watched the plane disappear into the clouds with my heart and the only woman I loved. Fatou Koma brings joy to me like a child's first exposure to magic.

When I hear her speak it is always positive and she speaks with candour and humour. Fatou is a delight to be with. It is feeling I never felt until I came across her. Oh, no, no do not rashly conclude my feeling for to be that of an infatuation love. No that fades while ours sprouts daily and full of joy. Fatou Koma is love and gift from God to me.

You can laugh at me if you wish but this how I feel about her and she feels the same or more about me. Now that my Fatou Koma-Ceesay was gone I embarked on bracing myself for the task of getting out of Montserrat and completing my pre-clinic courses. I was in Montesrrat the next day and in solitude lonelier than the grave.

A word or two about Miss Gayle Baumgardner would now befit the saga of my current life after hurricane Hugo. Gayle had, according to friends, devoted all her life to teaching and sharing her day with others. She is nicknamed the mother Theresa of Montserrat.

Like a missionary she was literally known by almost everyone and was always helping the needy.

Gayle was a giving heart that yearns and beckons people to allow her hem lighten their burdens just as inscribed at Liberty Island. Gayle seems to say, "Come to with your laden hearts. I shall do my best to lighten your load."

Miss Baumgardner was unique, for at the condominiums she was duped, "Primary Manager" for she knew everything about the place and how to

get problems solved quickly better than the then designated manager of a place. All one had to do was to ask Gayle about something relating to the condominium and the answer would spew out as if it is from a well organized computer. Gayle knows were to find things better than any on the grounds. Rain or dry this heart of gold is on the move helping others.
When asked, Gayle where next? She would calmly and with a broad smile, reply, "I was just going to visit an old friend and help restore so and so thing for him or her." Gayle works from dawn to dusk with a capacity unique only to Gayle Baumgardner. Having worked with her and as well as observed her, I at times wished I had a way of keeping her rested just for twenty four hours a week.
But rest makes her miserable as she once told me. I do not want that to happen to her for boredom would mean suicide for her. It will be too anguishing an experience for this princess of Montserrat. Gayle Baumgardner was a jack-of-all-trades, teacher, carpenter, a junk sales person, and above all, a devoted philanthropist.
My Miss Gayle Baumgardner like mother Theresa was a living example of sharing and caring in the literal sense of the word. This angel was happiest when helping others and restless if not engaged in some form of work. She was true and trues the most holy workaholic. I hope this short synopsis gave a bird's eye view of the lady of Montserrat.

Meanwhile the Deschners, Derby and Steve, became interested in helping me go to the USA as we became more and more acquainted with each other. Dr. Ronda Cooper arrange my meeting with the Skeletal staff who were about to depart for America to join the rest of the students at the Wayland Baptist University in Plainview, Texas, left on the Island.

They tried all they could to travel with me but again visa and money problem blocked that effort in my behalf. Hence it was agreed that I stay with Gayle Baumgardner and my exam papers would be sent periodically to an official to proctor while I take the exam.

Time came when the Deschners and other teachers had to leave. We had developed strong bonds and they too will soon be away from me. I thank God for making them care and they became the lifeline between the University in Texas and I in hurricane ravaged Montserrat.

They made certain that all the agreed arrangements concerning my exams were carried out in time by the administration of the medical school. The Deschners also solicited funds for me while in America so that I can complete payment of my fees to the American University of the Caribbean.

It is said that our genetic endowment may well limit our heights and intelligence which we can attain, but it is our environment and experiences, which determines to what extent our potential can be reached or realized. Hence, their agreeing to keep the channels of communication open while at Texas was indeed a benevolent act for which I was most grateful to this very day. This gracious couple, despite delays and unforeseen complications, left their doors and hearts open to me. They relayed requests and messages to the Dean and professors while AUC piggy bags at Wayland Baptist University.

Fatou and I certainly look forward to the day we can gather all these immaculate wingless lovely angels at our villages and the banks of the River Gambia where my villagers will be able to serenade and thank them for helping me fulfill my dream of providing needed medical aid to the villager.

It was during this sad and lonely time that another blow was dealt to me. News reached me from the defunct Ceesay Committee at Diocese of Michigan that my angel, Mrs. Patricia Koblyski had died. Pat, as everyone calls her, was the Refugee coordinator for the Diocese of Michigan in Detroit, and the first person I spoke to upon arriving at the Diocese center.

She devoted her life to helping people and became my best friend and confidant. She along with Lois R. Leonard fought very hard for me during our discussions and had always come up with brilliant ideas on how to go about bringing a solution to my crisis. She brought lots of positive help to me and I will never forget the kindness and love she showed me before her cancer took her away from me.

I knew chemotherapy was not a miracle cure but that she would succumb so early took us all by surprise.

I cried for more than four days, being unable to stop my tears welling whenever I think about Pat Koblyski and kindness she represented to me. The feeling still persist in my heart. Could you imagine she cried along with me on the first day I met her and told her about my experience with the INS? I sent the following letter to Bishop McGehee and Diocesan Newspaper, The Record.

C/O Miss Gayle Baumgardner
The Condominiums
Plymouth, Montserrat
West Indies
IN LOVING MEMORY OF MRS. PATRICIA KOBLYSKI, DIOCESE OF MICHIGAN
Dear Editor,

I wish through your paper to express sympathy and sincere condolence to Mr. Bob Koblyski, his family and the Diocese of Michigan for the untimely lost of our dear friend and Sister Mrs. Patricia Koblyski. The departure of some leaves us bewildered, shocked and flushed.

We ask why at this time dear God? Mrs. Patricia Koblyski is now gleefully resting in the right hands of our maker. We will miss her. For me, a part of me

went along with her. She was a good friend and a true Christian heart that was dedicated to all of us God's children. Four years ago she cried with me and at that same time helped to wipe my tears. She gave hope of freedom and assistance to me and to entire villagers several thousand miles away. Patricia Koblyski knew none of them but like the rest of you she more than any was dedicated in seeing that we all breathe the air in peace and walk together side by side in freedom on mother earth. Pat, thanks a million for having lived a full Christian life and for all of us. Our profound gratitude and indebt ness goes to you for being our Good Samaritan. The only befitting legacy I have for you and my villagers is returning to serve rural Gambia and especially the villager you fought for during these last minutes of a full Christian and a wonderful life of giving to others.
We will never, never forget you and May your soul rest in eternal peace by the right hand side of the Almighty God. Amen!!
Your everlasting Friend
Alhasan S. Ceesay

With Fatou Koma-Ceesay back in the Gambia I continued my scourged or blighted life at the condominiums. I stayed in Montserrat like an orphan working all day and studying up to 1.30 A.M every night for four good months before being join the rest of the students at the Wayland Baptist

University in Plainview, Texas. In that interim I chanced to make a lot of friends at the condominiums. Most rewarding of all was the bond that developed between Rudolf and Sophie Kurt; retired German couples who had come to make this nation island their home away from home.

The rumor about a marooned American University of the Caribbean's student on the island needing urgent help spread in town and around the business community like a wild fire making me even more embarrassed to go to town.

So on December 19, 1989, I decided to take a break from my studies and be with Rudolf and his wife Sophie Kurt for a chat before they retire for the night. I will come back to this day later.

Cousin Rohey Yata Sey-Corr, Fajikunda, Gambia

Chapter Seven
THE SEARCH FOR A SPONSOR

The death of Mrs. Patricia Koblyski left me devastated and concerned. She meant a lot to me and her sincerity and determination to free me was unsurpassed by any other member of the Ceesay Support Committee. Her death was indeed a tragic loss to my villagers and I.

We pray and mourn her passing. Mrs. Lois R. Leonard's statement summed up my feeling about Patricia A. Koblyski when she wrote, "It still seems terribly strange to go in that building (meaning the Diocese) and not see Pat Koblyski." I missed her very much. Her death ushered in pain and a sense of great loss for me. May she rest in peace with God in heaven.

Patricia Kolinsky was one of those who fought vehemently against the intentions of Richard Smith effort to stop my going to the Caribbean. Instead, Richard wanted me to do nursing because we fail to see eye to eye on most points he raised during our meetings. It was as though he felt a black should not challenge ideas he tabled.

This became great snarl between us with Lois enjoy the tug of war going on between Richard and I. Still determined to stop my getting help from the Diocese Richard managed to get himself selected to pay a surprise visit to AUC medical school in Plymouth, Montserrat, West Indies.

He was eager come and check on my performance and to use any negative aspect of it to derail me. He now had the opportunity because some of the staff like David Breidenbach was not happy with me. This was Richard's chance to drown me into oblivion to the bottom of the Atlantic Ocean. Hence on December 1, 1987, I received a departmental notice from Dr. G. F. Breidenbach, assistant dean of the school telling me that Richard would be on campus shortly. The memo ushered an ominous sign of anxiety akin to surveying the forest before walking among the trees. It exacerbated the paroxysm that caused a retrogressive dream for me. It brought all the arguments we had fresh in my mind.

It was a Delphien memo that foretold a bleak future for medical education and aspirations. The memo simply read, "A Mr. Richard Smith, who apparently is one of your sponsors, will be on Montserrat and AUC on December 11, 1987.
He will be meeting me 9.00 AM. Please let me know where you will be contacted between 9.30 and 11.30 A. M on that day. I met Breidenbach the same afternoon to let him know where I would be on said day of Richards visit to the campus.
I was not happy meeting the man who fought against my coming to AUC for he had expressed such opinion too many times during our debate about alternative route to relieve of my torturous INS experience.

Richard cared little about time it would take for my INS Appeal Board appeal to come through. Age and time were not going to wait for me. Richard Smith did not care about stressed my life went through in the past fours of exile in skid row America.

He might have construed a drug rehabilitation center to be a palace for an African like me. He did not care about the rebound effects of being constantly turned down by the INS would have on me nor what it meant living with addicts and former convicts at Ledyard.

All Richard Smith cared was to reverse the decision, which sent me to Montserrat in the first place. This being his primary intention, chagrined Richard Smith showed up on campus on December 4, 1987. I had gone to town to mail letters that day. He was only able to meet my ach enemy Breidenbach and some staff to reward him with false ammunition and negative information he wishes to take back to maligned me to what was remaining of the Ceesay Support Committee.

Richard Smith, though a newcomer to the committee want to run the show and got angry with me when he found me nut manipulability.

He disliked the Diocese sponsoring me and fought it very subtle ways at time trying to illicit hot tempers from me. After meeting the staff at the American University of the Caribbean Richard Smith went on a tour of the Islands or what I apply duped "Island hopping."

We finally met at 7.45 pm in a very hostile encounter and animated indeed, which was punctuated with angry argumentative discussions between us. At the end I assured him that he was no God and did not leave my life and I do not wish him such an experience in his lifetime.

I made it clear that I was not going to worship him or any other human being for that matter in other to get to where I want. I left him fuming at his hotel and had a word with Breidenbach for untrue statement he spewed to Richard Smith.

David denied most of it but I know better for everything happened in my absence and I now did not care what Richard plans. I made up my mind to transfer to next-door medical school at Ross University if the AUC yielded to Richard Smith's dark plans. He went back to Detroit, Michigan armed to destroy me. I wonder if he were not originally deep from the South?

I learnt on the next day of his return he conveyed an emergency meeting of the Ceesay support Committee and gave them such scorching and negative report about me that the committee or what was left of it blindly swallowed his version wholeheartedly and felt obliged to cease raising money for my studies at American University of the Caribbean school of medicine.

He did his best and not being present to defend myself, he left my integrity standing on slippery grounds which lead to a surge of anger against me.

He even told them that I do not attend classes where as the only class I missed was when I had asthma and had to go to hospital three days. Breidenbach took that as my not wanting to attend his classes. All the remaining members, most of who were new members I never met, of then Ceesay support committee under Richard's wings, except Lois R. Leonard and those unable to attend that meeting felt that they no longer could solicited money for a cause that seemed to have some doubts or shadows in it being successful.

Mrs. Lois Leonard felt that or explained her reasons for dissenting with the decision of the committee as follows, "My reasons for voting against the rest of the committee was that I felt that we had made a promise and we were not keeping it. We promised to send you enough for five semesters.

And we stopped sending it before the time was completed." I finally heard from the committee current coordinator and one whom I have high regards, Rev. Hugh C. White. It said:

Diocese of Michigan
4800 Woodward Avenue
Detroit, Michigan 48201
December 28, 1988

Dear Alhasan
You are an important person to the many friends you made here in the Diocese area. The realization

of this makes what I am about to say difficult. From our vantage point following Richard Smith's trip to see you in Montserrat, and following two meetings of the committee earlier this month we have concluded that we must suspend any further financial help for the reasons that we cannot continue to raise funds for your medical school education at AUC.

By authorization of your support committee, and with the concurrence of Bishop McGehee, we have deposited to your account at Barclays Bank in Monttserrat, a check for $4121.00, which represented the balance of the funds. You may use these funds towards your fourth semester at the school or you may use them for whatever purpose you see fit for your future interest.

Please know that this decision was difficult for us to take. Also know that we have some understanding of the pressure and stress you have been under in attempting to make way through medical school. If any additional funds are obtained for you in the immediate weeks ahead, we will forward them to you personally.

Such additional funds are not likely to be in any significant amounts. The one dissenter on the committee to the action outlined in this letter was Lois Leonard. She hoped that we would make an effort to raise the necessary funds for the balance of your studies.

It was the judgment of the committee that such an effort would not be credible or successful in the face of your situation and record. We hope you will let us know how you made out in the light of the action, which we have taken. We live in remembrance and respect of you.
Faithfully,
(The Rev) Hugh C. white
This note brought melancholy, darkness and grief to me and I grew more depressed and frustrated with life. I made several attempts to put forth my side of the story. It fell on deaf ears and failed to reunite me with the Ceesay Support committee.
Close sources told me that negative report given by Richard Smith made it very difficult to convince or convene a meeting even if Hugh White were willing to try to call one after his convention project was over.
Under the circumstances I will not secure a visa to the USA to rally the committee into some sensible direction. Richard Smith had fired the first short in this war and I shall return mine with having the doctor of medicine degree confirmed on me.
I manage to talk to Bishop McGehee by telephone but found his head buried in sand like an Ostrich. He was eager to get to the Lambert Conference in England than deal with my case.
He did ask Hugh White to look into the affair and in reply to my inquiry Hugh White wrote but I never receive his letter.

However, I received the following separate surprise not from the administrative assistance to the Bishop.

Diocese of Michigan
4800 Woodward Avenue
August 12, 1988

Dear Ceesay,
This will acknowledge receipt of your note dated July 27, 1988 to Bishop McGehee requesting more funding for your studies. The Bishop is vacationing in England and will return to the office September 6, 1988, at which time he will receive your correspondence.
In the meantime, I refer you to previous letters written this summer concerning your finances. The most recent of which is the letter dated July 28, 19888 from Hugh White informing you that the Episcopal Diocese of Michigan does not have the ability to raise any more funds for your continued support.
Hope you are able to re-think your situation and work towards another goal that will not only give you satisfaction, but also help others in need. You have come too far and your spirit is too great to give up completely.
I urge you to find some one there who will be able to assist you in the getting on with your life. You do remain in the thoughts and prayers of the people of Diocese of Michigan. Peace.

Mrs. Sheila Gardner
Administrative Assistance
To the Bishop

The raw truth was that, for many of my friends interested in my struggles, their participation ended with my decision not to wait for the ruling of the INS Appeal Board. I have always believed that God's ways were the best solutions.

The waxing and waning of interest plus the fact that distance makes the heart fonder helped Richard Smith in landing his final knock out blows to my cause at this crucial moment in my life.

I certainly forgive him and hope that the outcome, as it is today, will let him know he was no God and faith and hard work can indeed overcome the most difficult challenge one may be faced with in a given moment in time

The core outcome of all these were that I found myself totally marooned, like Robinson Crusoe, in tiny Montserrat which only God and very few people or organizations to turn to for help.

I again refused to allow this hillock God placed on my way to stop my journey. I had faith in God, hard work and the goodness of man. I swallowed my pride and made a lasting ditch attempt, after offering prayers, for God to be on my side, to contact the committee.

I knew a lot of them cared and that time might turn the tide to my favour. I could not nor would I accept that my good friends and foot solders at the Diocese

of Michigan would throw me to the wolves as easily as they it occurred. There were friends and good Christians who struggled and fought along my side all those trying years to help me realize my goal. What has Richard Smith, my Brutus told the Committee?
Why would they not have patients knowing that we are not far from the end of the road? And the triumph of giving and receiving would have taken happen for the villagers. I dispatched the following.

School of Medicine
American University
Of the Caribbean
Plymouth, Montserrat
West Indies

Dear Support Committee,
The suspension of your aid for my studies at the above university was brought to my attention by your December 28, 1987 and July 28, 1988 letters, which were duly received.
They are humbling notes by special friends of good will. Suffice it to say the loss of confidence of such special friends is indeed agonizing albeit challenging.
For me it was God's dictum and in humanistic terms a simple misfortune and coup de grace of a permanent festering sore. It marks another sad pivotal stage in my life and experience.

I owe to all of you profound gratitude and highest regards for the noble deed. The money sent has been paid to the school to fulfill the intention of the Church and Christ-like donors.

Please tell your envoy, Richard Smith, that the shouts and inanimate discussions and anger he displayed when we met were all a burst of caring and his desire for me to get something good out of the venture. I thank him but sadden that he took back wrong information and impression to the support Committee.

Hence, the untimely decision has not only compromised and compounded my problems but made it very complicated. God's will has it that we are healed by our strive and made stronger by faith in Him and our sufferings will be painless.

I will believe that God love all of us and be assured that I will not let you down. All of you sought to be Christ like and have opened your arms and hearts to me. We are all God's children and I have no better friends than you.

I will surely continue the struggle to the end. Thanks for letting me touch the core of your hearts. May God continue to be our guide in todays light and tomorrow's darkness. Again all of you have my admiration and respect.

My family is greatly indebted to you. I will do all I can to bring joy to my country and your hearts. I will look for solutions and do ask for your sincere

prayers. Thanks a million and keep in touch.
Goodbye for now.
Yours Sincerely
Alhasan S. Ceesay

This letter and many more fell on deaf ears. Some wrote to say how unduly influenced the committee was by Richard Smith's negative report and others expressed the feeling that the Church has disappointed me.
Needless to say my goal suffered further delays under the circumstances as I worried more about my dwindling finances and the state of my family in the Gambia. However, I never lost faith or direction towards my goal.
I sent appeal letters to anyone, except the Diocese of Michigan, that I thought would reciprocate kindly upon hearing my plight. Among these was Dr. Nelson Herron, a friend and former colleague at Alpena Community College in Michigan. He wasted no time in recruiting interested friends like Ms. Deirdre O'Leary, of Dublin, Ireland.

They sent me $400 and contacted the Medical Missionaries of May in Drogfield, Ireland seeking assistance for me. The Mission responded favourably as can be seen in the following letter to Ms. O'Leary.

Dudou Ceesay, in green, with family

Dear Deirdre,

In reference to our telephone call of last evening, I am happy on behalf of Medical Missionaries of May (M.M.M.) to enclose a check for IR500.00 towards Alhasan Ceesay's final year medical fees.

I hope and pray that he will be successful in his exams. May his years as a doctor in his country of the Gambia be fruitful and rewarding for him and his people.

Thanks for your concern for him and his many difficulties and wishing you all the very best. With kindness regards and with every good wish.

Yours Sincerely

Sr. Rosemarry Mohan, MMM

Central Business administration

God has His own ways of solving the impossible moments, which are incomprehensible to man. Help in small amounts continued to reach me from Mrs. Lois R. Leonard, Judge and Mrs. Viola S. Glennie, Dr. Charles T. Egli, Mr. Cloyd Ramsey, Mr. & Mrs. Bill Johnson of Birmingham, Michigan and many more who wish to remain anonymous donors. Despite all these inputs my financial obligation to the Medical School could not be met because of an increase in tuition fees. The donations amounted to drop in the bucket with regards to what I owed the medical school, rent, and student permit fees to the government of Montserrat.

I tittered upon the brink of starvation. I got my meals by picking fruit and berries from nearby hills. My over abundant pride made it impossible for me to beg for food from the street or from the students. The weight of the burden became unbearable to make breakdown and lost my guard when I revealed my state one of the very reliable group of students. Rodney G. Carter, being one of them, was moved to tears and offered me whatever food was left over in his refrigerator and pantry.

We became great friends and he has since become one of my advocates and had spoken to lots of people in Alabama in an effort to raise more funds for my studies at the American University of the Caribbean

Aside from this, he helped me type all my correspondence to various organizations, individuals, Embassies around the world and part of manuscript when he was not studying. My deepest appreciation goes to this kind human being with great concern for needy people.

My spirit never waned. Only my body started to shrivel and to give up for lack of rest and food. I lost tremendous weight and looked like a living ghost among the students.

I became a feather of less than forty kilograms that avoided strong winds and walked near walls during storms to avoid being swept away into the Ocean. Things got worse when money stopped trickling down.

I no longer could pay for rent, light bills or buy gas to cook with. William Ryan, my landlord turned out to be a kind and exceptional being, felt sorry that I had to undergo such brutal hardship away from home. He empathized with me know all that had transpired in my case since the suspension of my grant by my Detroit sponsors.

Willie Ryan assured me that I could stay as long as I needed and pay him whenever I have money or working at one of the hospital somewhere. In addition to this benevolent act he would once on a while bring food to me when it seemed to him that I have not had food for days.

Mr. Willie Ryan is my Montserrat just as Gayle Baumgartner was to me during hurricane Hugo. He has always been generous and kind to me. I look forward to the day I can reciprocate to him and his family for kindness rendered me.

Not many in Montserrat bestrode such generosity to me. In my experience, when it rains, that is when I get woes, it pours and does so with vengeance and incessantly. My life looked like an endless struck or string of bad news upon bad news.

Coming to think about it; who would have expected the Ceesay Support Committee to be so easily bamboozled by some one seemingly from the South, who in the first place was not in support of my leaving the USA for the Caribbean.

With these roadblocks the Registrar, Mrs. Mary Rose Tuit (bless her heart) assisted me by releasing the following letter to potential contributors or donors to help alleviate my financial debts at the America University of the Caribbean.

America University of the Caribbean
School of Medicine
Plymouth, Montserrat
West Indies

TO WHOM IT MAY CONCERN

Mr. Alhasan S. Ceesay, student number 24026, is a student at the American university of the Caribbean School of Medicine, situated in Momtserrat West Indies.
The school is listed in the Directory of the World Health Organizations (WHO). This student is in need of financial assistance to enable him complete his forth and fifth semesters at the School.
The tuition fees for a semester now is $4600.00
Any courtesies extended to him will be greatly appreciated by the administration of this Institution.
Respectfully
Mrs. Mary Rose Tuit
Registrar

The school failing to receive any payment in my behalf made the administration and Finance office pursue me with constant reminders that my tuition payment deadline had long passed.

Finally, on October 12, 1988, I was asked to see the registrar no later than 4.00 P. M. that day. I went with full knowledge of what was about to befall me. I was told that the school had waited patiently and long enough and that no substantial payments were made in my behalf.

In view of this I was advised and instructed to take a leave of absence from the university and try to raise the money for the rest of my studies at the medical school.

With a leaden heart, I spoke to the Dean about my problems and other friendly faculty and I was advised no differently. I should have known that the Registrar was just an escape goat in the whole affair. Anyhow, I thought it senseless to have to stop schooling in the middle of the semester.

If allowed to complete the term I would only have to attend the next semester to complete my basic sciences.

I went home and thought through about it and then concluded that perhaps explaining my situation to Dr. Paul Tien, owner and president of the university, in a desperate last minute ditch might lead to some type of reprieve if not a deferment of payments or new scheduling of payments.

He hopelessness of the situation was such that *wrote* the following with my tears to Dr. Tien.

American University of the Caribbean
School of Medicine
Plymouth, Montserrat
West Indies

Dear Dr. Tien,
Most likely my situation has been brought to your attention. I will be most grateful if you would kindly grant me audience to explain the cause of the delay in my payments.
Briefly, I lost my original sponsors in early part of the year but was able to recently get the Catholic Mission in New York to take over sponsorship the rest of my studies at the America University of the Caribbean.
This has just been recently approved and they promised to send an initial payment of $4500.00 within the next fortnight for me to pay some of my outstanding Bills at the school.
Also, I have just received my application forms from the World Health Organization that has been completed and sent to Geneva. The fellowship will cover the entire cost at this school and clinical rotations.
Meanwhile, most of the embassies I contacted have promised to help me upon consultation with their home based offices. In view of these developments I

am kindly pleading that you give me 45 days extension on my payments. Again, I sincerely regret the delay and do promised to continue to make certain that such delays never happen again. Greetings and I am waiting anxiously waiting and looking forward to your kind considerations in this matter.
Sincerely
Alhasan S. Ceesay (4026)

Dr. Paul Tien was a forthright man and he granted me the audience I requested. We met and discussed my case thoroughly and I left that meeting with the impression that he would let me finish the current semester but may not be allowed to register for the next semester if no money appeared.
Two weeks later the Catholic Mission's promise failed to materialize because someone told them of the difficulties I had with previous sponsors from Michigan.
Whoever spoke to the Catholic Mission got to Dr. Tien for I shortly there after received the following thunderbolt memo from him in a memorandum directed to, copied to the registrar and the staff.
It simply said, "We inform you that you will have to leave the school if all outstanding payments to the American University School are not paid by November 18, 1988."

By now I have weathered many thunder storms in my life but I have to admit this was the mother of them all and this bombshell did more than ruffle my feathers. My plight magnified many fold.

If I leave where would I head? I was not able to return to USA nor was it possible for me to return to the Gambia at the time. It was too close to my asylum fight that they would not be willing to look the other way.

Montserrat was not a place to be stranded for help was certainly not going to come from a small poor island nation like it. My having told school officials the risk I would be at if were not allowed to finish my education until the promises show up made them worry more for fear that I may after all not be able to get help with the payments needed to clear the outstanding bills.

The school was not going to continue with the build up of unpaid bills surrounded by uncertainty that help may not surface sooner. My fighting spirit was rekindled and I fought back with the only means at my disposal, my mind, pen and paper.

I wrote endless letters to America, Britain, France, Canada, Russia, Saudi Arabia, United Emirates, Japan and numerous other countries embassies appealing for assistance to complete my medical training. I emphasized the need to help me out of my precarious state my standing was at AUC in Montserrat.

The saying that, "A drowning man will hang onto any straw for dear life" Was very true in my case. I would write to any name or organization suggested to me. For some reason I was confident that Britain, Canada, France USA or Japan would come to my rescue.

Why? I guess it was just a hunch and out of admiration for these countries and their stand against injustice and currently having done a lot for people in Africa.

Initial responses from the British, American, and Canadian Embassies suggested that I write to their counter part embassies based in the Gambia for these administers assistance program available to the Gambian national.

It dashed all my hope of getting help as long as it had to involve Gambia or emissaries located in the Gambia.

If the Gambia were able to influence the state department as the ambassador did in my asylum case, what would it not do with people next door and in the Gambia?

Nonetheless, the embassies wished me good luck in my search for financial relief and continuance of my medical education. The replies were copied to their respective offices in the Gambia. The Japanese embassy said it was unable to help at that moment. Meanwhile the medical school campus reeled with the news of my financial plight and the termination of my schooling until when I can pay up all

outstanding bills to the American University of the Caribbean.
The students rallied and collected donations in my behalf without my knowing for fear that I will feel obliged to them or feel pity for myself. I will never ever forget their kindness especially Robert G. Carter, Luis Shone, Mohamed Saleh, and Nahil who spear headed the whole affair in my behalf with tact and respect.
With the donation I bought food and reduced a portion of the outstanding bills. It neither dented the amount I owed the school nor gave me leeway to continue my schooling for that semester. I continued to be embattled by unforeseen events while time flies. I kept on pleading for help worldwide.
Finally I met the Dean and accepted to take a leave of absence effective from October 12, 1988 to January 1989 with hope that enough money would be raised to allow me to register for the upcoming semester.
January 1989 has now become the new deadline but I cannot attend classes until then and only if all outstanding bills were paid by registration day. Worse, I have to repeat the fourth semester all over as it was going to be erased from the record that I attended it.None of the exams I took during the said forth semester were acceptable for recording because of none payment of tuition fees.
I left the Dean's office with tears welling uncontrollably down my cheeks. What a life! I said

to myself. I thank God for the challenge and asked for His guidance. The students felt very sorry and sad for me and feared the worst.

There were those who seriously believed that I might end up taking my life because of the effect of series of disappointments from organization, churches and governments. Hence the students made certain that someone was around me most of the time chatting or bringing notes for me to copy and read ahead of the coming semester.

They reassured me that some have written to their parents requesting money earmarked for me to lighten my burden. Yes, the human heart is good for all these acts of kindness were done without my knowing them taking place on my behalf. They certainly did their utmost in trying to enlighten and lighten my spirit.

The propensity to sudden roadblocks, some how, seem to be the ordain way for me.

Nonetheless friends like Mr. & Mrs. Bill Johnson of Birmingham, Michigan, Lois R. Leonard, Ferry Burns, Cloyd Ramsey and Nelson Herron among others became very special as they brought cheers to my life and accorded me all the moral and financial support they could give at the time.

Here are the synapses of the angels who made life bearable foe me the time. Jerry Burns and I met through a mutual friend and had since then built up a very unique friendship. He is a nurse and former Peace Corp who served in Niger during the John F.

Kennedy era. He fell in love with Niger and her people who inundated with kindness.

He liked their culture and systems, their good nature and hard working of the Niger Fulas. He developed strong bond with the Niger people. Never did two have similar philosophies, religious tolerance, and political views than he and I. We are just like twins living in distant lands both with nursing backgrounds and are committed to being our brother/sister's keeper.

We always had lively and cheerful meetings in which we discuss trends and shifts of values, global politics, governments, schools and at times about as flimsy as the decadence one sees at certain parts of Detroit' Cass corridor. He helped relentlessly to lighten my plight and we remain in contact to today.

Mr. & Mrs. William (Bill) J. Johnson came to my sphere through their son Bill Johnson, jr. who was at the time a class mate of mine at Wayne State University in Detroit. There an unbelievable bond of friendship developed between Bill jr. and I. Biochemistry graduate level was not a forum where most make friends. But for Bill jr. and I it started here and never faded. My forty-third-birth day was just two weeks and because of it Bill calls me the grand daddy of the class.

I was the oldest and poorest in that class and very soon our classmates relaxed about my age. The Johnson's were very kind and friendly people and cared a lot about plight of others. Bill Jr. was intelligent, gentle, compassionate and alert to current affairs.

Come my birthday he crowned the occasion with a special gift. He met me at school and in his modest and gentle way quietly and simply said, "Please accept this little token to remember your day with." I was happy and grateful for we had only casually known each other less than a month and here was Bill sharing my day as he showers it with kindness. The moment and graciousness of the act remained indelibly etched in my mind to today.

Bill works part time for a mining company and anted school on part time bases. Our conversations ranged from the spiraling downward education, politics, the developing world of Africa, people's basic needs and how to meet these to bring relief to recipients.

We believing improving the lives of others, in due course, improve our own. Upon learning about my difficulties at the American university of the Caribbean Bill Johnson, Jr rallied to assist me in my endeavors.

His parents generously donated one thousand dollars in addition to the two advanced donations of five hundred dollars Bill just sent me. The Johnson's continued to touch my heart with tender hearts of generosity and sharing I will never forget.

I visited the family few days before heading for Montserrat during which time they spoiled with gifts and dinner fit for a king. They tried to stuff me so as to put some pad of fat on my skeletal frame.

It goes without doubts that I engorged myself to the ears and yet remained the featherweight I came in with.

Most of the discussion centred on my plight with the Gambia, my determination to over come it and return as positive contributor to the Gambia.

They told of having wonderful time and had lots of friends during their diplomatic tenure in Africa.

It is William J. Johnson's believe that the third world needed more aid from America then been forthcoming in recent times.

I left them with full appreciation of the humane concerns for other and the wish to help the developing world. Bill Jr's father Mr. William J. Johnson was U.S. Ambassador to Kenya during the Kennedy presidency. He too fell in love with Africa. He and lovely wife Majorette Johnson made many return trips to Kenya and other neighboring African states. Hence, I was family from day one of our meeting to new.

Despite the fact that I have been away from the USA for years we still write to each other and they continued helping me find solutions to the seemingly endless financial woes that beset my life and educational pursuits.

Hence, when AUC threatened to end my schooling, it was through kind contributions of the Johnsons' that helped pay an outstanding bill of three thousand dollars to the American University of the Caribbean school of Medicine. This came in at the nick of time or at very critical moment for me in my adventure to gain medical education and return to serve the Gambia.

AUC was taken by surprise in manner I cleared all outstanding bills in time to reregister for the forth semester I lost during the financial fiasco of 1988/89 academic year for the basic medical sciences courses.

Both AUC and I send a thank you note to the William Johnson and family for magnanimity and kindness shown by their helping out at the school. Praises be God's for letting such kind people come to my rescue at the nick of time when everything looked hopelessly bleak.

Germane to my survival were insistence that failure be not the last chapter in the saga of my experience and that the Gambia be the benefactor in all these mesh, which will remain in my mind for some time. The most rewarding element was the steadfastness with which my friends backed my seemingly never-ending stride towards the Doctor of Medicine degree (MD).

Amongst these were long time friend and colleague at Alpena Community College (1967 – 69) in Michigan Nelson Herron, who became unique friend since we met at Alpena. Upon hearing about decision of AUC regarding my medical training, Nelson Herron, out of kindness and concern for me, voluntarily lent me another $4600.00 to reduce the huge bill I then owe the school and to advance towards my registration fees.

Without these inputs from the Johnsons and Nelson Herron my medical education/training at AUC would have come to an abrupt nose dive for oblivion or catastrophic end as envisioned by Richard Smith and his followers. No matter how brilliant one is, going through uphill challenges the way I had was, to say the least, frustrating, challenging, and worse way to have to go through competitive medical school in such a fashion. I was never sure if my registration would be completed, cancelled or where the next penny was going to come from to help me finish my schooling.

By this time my pride gave way and I turned into a beggar as I had very little choice or control over events that kept unfolding in my path. Like a mule leaden with bags of salt, I struggled under the yoke of poverty being buoyed only by constant surge of inextinguishable ambition to forge ahead for the Gambia and my fellow men.

To this were the phenomenal encouragements I received from Americans. Channing Poiock said, "The only good luck many great men ever had was being born with the ability and determination to overcome bad luck." My life at this stage had blossomed to one percent inspiration and ninety-nine percent perspirations.

Things were not relenting and I could not help my wife or parents back in the Gambia. Remember, our cultural norms and obligations made it obvious that a forty plus male should be able to care not only for himself but also for his aged parent and others, rather than being stuck in class at a desolate impoverish island like Montserrat in the West Indies.

Dr. Ceesay receiving UK Resident Permit from Dr. Angela J. Stull of Loydslaw Firm, Manchester, 2013

Bellow is samples of requests and replies that trickled by after a lengthy wait and hope of getting help.

World Health Organization
CH1211, Geneve 27, Suise
March 29, 1088

Dear Mr. Ceesay,
In reply to your letter of March 8,1988, we would inform that WHO fellowships can only be awarded at the request of the candidates' national Health Authority.
We would advise you, therefore, to write to the Gambia Ministry of Health asking to be nominated for such a fellowship.
You will receive the relevant application forms from the Ministry if they are willing to sponsor your candidature.
Yours Sincerely
Mrs. B. J. Amara
Fellowship Division of
Health Manpower development
This was sent after I told them my predicament with the Gambia. The Canadian version ran thus

Bureau Des Conseillers Technique
De La Cooperation Canadiene
P. 3373, Dakar, Senegal
December 5, 1988

Dear Sir,

This is to acknowledge receipt of your letter of September 21, regarding a scholarship from the Canadian International Development Agency. The number of scholarships available is extremely limited and all applications are coordinated through the Ministry of Education of the Gambia, North American scholarships.

Thus we suggest that you contact the Ministry in Banjul for information on current scholarship programs.

Thank you for your interest in studies in Canada.
Yours sincerely
Alime touzim
Coordinator Des bourses ACDI

The only reply that shaded light of hope was from the British High Commission in Banjul, the Gambia of all places. Upon getting my letter the staff of the Commission got in touch with the Gambian authorities and after softening things, sent me the following response.

British High Commission
P.O. Box 507, Banjul
The Gambia, West Africa
November 29, 1988

Dear Mr. Ceesay,

The High commission has asked me to thank you for your letter of September 22, 1988, which did not arrive here until November 17, 1988.
We were sorry to hear your financial predicaments. But unfortunately we are unable to help you as scholarships scheme is run as government to government basis only. In other words, you would need to receive official backing from the government of the Gambia before we may consider sponsoring you. However we have spoken to the Ministry of Health. I do hope that you were able to find a sponsor in time.
Yours Sincerely
Paul Chart

These and many more like in kind from world embassies and countries left one thing clear to me that destiny is not a matter of chance it is a unique question of one's choice.
And medicine is my committed choice for which I am willing to continue the struggle to the day I get the MD degree and eventual return to serve the Gambia as a dedicated physician.
I have always been convinced that all good things start in difficulty before becoming easy and rewarding.
I again, in desperation, lunched another barrage of appeals and even contacted Mr. Paul Chart at the British High Commission in Banjul as if though his last letter of November 29, 1988 never reached me.

Paul replied reiterating reasons in this previous letter and made it clear that the High Commission will not sponsor me. He concluded by saying, "However, I have taken the liberty of mentioning your predicament to Dr. Hatib Njie, Director of Medical services at the Department of Health in Banjul, in hope that he may be able to suggest a solution to your problems."

Here you have it. The Pandora's box opened by Paul Chart's discussion of the matter with the Director was the following:

Medical and Health Department
Medical Headquarters
Banjul, The Gambia
February 21, 1989
Reference MED/109

RE: application for sponsorship
Dear Mr. Ceesay
I write to inform you that Permanent Secretary Management Office is the person in charge of training at home and abroad. You may therefore apply directly to him for sponsorship. Send your application to him as quickly as possible.
Yours Sincerely,
Signed for Director
Medical services
The Gambia

At this juncture small opportunities like this one were not left alone or unexplored. I at the back of my mind was expecting nothing to come out from the Gambia. However I wasted no time and prepared an application with the following letters of support from various staff and current Dean of Medicine at the American University of the Caribbean School of Medicine in Montserrat, West Indies. Here are a few of the letters sent along with my application.

American University of the Caribbean
P.O. Box 400
Plymouth, Montserrat
West Indies
March 23, 1989

TO WHOM IT MAY CONCERN

Mr. Alhasan Ceesay has requested that I write a letter in support of his request for financial aid in completing his medical training. I have known Mr. Ceesay for several years as his professor in Physiology and as the Dean of the Medical sciences. Mr. Ceesay is a very personable and articulate man who interacts well with both the faculty and his classmates. He is a hard working student who is totally dedicated to becoming a physician and practicing medicine in the Gambia.
Thus far Mr. Ceesay has had to endure major financial problems in his pursuit of a medical

degree. I feel Mr. Ceesay is very deserving of financial support for the remainder of his training and will become a compassionate, competent and caring physician for his people.
Sincerely
Robert J. Chetok, PhD
Professor of Physiology
Dean of Medical Sciences

Another letter was from. Dr. D. E. Vonwomer, my professor of Pathology and retired former Dean of the College of Medicine, AUC.

American University of the Caribbean
P. O. Box 400
Plymouth, Montserrat
West Indies
March 25, 1989

TO WHOM IT MAY CONCERN

Mr. Alhasan Ceesay has asked me for a letter supporting his application for financial support for the remainder of his medical schooling.
Mr. Ceesay is a hard working student and who spends many hours preparing him to become a physician.
He is highly motivated and spends most of the hours of his day studying so be might become a physician to serve the people of the Gambia.

Mr. Ceesay is extremely consciencious, very diligent in his work, and is also very pleasant cooperative young man. He is well liked by his fellow students and his professors and gets along well with all.
This young man has a very critical financial problem. And he needs financial support to continue the last half of his medical school curriculum.
I hope it is possible for someone to assist this dedicated man so he will be able to return to his country and practice medicine.
Sincerely
D. E. Vanwormer, MD
Professor of Pathology
Advisor

The final addendum from the American University of the Caribbean to be sent to the Gambia was a note from the Registrar of the university, Mrs. Mary R. Tuit, Who sent the following.
American University of the Caribbean
School of Medicine
Plymouth, Montserrat
West Indies

RE: Application for financial Assistance

Mr. Ceesay is 5th semester student at the American university of the Caribbean School of Medicine. He will finish basic sciences in August 1989.

Mr. Ceesay is expected to take up clinical assignments at the East borne District General Hospital, England coming September 1989.

The administration of the school will be grateful if you will facilitate financially his continuance of his studies. Any further courtesies extended to him will be greatly appreciated. Clinical in England will cost another $6450 per semester.

See enclosed breakdown of payments.

Respectfully

Mary R. Tuit

Registrar

These and lot more from my professors at the university were packaged and sent registered mail to the Permanent Secretary, Personnel Management, Banjul, the Gambia, as advised by the Director of Health's letter of February 12, 1989.

The school staffs were relieved and confident the financial burden would soon become history and be off my shoulders since to their expectation the letters of support were going to be the barometer of my progress and for the scholarship committee in the Gambia to look at in making final decision on my appeal.

Knowing what I knew and have gone through from the hands of the Gambia government, I just prayed for the reversal of tides in my favour so that I can move forward with my objective of serving the Gambians.

My fears and expectations were brought to light three months later when I received the following reply from an official in behalf of the Permanent Secretary, Personnel Management Office. Here is the full text of that heart-wrenching missive in reply to my request for financial assistance at a crucial stage of my medical training.

Personnel Management Office
The Quadrangle, Banjul
The Gambia
West Africa
June 13, 1989

EST/X811E/TEMP/C82

REQUEST FOR SPONSORSHIP TO UNDERTAKE A
MEDICAL DEGREE: MR. ALHASAN S. CEESAY

I wish to acknowledge receipt of your letter dated March 28, 1989, in which you requested this office to seek assistance on your behalf from the British government in the form of scholarship award, so as to enable you to complete your medical degree at the American University of the Caribbean School of Medicine.
In this regard I am directed to inform you that our 1989/90 overseas Development Training Program has been finalized and it is therefore too late to make any provisions for you in the aforementioned

program. Sorry for our inability to be of much help to you in this circumstance.
Sincerely,
L.T. Jorbateh
For Permanent Secretary

If I had not applied prior to writing then doubts wound continue to linger between the Gambia Ministry of Health and I. I had prior to applying for financial assistance asked the Director if the said Overseas Development Program was then still available. I was told by the Director to send my application quickly for he had had a word with the Permanent Secretary of the Personnel Management Office.

Anyhow, if adversity reveals genius now was the time for something to happen for me. I had already been assigned to a hospital for my clinical training and now the last straw of hope and source of financial relief I expected slipped by in thin air. Like before, I accepted my fate and said, "God I know you care and love me and you will help me solve this difficult hillock. No one can stand the assault of sustained challenges.

I will endure as ordained by your wish." Louisa May Alcott said, "Far away there in the sunshine are my highest aspirations. I may not reach them, but I can look up and see their beauty, believe in them and try to follow where they lead."

Is it not true that obstacles are those frightful things we see when we take our eyes off our goals? No hillock or crisis like this development will ruffle my feathers.

I continued to swim towards my ship, instead of waiting for it to come to me. I braced up again and wrote several letters and asked friends to write in my behalf to any organization or government they think would come to my assistance for the medical degree meant a lot not only for me but the villager whom I intend to provide modern affordable medicines.

In this desperate state of my life, Jacob Riis' statement said it best for me. He said, "When nothing seem to help, I go and look at the stonecutter hammering away at his rock perchance a hundred times without as much a crack showing in it. Yet, at the hundred and first blow it will split into two, and I know it was not that blow that did it, but all that had gone before." I am another stonecutter, mine comprises of humans, the most harden element on earth, so to speak, that I will be relentless with my unyielding rock, the MD degree, for my people, until I receive the right to practice in Gambia and Africa.

Each day is a specific thrill that leads to that exhilarating moment of victory for Gambia and mankind. It is a hard march toward the day I will be able to serve the Gambia as a physician.

I feel favoured, if not blessed, having Mrs. Lois R. Leonard on my side. I became her potage when she came to discover my strength, perseverance, and endurance to face very difficult challenges.

She was the only member of the remaining Ceesay Support Committee that did not throw the towel at my face, present at the backstabbing meeting held while my friends Richard castigated me.

Lois shared my agonies and ecstasy as events unfolded during my stay in Montserrat, West Indies. She and a few others were source of relief and blessings to me. Lois Leonard would once on a while send me fifty dollars to put food into my dying body held by skeletal frame that refuses to be dismembered by starvation.

Upon hearing about my assignment do clinical rotation at Eat Borne she rallied friends and collected seven thousand dollars to help me start my clinical clerkship. Unfortunately the money had to be applied to clear unpaid past bills I owe the school.

The university would not let me move without the remaining financial bill being cleared. This development adversely affected my classes for that semester. However, I remained obliged to Lois Leonard even though she was no longer able to help since she had exhausted all resources and contacts available to her, which she lamented. On hindsight had the Gambia not fought back my clinical clerkship would not have been delayed or postponed to September 1990 the very least cost went higher as tuition was increase to $4600 a semester.

Henry Forth said, "Failure is the opportunity to begin again more intelligently." So like Abraham Lincoln who said, "I will do the best I know how, the very best I can, and I mean to keep on doing it to the end. If the end brings me out all right, what is said against me will not amount to anything.

If the end brings me out wrong, then ten angels swearing I was right would make no difference."

Miss Famatanding Ceesay, daughter

Chapter 29
Welcome to United States:Texas

Let our narration detour in time to bring other events I passed through before the above developments. The kaleidoscope, which followed hurricane Hugo, only multiplied the whirlwinds of worries that were running through my head.

I had just finished three courses and had taken the last of nine exams I was assigned and needed $18,000 us dollars to enable me start the clinical phase after my last semester at the Texas Campus. A void followed despite a series of telephone call to would be sympathetic persons in the USA and Canada.

I waited for days and weeks and nothing seem to materialize to allow me start the clinical clerkship after Texas. On December 19, 1989, Rudolf Kurt and his wife Sophie Kurt invited me for a chat and lunch with them. This day was another pivotal one in the saga of my life.

After lunch and a detailed history of my case, these aged German couple, turned events around for a good start in my career. As reneged will have it, one thing lead to another until when, to my delightful surprise, Rudolf and Wife Sophie Kurt, revealed that they have agreed to lend me $6000.00 (six thousand dollars!) to help me start my clinical studies in England.

Rudolf went cross and brought a checkbook and made two separate checks of three thousand dollars each to the American University of the Caribbean. One was to be applied toward completing the outstanding tuition bills and the other to be used directly towards my clinical training in the United Kingdom.

I, in utter disbelieve shrouded with gratitude, hugged and thanked them several times and promised them that they will never regret helping me.

I was released to go and I ran from the condominium to the American University of the Caribbean financial officer, Mr. Soong, supervising the renovation of the campus. I made the payments to the University's account at the Barclays Bank down town Plymouth and he issued receipts to that effect and cleared my outstanding bills with the university.

Mr. Soong then called Texas to AUC allow me join the students at Wayland Baptist University where AUC is piggy bagging the after effect of hurricane Hugo, in Plainview.

The following letter and events after them signaled some relief in my blighted life. Some earlier appeals for sponsorship yielded enough to allow me start arranging for a visa to travel to the United States to complete my basic medical sciences.

Two days after I made those payments and for some reason the owner and president of the American University, Dr. Paul Tien, showed up on campus with engineers to estimate the cost of rebuilding the university. I wasted no time bringing my newfound luck to light and went to meet him as soon as friends told me of his being in the Island.

I requested that he add his weight to my attempt to secure a visa from the American Consulate at Antigua for me to travel to Texas and join the rest of the students at the campus of Wayland Baptist University in Plainview.

He was very happy to oblige. When he finished he school my hands and said, "Ceesay, you are a good fighter. You have my respect and good luck in your clinical training." This was what he told the US emissary:

American University of the Caribbean
School of Medicine
P.O. Box 400
Plymouth, Montserrat
December 20, 1989

Consulate
Visa Section
U. S. Embassy
Antigua, West Indies

Dear Sir,

This is to inform you that I support the request for a visa application made by Alhasan S. Ceesay.

Mr. Ceesay is a student of the American University of the Caribbean.

He wishes to enter the United States in other to take the last classes of the basic sciences before proceeding to England for his clinical experience. Upon completing his residency program, he will return to practice medicine in the Gambia. All assistance to him to enable him complete his studies would be most welcomed. Thank you for your help in this matter.

Sincerely
Dr. Paul Tien
American Univ. of the Caribbean

The following day I bravely held onto my letters and flew to Antigua and reported at the visa section of the U. S. Embassy 8.00 A.M the next morning.

I was among first to be interviewed and I imaged smiling gleefully for a visa had been granted and affixed on my passport.

I can now join my colleagues four months after hurricane Hugo and very laborious work at the condominiums. I boarded TWA and headed once more for the United States of America. This time I landed in Miami International Airport in Florida and took a shuttle flight to Lubbock airport in Texas.

I was expecting to meet Dr. Steve Deschner at this Airport but he failed to turn up because of changes in his scheduled lectures and that of my flight. This posed no difficulty for me, having been in America as long as I did.

I just went to the bus stand and took the one marked Plainview. I arrived at the Wayland Baptist University in Plainview, where the American university of the Caribbean had temporaly relocated after hurricane Hugo. I lodged with a student until the next day when I completed the formalities of registering for my last basic medical science courses. The office used money lent to me by the Kurts of Montserrat to cover areas I thought had been taken care off.

The officer insisted that the previous semester was not fully covered even though I showed that three thousand us dollars was paid in Montserrat. This stalemate put me back into square one and only worst I had no one to turn to in Texas except the Almighty God.

I still feel cheated by AUC for having to find that my payments were not regularized to erase the outstanding bill on record. The financial nightmare of my life surfaced at a very difficult transition time for me. Again, I accepted that one must whittle today for a rewarding tomorrow.

All that mattered was for work and struggle to go on, the curse endured, hope still lives and that my dream shall never die. I am part of all that I have endured and met. I will strive to seek, to find and never yield to challenge. I made a concerted effort to visit churches and tell whomever I meet on the way what my plight was and that I desperately needed a loan to help me finish my medical education.

It was during one of these trips that I came across an angel from the blue, in the body of Rev. Mark D. Meyer. He was then in charge of St. Mark's Episcopal Church on 710 Joliet Street, Plainview, Texas.

I found him at the entrance of St. Mark's Church just about to leave to minister to an old man, a member of the Parish who was under the weather. One look at my faced made him decide to listen to my narrative and about the urgency of it.

He expressed dismay at the fact that I was left stranded for four months in tiny Montserrat hopelessly destroyed by hurricane Hugo. He could not believe the heartlessness of not being evacuated along with the American students.

The American University of the Caribbean just abandoned me to find my way out of Montserrat while the American Consulate flew American and Canadian students back to America.

The end result of the short conversation was an extensive interview about my goal and utilization of my training was an invitation with his Sunday service group on the following Sunday.

He revealed, during our meeting, that he too was a medical aspirant but changed his vocation to the Priesthood before getting too far into the art of Medicine He also said his father was a doctor and a member of the board of the American Medical association.

My eyes opened widely hearing that I now have someone interested in me whose father's recommendation to any medical school would give weight for consideration by admission committees. I therein and then prayed silently for God's help so that this angel of His would heed my plight.

Rev. Mark D. Meyer turned a God sent relief to my challenge. He spoke to his congregation and came to Wayland Baptist University and made a down payment of $4200 (four thousand two hundred us dollars) in my name as a loan.

He contributed one thousand and the rest came from Church funds. Another member of the church, Mr. John Morse gave $500 as a personal gift to me. Rev. Mark D. Meyer's efforts did not end here for as the year waned and my financial blight remained unbearable, he asked me to stay with him at his residence on 1409 Garland Street, Plainview, Texas. I stayed there with him until it was time for me to proceed to do my clinical clerkship in England. Through him I made a lot of friends in Plainview among who were Dr. Thomas Allen of Grace Presbyterian Church, Dr. Hoyt Huff of First Christian Church, Dr. & Mrs. Douglas E. Kopp and

(The Rt. Rev) Bishop Sam B. Hulsey, Bishop of the Episcopal Diocese of North West Texas at Lubbock, just to name a few of Christ's modern day disciples who came to my aid while I was in dire financial state in the last leg f my basic medical sciences.

In response to the overwhelming generosity and Christian stand these people took in my affairs I wrote the following note of appreciation for the uniqueness of their gesture towards me and for enabling me move forward in my aspiration to serve the Gambia as a physician.

In the mean time various small gifts kept pouring in to keep me happy. Many invited me to their homes to meet with their families or have some meal with them whenever convenient.

Plainview was my Texas and rev. Meyer my redeemer from earthly hell. We refer to each other as brother in Christ and humanity. He solicited help for me from groups like the Domestic and Foreign missionary Society of the Protestant Episcopal Church in the United States and numerous other church organizations in the USA and England. Between us we used to write more than twenty-five letters a day appealing for help to enable me meet my goal for the Gambian villagers. Rev. Mark D. Meyer and I have same objective in life, i.e. to seek piety, by having strong faith in God, to gain knowledge to better serve our fellow human being by providing hope and relief to those we may come across in this life and finally to live a simple human trail of love and commitment to peace and good will to all on earth. It entailed a life of sacrifice, devotion to our faith and commitment to move forward despite deterring challenges and roadblocks we may come across. Rev. Mark used to jokingly say to me, "Ceesay, if all Muslims were like you then the whole world would be one big Christian brotherhood."

This told more about our sense of oneness that a dictionary could define in a billion words closeness of two earthly creatures of God. Here is the letter I mentioned earlier on.

American University
C/O Wayland Baptist University
Plainview, Texas, USA

Dear editor and Friends,

Sometimes god has a way of stepping into our lives when we least expected it. Such was the state which Rev. Mark D. Meyer and I. He steeped forward at a critical time of my plights and was kind and generous also helpful to my mission to serve the Gambia as a physician.

Without further adieu, I humbly and most gratefully acknowledge the loan he got for me from his kind congregation and other interested persons in Plainview. Your kindness has touched me deeply and made me more determined to succeed and return to my country, the Gambia, in due course.

Rev. Mark D. Meyer and I have become good friends and brothers in Christ. I am most grateful to all of you for this continued contribution to the Gambian people.

Please convey our profound gratitude for this unique assistance to not only members of your church but to all those who one way or the other, in various gestures of generous acts, have helped to make my path a little bit easier to walk on.

You are very special to me and in the hearts of my villagers. I will certainly return to provide much needed modern medical service to the villages in the Gambia. We are indebted to all of you. Please come visit us.

The villagers are itching to meet you and serenade you for kindness and your willingness to share generously with us so as to bring hope and relief to people in rural Gambia.

Finally, God bless you and be rest assured that I will keep you informed of my progress wherever I am. Please continue to pray for my success and eventual return to serve my people in the smiling cost of the Gambia, West Africa. Cheers and regards to all
Your friend
Alhasan S. Ceesay
Gambian/AUC student

This letter ushered in more friends from far and wide of Texas. I had people asking me to meet with them as far away as Huston, Dallas and other heartland cities in Texas.

It was also while at Garland Street that our discussions vied onto my idea of a village clinic in the future with which to fulfill my dream of bringing modern medicine to the forgotten and neglected villager's health care needs.

Again, we went into full gear and wrote to hundreds of charity groups asking for ideas and assistance on how to get started on what would later be the present Manding Medical Centre at Njawara village, The Gambia, West Africa.

Most of the replies stress that only local organizations were eligible for possible funding and that most were already too committed to take on any other aspirants like my clinic.

These negative replies had a little dampening effect on our drive but we pushed on as hard as can be to raise funds for the future Manding Medical Centre. We did developed friendship with architectural group, L. James Robinson and Associates, located at 205 West 4th Street, Plainview, Texas, 790723, headed by Mr. L. James Robinson.

This friendly rapport led to the first architectural plan of Manding Medical Centre. We only altered few parts to suit the Gambian environment and the board and any who saw it had unanimously adopted the plan. The above made a unique hospital plan that would when completed will stand the test of time and will serve its intended purpose.

Time flew fast and soon came the most difficult event between two that have become one in spirit. My basic medical courses ended in July 1990 and arrangements were afoot for me to proceed to either Kinston Hospital, Kingston upon -Thames, or Essex County Hospital, Colchester, England by September 1990 to do my clinical clerkship.
The last week was very intense for both of us. Leaving for good or for a long time was unbearable. Rev. Mark D. Meyer had, like Mr. L.A. Bouvier, become the ideal friend and an honest person to turn to. We are totally devoted folks to our belief and causes and we care a lot about plight of the downtrodden of life.
Meanwhile, the American University of the Caribbean sent the following letter to Mrs. Mickey, Program Coordinator, Kingston Hospital informing her about my plans to do my clinical clerkship at their hospital.

American University of the Caribbean
School of Medicine
P. O. Box 400
Plymouth, Montserrat
West Indies July 14, 1990

Mrs. Mickey,
Program Coordinator
Kingston Hospital

Gals worthy Road
Kingston Upon Thames
Surry KT2 7BE
England, Uk

Dear Mrs. Mickey,

This letter is being sent on behalf of Alhasan Ceesay, a student of the American university of the Caribbean School of Medicine. Mr. Ceesay is a citizen of the Gambia and in other to obtain his visa to come to England the British Consulate requested a letter be sent from you stating that he has been accepted into your clinical program.

I have spoken with Dr. Youel in this regards and he has informed me that he will be assigning Mr. Ceesay to your program to begin on September 3, 1990. I have sent the student a letter to this effect to take to the consulate's office. However, they also require a letter directly from the hospital.

As the US visa will be expiring in July, at which time he will need to relocate to England, will you please send a letter as soon as possible to the British Consulate-General, Suit 2250, Dresser Tower, 601 Jefferson, Huston, Texas 77002, attention, Mrs. H. M. Tanks, British vice Consul.

We appreciate your assistance in this matter. May I also request that you send a copy of the letter for me to place it in Mr. Ceesay's file. Thank you.

Sincerely
Jackie R. Allen

Secretary to Liaison Official

Another letter dated September 1990 was sent to Essex County after an unforeseen delay in hearing from the British High Commission in Huston, Texas. It read,

American University of the Caribbean
School of Medicine, P. O. Box 400
Plymouth, Montserrat
September 6th 1990

Dear Dr. Peter R. Wilson,
Alhasan Ceesay has been assigned to begin clinical clerkship at Essex County Hospital, Colchester on October 8, 1990.
This is to certify that Mr. Ceesay is academically qualified and administratively approved to begin the clinical clerkship program at the American university of the Caribbean School of Medicine as a third year medical student in September 1990.
Signed: David Bruce Youel, MD
Dean Clinical Sciences
Robert Chertok, PhD
 Dean of Medicine Sciences
 I took this last with me to Huston and after a lengthy interview disproving allegation I choused England to emigrate instead of just doing my clinical. I made it very clear that had that been my

intention I will not select UK being already on American soil. The officer after few minutes of reflection concord and offered me student visa to attend Essex County Hospital's clinical program in Colchester, Essex, England in October 1990.

Gorgeous Fatou Koma Ceesay, Oldham, UK 2018

Chapter 30
England at Last Clinical Training 1990

I flew to the British Consulate at Huston, Texas to be interviewed for a visa to enter the United Kingdom to do my clinical clerkship at the Essex County Hospital in Colchester by October 8, 1990. No, my financial curse never left me.

It was a dragon that would show its head again and again while I was in England. Rev. Mark D. Meyer went with me up to Lubbock airport on the day of my travels to the UK. At Lubbock airport, we prayed and hugged each other, with eyes full of tears, several times before we could say our final goodbyes.

I left Huston with a student visa and boarded BA flight 0224 on the September 12, 1990 heading for Heathrow International Airport, London, England. I landed at Heathrow on Wednesday September 12, 1990.

My impression of England and her people never disappointed me. The people were friendly but much more business like. The immigration Officer received my document and placed a call to Essex County hospital to verify status as student with them.

This done a leave to remain in the U.K was stamped onto my passport and allowed to proceed to my final destination, Colchester. Arrangements were made for me to stay at a hotel call the George located at the High street down town Colchester, Essex County. The hotel staffs were very kind and helpful as they brought food from nearby restaurant because the hotel kitchen had closed for the night when I arrived at o1.35 a.m.

The following day at about 8.30 am I reported to Dr. Peter R. Wilson's office, clinical program director for the American university of the Caribbean, at Essex county Hospital in Colchester. I later on that day met Mrs. Penny West, a very kind lady, the program administrator for further briefing of our program and what was expected of us while in England.

There I met two other Americans ladies and two gentlemen students from previous classes at the American university of the Caribbean School of Medicine, who also came to do their clinical clerkship at Essex county Hospital.

I was moved from the hotel to flat 2 Kensington Court, 47 Roman Road, Colchester administered by the Pullars estate agents. We went through one week of orientation and familiarizing ourselves where about the shops and postal services, bus stations for the National Express services and many other things of interest in the city.

We were then issued schedules and units and department/ assignment to begin our clinical training. I was only able to pay for the first semester of the training because promises to help me finish failed to materialize.

This led Rev. Mark D. Meyer to lend me another $2000 (two thousand us dollars) on March 6, 1990 and again another personal loan of $900 (nine hundred us dollars) later.

These monies were deposited to the university in my name but the cost per semester was $4600 leaving me $1700 short of meeting my financial obligation to the school for the second semester at the clinics. It was during those frustrating moments that I decided to bite the bullet and called a long time Gambian friend of mine, Dr. Ebrahima M Samba, to come to my rescue.

This he did by promptly calling his bank in London and authorizing them to send me three thousand seven hundred pounds sterling loan to help me complete the semester. I received it with gratitude and humility. Praises be God's for only through Him have miracles been happening for me. Two weeks later the same bank sent another equal amount allotment from Dr. Samba.

In my acknowledgement letter I thanked Dr. Samba for the two disbursements and told him that the University had already debited them to my accounts to clear the outstanding bills.

Later that week the bank called and wrote to say they made a mistake by sending me the second allotment from Dr. Samba's account and that I should return the money forthwith.

At the time all monies sent to me had already been applied toward my fees at the American university

of the Caribbean. Dr. Ebrahima M Samba kindly intervened and blamed the bank for the mistake and let me now owe him Four thousand four hundred pounds sterling instead of the original approved three thousand seven hundred pound sterling.
No other Gambian would have acquiescence other than this angel friend of mine.
He proved to be true and true real friend in need and in good times. I will reimburse him all monies I owe him whenever my earnings improve. This saga allowed me to sail on through until November 11, 1991.
The bubble busted again. AUC threatened to throw me out of the program upon my failure to meet payment of the balance of my areas with the school. This treat lead Dr. Peter R. Wilson, Program Director for AUC at Essex County Hospital to intervene with the following letter to Dr. Bruce Youel, Dean of Clinical sciences for the American university of the Caribbean.

Colchester and North Essex
Postgraduate Center
Essex County Hospital
Colchester, Essex CO3 3NB

Dr. Bruce Yuoel
Dean of Clinical Sciences
American University of the Caribbean
April 24, 1991

Dear Dr. Youel

RE: Alhasan Ceesay

As Director of the AUC students in Colchester I take exceptions to the highhanded and unreasonable attitude in regards to this trainee doctor who has hitherto given you no cause for anxiety in respect of his funding and through no fault of his own has found himself in dire financial distress because his government has in some way delayed funding.
I am making every effort on his behalf to find someone to help him financially by contacting the Gambia High Commission etc and I expect you to allow him adequate time to sort out his finances.
I shall continue to provide him with clinical training here and I expect you to honour that and I shall be in touch with you before the end of May to see if we can reach suitable compromise.
I would like you to decide whether you can offer any financial help yourself and when and what scholarship you are prepared to offer him.
Yours Sincerely
Dr. Peter R. Wilson
AUC Program Director
Colchester General Hospital
Dr. Peter Wilson not only looked for more sources of help to alleviate my situation but he generously donated one thousand pounds sterling from his bank

for me to pay AUC and the rent at 47 Roman Road in Colchester.
Among other letters seeking financial help for me was one sent to the student adviser, Mr. Peter Bird, of the African Education Trust on 38 King Street, London on March 20, 1991.

Dr. Peter R. Wilson
Program Director for AUC
Essex County Hospital
Colchester, Essex CO3 3NB

Mr. Peter Bird
Advisor
African Education Trust
38 King Street
London
March 20, 1991

Dear Sir,

RE: Alhasan S. Ceesay

I enclosed confidential letter of recommendation for the above student for you consideration. Please do not hesitate to contact me if you feel I can be of any further assistance.
Yours faithfully
Dr. Peter R. Wilson
AUC Program Director

CONFIDENCIAL LETTER OF RECOMMENDATION FOR MR. ALHASAN S. CEESAY

Alhasan is an extremely conscientious and competent man, determined against all odds to complete a Doctorate course in medicine, so that he can return to use his knowledge to serve his people. I have no doubts about his sincerity of his purpose nor of his dedication and hard work and various scholarships he had earned en route.

He managed to be one of few rural students without financial backing from his family or government to receive secondary education and gained one of the extremely rare university entrances and took a masters of Science degree before embarking on his medical studies.

Enrolled after years of hard work in the USA trying to save enough money during his undergraduate career in science in the states, he joined the American University of the Caribbean as a matured student for his clinical training and funded himself through the first five semesters of this course.

He applied to come to England as do many students from this university in order to gain his clinical experience in an English hospital and was assured by the Gambia high Commission that he had been warded a Commonwealth Foundation training scholarship for the remainder of his clinical training.

Only after beginning his training in the UK did he discovered that the Commonwealth foundation Training body were unable to fulfill their apparent promise to the Gambia High Commission and since then he has been desperately borrowing money from those who sponsored him during his training hitherto and has written many letters since then begging for help from the Gambia Ministry of Health and Education Department.

He has been unable to any more than token financial help. Anything you can do to help now will enable this very conscientious man to complete his course. It would be tragedy if he were not able do so. He has, to my knowledge, many letters of support to back mine, which he will also be submitting to you. I have no doubt.

Peter R. Wilson
Program Director
Severals' Hospital
Colchester, Essex

On February 22, 1991 the Bishop of Colchester, The Rt. Rev Michael E. Vikers, sent the following appeal in my behalf to Hon. Bakary Darboe, Vice president and Minister of Education, Banjul, The Gambia, West Africa. It read:

Dear Vice President/Minister of Education
RE: Mr. Alhasan S. Ceesay

I understand from Mr. Ceesay, with whom I have been speaking this morning, that he was on the telephone to you either yesterday or the day before, about the financial crisis, which threatens to place the completion of his studies in jeopardy and end the possibility of his returning as a trained physician to the Gambia.

I have been drawn into Mr. Ceesay's situation over the last four months, partly through a colleague in the United States who was able to give some assistance and encouragement during an earlier stage of his studies.

I can vouch for the critical nature of his present situation and I am sure that you will wish to do anything that you can to assist him.

His university has recently told him that, unless he is able to pay the tuition fees due, $5200 (five thousand two hundred us dollars) by the 5th of April, 1991 he will be placed on a financial leave of absence during which time he will not be permitted to continue classes. With best wishes

Yours sincerely

Bishop Michael E. Vickers

Some help surfaced but not from the Gambia government. A Liza Gilbert replied to one of several appeals both Dr. Peter r. Wilson and I sent to The Africa Education Grant Advisory Service in London and gave the following good news for decades.

Assistant student Advisor
African Education Grant
38 king street
London
May 23, 1991

R-L: Abdoulie Ceesay, MP and Alagie Mama Ceesday at the train station in Germany, 2018

Mr. A. S. Ceesay
Flat 2, Kensington Court
47 Roman Road
Colchester, Essex CO1 1UR

Our ref: EG91/0123

Dear Mr. Ceesay

Further to your case I am pleased to inform you that the Education Committee of the family welfare association has kindly agreed to make you an award to assist you in your present difficulties.

A cheque in enclosed made payable to your place of study as previously explained. I would be grateful if you could acknowledge receipt of this check.

It you take the enclosed cheque to the finance off ice of your college they will be able to administer it for you and will either draw up a further cheque or pay the grant in cash.

Enclosed is two thousand six hundred pounds sterling for fees. The committee has asked that if the ministry in Gambia do eventually pay the fees, they could be re-embossed but do not expect repayment otherwise. With best wishes for the future

Yours Sincerely

Liza Gilbert

Assistant student Advisor

Prior to the above letter I had applied to Dr. Peter R. Wilson to contact the Postgraduate Committee in my behalf for possible assistance with an emergency loan of six thousand five hundred pounds sterling to enable me pay the rest of the remaining two and half semesters of my clinical training.

Rev. Mark Meyer and Mrs. Lois R. Leonard also made efforts to collect money for me. Mark sent $500 on 28/10/91 followed by another $2600 on 25/11/91 and finally $900 on the 27/3/92.

All these monies went into payment of tuition fees and rent. To add fuel to fire, the university increased its tuition fees up 6% throwing students like me into more financial crisis than can be imagined.

Dr. Peter R. Wilson was also successful with his appeal from the Postgraduate Committee to which amount he added his own one thousand pounds sterling as a loan to me. He informed me of the grant from the Postgraduate Committee thus;

Colchester and North East Essex
Postgraduate Medical Center
Essex County Hospital
Colchester, CO3 3NB
May 10, 1991

Ref: PRW/PAH

Mr. Alhasan Ceesay
Flat 2, Kensington Court
47 Roman Road
Colchester, Essex

Dear Alhasan,

I am able to give you good news. The Medical advisory Committee of the hospital agreed to my recommendation that you should be offered immediately a loan, interest free, of six thousand five hundred pounds sterling to enable you to complete your studies in medicine and take your degree as you had hoped to do.

The M.A. C. recognize that you have studied conscientiously and I do not believe you would have receive this offer unless several of the tutors with whom you have had contacts had not spoken up enthusiastically in your support on knowledge of your conduct. The M. A. C. recognize that you are in no position to guarantee repayment of this loan and in any case do not expect you to begin repayment until June 1994 when they hope you will be in a position to do so.

I would strongly recommend that you advise your friends that you would have completed your studies and then give them priority in repayment. At least two of the consultants in this district know the Gambia intimately and are aware of the effort you have made in your efforts so far to get in your course and training and all wish you well in fulfilling your ambition to become a doctor and serve your people as I am sure you will be able to do.

We shall expect you to complete your clinical training including the electives in the near future. Please come and see me.
Your Sincerely
Dr. Peter R. Wilson
AUC Program director

This was a historic relief anointed by the Gods on mount Olympus. It marked a pivotal point in my quest for the elusive medical degree for the Gambia. Needless to say I was flabbergasted, more than delighted and terribly relieved that the tuition fee problem has now been laid to rest forever.

Wife and I prayed for all, especially for Dr. Peter R. Wilson and M.A.C. We felt eternally indebted and profoundly grateful for their generosity, understanding and stand to see me get the medical training I want to serve my people with in the future. I sent the following note of thanks and appreciation for the good will to the Postgraduate Committee at Essex County Hospital in Colchester.

Flat 2, Kensington Court
47 Roman Road
Colchester, Essex CO1 1UR
May 20, 1991

Mr. Kitchen, chairman
Medical Advisory Committee
Postgraduate Medical Center
Essex county Hospital

Colchester, Essex CO3 3NB

Dear Committee,

RE: In Appreciation/grant

This is to acknowledge receipt of the six thousand five hundred pounds sterling loan you approved to help me complete my clinical training here at Essex County hospital in Colchester.

Thank you is awfully inadequate and words cannot aptly convey to you the gratitude and appreciation Gambia and I have for the help you so kindly rendered us.

We are profoundly grateful got this kindness and generous contribution in our behalf. Rest assured that the fruits of this benevolence would be fully shared with the sick and needy villagers.

This humane gesture now makes that venue more certain. Finally the six thousand five hundred pounds sterling loan will be repaid in full and in time. I will return to serve the Gambia, especially villagers. I will keep in touch with most of you, especially the M.A. C.

Again, God bless and a million thanks for being so helpful to us. I remain ever so grateful to all of you. Cheers and regards.

Yours Sincerely

Alhasan S. Ceesay

Gambian Medical Student

I met Dr. Peter R. Wilson the next morning and we had a cordial and memorable chat that day. He was very relieved that I could now work toward serving my nation and fulfilling my dream fro my people who are desperately in need of medical care.
I gave him a note of thanks for him and his staff who worked acidulously to help me resolve my financial woes. I felt happy with Mrs. Penny West, Mrs. Hornby and all those who assisted to bring hope to my venture. It simply said:

Flat 2, Kensington Court
47 Roman Road
Colchester, Essex CO1 1UR
May 20, 1991

Dear Dr. Wilson,
Thank you for your May 10, 1991 letter informing me of the six thousand five hundred pounds sterling loan the Medical Advisory Committee approved in my behalf through your relentless kind initiative efforts.
I am most grateful to you and the committee for this humane gesture as such critical state of my medical education. It is very kind and generous and the Gambia and I remain touched by it. You have again extended your healing hands to touch us in the Gambia. Wife and I remain profoundly grateful and feel privileged having you on our side and as a friend.

Secondly, we thank you the trip to Hartfield House and the dinner with the Rotary Club. It was our first time out of Colchester and we really fully appreciated the gesture. Hartfield House is an appreciable history of English Monarchy.

The loan will be fully repaid within the stated time. Finally, kindly convey sincere thanks to the Committee, Mrs. Penny West and Mrs. Horny and all the staff for their love and kindness showed us. It was an admirable ceaseless effort from all of you that brought light at the end of the tunnel for the Gambia and I.

Wife and I are deeply touched. I will be at your office for us to plan the rest of my medical training. Cheers and regards. God bless you, my friend.

Yours Sincerely

Alhasan S. Ceesay

Gambian Medical Student

This phase of my life in Colchester will be incomplete without mentioning of few other angels wife and I met. Our first friendly contact, aside hospital staff, was an unusually easy going old lady, Mrs. Maureen P. Smith, who lived across our building on Roman Road.

She was the first neighbour who came to visit with us and we hitherto formed the warmest long lasting bond of friendship with her. We tease her as UK's deputy ambassador for Africa and Japan.

Why? Shed had friends from all over the world but more so of Japanese and she spends nearly all her holidays in Japan. We loved her for breaking the social ice for us and through her we met lots of other good people in Roman Road. I first met Nurse Lorna V. Robinson while at my surgical rotation at the Colchester General Hospital.

She had just returned from vacationing in the smiling coast, the Gambia. She came to see me at the surgical ward the moment she was told of a Gambian student doing his clinical training at the hospital. The meeting was brief but I found her friendly and we decided to meet my wife at the end of the day.

The meeting will not be until the birth of our first daughter, Famatanding Ceesay, on the 17/9/91 that Lorna and husband turned up at the Colchester Maternity Hospital to congratulate us.

Lorna Robinson took the most important photograph; baby Famatanding Ceesay, in the history of my family. Meanwhile she and wife got on as if they had known each other for centuries. They became sisters since that meeting. The two visited each other frequently and we maintained links with Lorna Robinson.

Last but the least was friendship we built with the Gassons of the Causeway, Boxford in Colchester. We met this lovely family through my contact with one of their sons, Daryl Gasson, who was then working at the Colchester General Hospital. He was interested in the Gambia and hence invited to meet with the rest of the Gassons at Boxford.

At Boxford the Gassons were more than delighted to meet wife and I. Everyone wanted to pick baby Famatanding and we had exhilarating and memorable two days with this family before returning to down town Colchester.

We really cherished friendships we built with countless families in the Colchester area and did try to keep up with all after leaving friendly Colchester in 1992. As time passed we lost contacts with some friends but Lorna Robinson became our extended family in the UK. She visits us while in the Gambia during her summer holidays.

My daughter, Famatanding Ceesay, calls her "Auntie Lorna." We always look forward to her next visit to the Gambia. Her personal contribution to my family is immense and we remain grateful to her untold number of kind gestures to the family.

Being interested in helping others and having observed my work with the villagers, this lady took interest in it and agreed to help me get drugs, equipment, and to sensitize would be interested sponsors of a village health organization, when she returns to Colchester.

She did as promised and had for years sent numerous packages of materials donated to Manding Medical Centre at Njawara village.

She visited Njawara, my home village, in 1995 and saw how much need there was for the contribution to help provide much needed medical service to the villages.

She was swamped at the village by throngs of villagers wishing to thank her for being kind to them and for helping in their medical care needs.

Moved by this show of gratitude from villagers Lorna Robinson braced to do even more and today there is the usual, "Gambit Night" or Gambia Bazaar fund raising activity every weekend at Colchester.

Through her efforts we today have the Colchester friends of Manding Charitable Trust, which is and extended arm of Manding Medical Centre and serves as our liaison for the UK and the European Community countries.

The Charity was formed through her relentless efforts help of a solicitor the Charity Commission has registered the friends of Manding as a charity in England and Wales since August 21, 2001 to further the objectives of Manding Medical Centre at Njawara in the Gambia, West Africa.

As far back as June 6, 1993 Lorna Robinson released the following flyer on behalf of Manding Medical Centre. The appeal read thus:

82 Finchingfield Way
Black Heath
Colchester, Essex CO2 OOAU
England
6/06/93

Dear Friends,

I am writing on behalf of Dr. Alhasan Ceesay of the Manding Medical Centre at Njawara village in the North Bank Division of the Gambia, West Africa. My husband and I are helping Dr. Ceesay and the villagers establish a hospital that is surely needed as the nearest hospital is some 70 miles away strewed with bad roads, and no ambulances or proper transport for the ill villagers.

It will provide valuable medical, surgical, obstetrics, gynaecology, Paediatrics and other ancillary medical services. We hence write to you to join us as a partner in this humanitarian venture. Fifty pounds will buy a tone of cement and we need about 480 tones to build the center.

Any help in the form of money, equipment, contacts etc will be more than welcomed. We want to contribute in a positive way by providing medical aid and facilities to the villages, which will generate interest with greater participation, form a healthy agricultural society that may lead to improved nutritional and economic gain.

Finally, your help in bringing this gift to the villagers will be more than welcomed and deeply appreciated. Please help us catch dream for the villager. Also feel free to contact me should you or any need further information on the above project at Njawara in the Gambia. Regards

Yours Sincerely

Lorna V. Robinson

These and many more Colchester human angels were picked on the way as the years unfold. It has been my home way from home and a support line, if not lifeline for Manding Medical Centre at Njawara village, the Gambia, West Africa. God bless all.

Abdoulie Ceesay, MP, in blue, meets Hon.Ousainu Darboe, In white at a UDP gathering, Gambia 2018

Chapter 31
The MD Degree, 1992: Home Sweet Home

If there remain any out there who happens to be skeptic or cynical disbeliever in the existence of a curse or anything like it, be warned not to become a convert by the following events that are about to unfold right before you in these pages.

These events herein cannot just happen or come out of the blue by themselves after all my life had gone through these twenty-five years. Every major step of my life had met with stiff resistance compounded by painful, wretched, ill fated, contemptible, if not unsatisfactory, bitter experiences.

It is unbelievably hard to contemplate the challenges and inhuman roadblocks I had to face in my life. Hence dear reader, I suggest that you take a seat and prepare to be mesmerized. My life seem to follow the path of a sailor who, no, not that of the ancient Mariner and his Albatross, nor would Barron Murchison's adventure match it or be more thrilling in nature, finds himself sailing uncharted waters of life without a compass.

Yes, I am sailing through this life as if though no other hell surpasses this very one I am traveling. Let me tell you what happened few years ago, in 1989, when I was in Montserrat. While there hurricane Hugo decided to sweep by the Island nation hitting it with such ferrous vengeance that the roofs of buildings, including one we took shelter at, were blown away to the Caribbean sea leaving only the sky our mantle. It poured torrential waves of rain bringing water up to our necks. The razor sharp wind blowing at 175 to almost 300 miles per hour speeds nearly took me to sea like a kite. Wife and I held onto a pillar all night with micelles flying from all directions pass us.

Each of those heavy poles, corrugated sheets or doors hitting us would spell our doom. Wife and I prayed and readied us for our survival and all those on the path of this devil hurricane with such ferocity and evil wind cum rain-washing away life.

We were lucky to survive that night but lost most of our belongings, including house we took shelter at. Why did I survive if I were not to face another holocaust of a greater magnitude? Do not worry this was just the top of the iceberg.

I hope I have wet your appetite and that you are braced or ready for what good old Montserrat would spew at me after graduation ceremonies. Like any aspirant completing medical school, I was excited and looked forward to a rewarding life of devotion to helping likewise bringing hope and relief to the sick and needy for the Gambia.

I had looked forward to the good life and leaving behind most of, if not all my woes and financial troubles and follow a new path of devotion to God and service to my fellow man. Life is full of choices and I made mine to do medicine.

All I ever yearned for was the simple contribution of what my skills and strength can for others. My heart yeaned for relief, but do you think the elements would let me have a little peace with which to appreciate family and the beauty of life?

Having completed my clinical training at Colchester General Hospital and having met all the requirements for graduation, I bid farewell to my Colchester friends and headed for Montserrat on March 21, 1992.

Check-in time was scheduled for 7.40 a.m. at Gatwick North Terminal, London. You guess it right, the car we were traveling with lost a wheel six miles to Gatwick and the spare had busted in two places the night before.

Luckily an observant traffic police officer noticed us and decided to come and find out what was going on or what we were up to and how he could help us. Being an unusually kind and nice Bobbie he decided to call a repair crew to come to our rescue. What an omen for a traveler!

I made it to Gatwick North Terminal at the last announcement for boarding British Airways to Antigua, West Indies. The departure for the flight was 9.45 a.m. Everyone at the BA checking-in counter rushed to help me get on board the plane, delaying the take off time another twenty minutes. Some of the passengers thought I was some diplomat or VIP, to cause the pilot to want to wait for my joining the flight.

This brought me publicity and attention I did not bargain for on board. Finally, BA flight for Antigua managed to take off and away we went into soon blue skies with jet engines purring like a tamed cat sleeping on a couch.

The initial first four hours of flight were perfectly calm but not for long afterwards. The plane started to experience all of sudden bad weather and steeply went into turbulent weather. Luckily the captain was an exceptionally good, good experienced and adept enough pilot to get us through very serious thunderstorm and lightening.

It was a frightening fifteen minutes before we were clear above most of the heavy clouds and on course to Antigua. We were relieved for no one sustained any injuries and the rest of the flight was bearably comfortable. We finally landed in Antigua around 3.45 P.M. an hour late but safe and sound.

I had no problem at Antigua International arrival terminal. I even recognized some of the old hand at the terminal. Hence after hour's airport formalities we boarded Liat 596 flight heading for Montserrat, now my favourate island nation in the West Indies. The flight took only fifteen minutes over the Caribbean Sea and we were at Montserrat Airport. I took a taxi to Plymouth, capital city of the island and very soon was reunited with my former landlord, Willy Ryan and other friends.

This was March 25, 1992 three solid years after hurricane Hugo and one could still see the scars of the then mighty Hugo. My landlord's house and many others were still in disrepair and only few strong buildings were worth to dwell. Hotels and Condominiums were in full gear and I was to stay at the residence of Miss Gayle Baumgartner until after the graduation ceremonies scheduled for the 28th of March 1992.

This was an unbelievable big day I had worked very hard for and nothing was going to spoil it for me. I planned to savour every minute of it as historical for the Gambia and my family. Sadly neither my wife nor any friend of notary could make it to my graduation because of the cost of transportation and lodging them in broken down Montserrat.

I was to secure a visa and head for the US to do my internship and residency programs after receiving the MD degree from the American University of the Caribbean at Montserrat, West Indies. What happened or followed next is worse than my other recent bad experiences.

It was like a dream, but let us for the meantime continue on about graduating. Every graduating student was happy when March 28, 1992 dawned. It was a day we all had dreamt of in our ambitious push to better our lives and those whom we touch on our path. As for me, I was ecstatic and more than thankful that God had let me see the day I will finally receive the Doctor of Medicine degree.

However mixed feelings emanated because not one of my friends showed up, despite having promised to do so, and worse of all my return to America was uncertain.

Being on the Island brought back all those bleak and difficult day seven months of starvation and solitude I had to endure in Montserrat before being able to join the students at Wayland Baptist University, Plainview, Texas.

We were on the graduation procession three days after my landing in Montserrat. There was a big fanfare and neon signs congratulating and wishing every graduate well and a mélange of blooming verities of roses in full glory and splendor. There were blooming verities of roses everywhere the eye can see on campus.

Like all graduations, whether in Plymouth, Montserrat or any institute of learning, long speeches mark the occasion. In Montserrat, it always shows the Governor at his best political cum academic jargon.

This was normally followed by advises of a few other dignitaries in attendance. We took the Hippocratic Oath with all its solemnity and I again thanked God for the favor He has done by allowing me see the day of my graduation from medical school. I renewed my covenant to return to serve the Gambia no matter how difficult it might be getting to my objective of providing modern medical aid for the rural Gambian villagers.

Very soon we dispersed and parents and friends of graduates wished us well and retired to their hotels. We had a graduation party that lasted through the wee hours of the night for some but I had to leave around 11:00 Pm because I missed my wife and family back in the Gambia.

Gayle Baumgartner was away in America and the room I currently occupy was already booked but another guest arriving on the March 29, 1992. It meant that I had to find a place as quickly as I can before the arrival of the people whose room I was at. I needed few more days to seek a visa from the US Consulate in Barbados before I can proceed to do my internship and residency program in medicine in America, or so I thought until when I got to Barbados, West Indies.

My former Landlord, Willy Ryan, tried to buoy me up by being overly kind and even helped me look for vacancy for me to stay until I sort things out from Barbados and could fly to the USA to start my medical program as hoped or worse head for the Gambia.

I left my luggage with Willie Ryan and flew to Barbados the next day to seek for a visa to enter the United States for the sole purposes of doing my internship and residency program in medicine before returning to the Gambia. At Barbados I met an almost impossible visa consular officer who insisted that I return to the Gambia and seek a visa from the American Embassy in Banjul, the Gambia.

I pleaded with her that I had at the time spent all my money and by so doing it would cost more to travel to the Gambia and I would loose my chance for doing the promised internship and residency program and other consideration that were taking place at teaching hospitals in America.

She called one of these hospitals in the US and was told that unless I am able to visit with the institute no further action in my behalf would be considered. Despite the fact that it was now made clear to her that my going to Africa would mean losing the chance of further training in medicine in a US setting earmarked for me.

The officer rejected my visa application request to travel to America. Unless I am able visit with the teaching hospital in America my dream of being an American trained physician is abruptly brought to rest.

No, her reason for rejecting my request to travel to the USA was not based on my having previously asked for political asylum in America. My voluntary departure from America in December 1987, removed that record from the books and immigration data, and hand had nothing to do with subsequent entries. On hindsight, I was even able to renter in 1982 and 1989 after hurricane Hugo to join the AUC students at the Wayland Baptist University campus in Plainview, Texas.

Previous visa counselors would have not let me in had the asylum request been a deterrent. I thanked her after several attempts to reason things with her and thanked God before returning with a laden heart to Montserrat. At which place I contacted Rev. Mark D. Meyer in Nebraska.

He and other American friends along with Congressman Doug Berreuter of Nebraska agreed to intervene in my behalf by writing to the Ambassador, G. Philip Hughes requesting favourable review and reconsideration of my visa application.

All my friends agreed with me that traveling to the Gambia to seek a US visa was an unnecessary expense and time consuming drill or venture in my own history with the Gambia I could afford at the time.

My brother and friend in Christ, Rev. Mark D. Meyer sent the following communiqué to the Immigration officer at Barbados.

St. Mark's Episcopal Church
1714 Grant Street
P. O. Box 72
Blair, Nebraska, USA
April 22, 1992

To: The United States Immigration Officer
From: Rev. Mark D. Meyer

Dear Sir/Madam,

I write on behalf of Dr. Alhasan S. Ceesay and appeal to you to please award him a visa to enter the United States in order to finish his internship.

Alhasan came to my office in January of 1990, when I was a priest at St. Mark's Episcopal Church in Plainview, Texas.

The campus of the American University of the Caribbean had been offered some vacant classroom and dormitory space at Wayland Baptist University in Plainview. Alhasan had then used up all his funds in coming to Plainview from Montserrat, and I was able to help him with room and board to finish his classroom training.

At the end of that time he was able to get the United Nations Scholarship for clinical training in England. He was forced to spend to spend four months in Plainview trying to get a visa into England to do that clinical training.

During that time, he stayed with me in a spare bedroom and I get to know him very well.

He is a devoted man and passionately believed he has a mission and duty to serve his people in the Gambia.

I am so convinced of that fact that I have spent over $10,000 (ten thousand dollars) of my own money to help with tuition, plane fares, and telephone calls to the Gambia government and the like.

My father congregation in Plainview added their own funds, as did the Roman Catholic Archdiocese of Lubbock, Texas. I understand your concern. I know how many foreign medical students end up staying in the United States.

My father is a former president of the Illinois State Medical Society and was at one time on the AMA Education Committee, and I heard a great deal about foreign medical graduates, believe me I also read the recent Newsweek article on the subject.

I know the problem. Alhasan Ceesay is not part of that problem. As a priest, I believe I have some degree of discernment of a person's devotion and I have rarely seen devotion and conviction to a cause as to his commitment to serve the villagers in the Gambia who are so medically under-served.

He has suffered a lot for that end and I stake much of my life savings on it, and countless prayers gone to his way in these past years.

Please believe Alhasan Ceesay when he says that his desire is to return to the Gambia and serve his villagers. He is telling the truth. His time is short to take the necessary licensing exams in the United States.

He needs a visa if he is to do internship here. I have little money of my own to send him for plane fares to Barbados or the United States and he has absolutely none of his own and is living from hand to mouth.

His future is very much in your hands. Please do not hesitate to call: home 403-553-2412, Church 403-462-2057. Thank you.
Sincerely
The Rev. Mark D. Meyer
Mark further wrote to his congressman, Honourable Doug Berreuter, who in turn sent the following appeal on my behalf to the US Ambassador G. Philip Hughes in Barbados, West Indies. It read,

Congress of the United States
House of Representatives
Washington, D.C. 20515
April 2, 1992

The Honorable G. Philip Hughes
Ambassador
U.S. embassy
Barbados, (PPT. Miami, Florida 34054)

Dear Mr. Ambassador,
This is a request for your service in behalf of my constituent, the reverend Mar. D. Meyer who has befriended Alhasan Ceesay, a young man from the Gambia. Alhasan Ceesay is a graduate of the American university of the Caribbean in Montserrat, West Indies. He is training to be a doctor and has completed his clinical work at Colchester General Hospital in England.

Alhasan must now do a year's internship here in the United States to complete his licensing training before returning to the work in the Gambia villages. I have been advised that his request for a visa was denied. Therefore, I am now asking that his request be given reconsideration.

What he needs at the time is visitor's visa with prospective student designation so that the internship can be completed. He will return to his country to practice medicine with his own people. We need to be able to assist him in this direction. Should you need to contact this young man he is Alhasan S. Ceesay, C/O Gayle Baumgartner, P. O. Box. 27, Plymouth, Montserrat, West Indies.

I call your kind attention to this request for its most sincere and any help accorded him will be sincerely appreciated. Best wishes.

Doug Berreuter
Member of Congress

Along with this were letters from Lois Leonard, and numerous others, which I packaged with the following, appeal, requesting to be allowed to enter the United States of America.

P.O. Box 27
Plymouth, Montserrat
West Indies

The Counselor
Visa Section
U. S. embassy
Barbados
West Indies

Dear Sir/Madam,
I am a Gambian self-sponsored student from Njawara village. I initially did my undergraduate and graduate studies in the U.S. A. 1967 –1973 before attending the American university of the Caribbean school of Medicine in Montsetrrat, West Indies.
All my previous schooling and recently earned M.D. degree came through the kindness and help of American friends and hard work on my part.
I am committed to my people in the villages and do seek your kind considerations to issue me a B2 prospective student visa for me to go and complete my training, i.e. do my internship and residency program in medicine, so that I can be proficient physician serving the Gambia.
Please take my word of honour that I will return to the villages as soon as I complete my residency program in internal medicine. This is my objective in life and I will not fail my people for there is an overwhelming need of proper modern medical service in rural Gambia. I will contribute towards that end in due course.

In brief, the villagers and I appeal for your understanding of our situation and real need for this assistance. We thank you for taking time to reconsider our request and do look forward to seeing you in the Gambia some day. Again, my obligation to the Gambia is supreme and I will return to serve people as soon as I finish the next phase of my medical training. Go bless and thanks a million for your considerations in this matter.
Yours Sincerely
Dr. Alhasan S. Ceesay
AUC/Gambian Student

It would not be until April 22, 1992 before a sinister reply came from the U. S. ambassador in Barbados addressed to Congressman Doug Berreuter of Nebraska, USA. The fight to and from Barbados had already dented the little money I had left with me. And the silence was like lead over my shoulders for every passing moment spells a tragic loss and waste of time.
Most inhabitants of the island were foraging for food and might or would not just be able to add mine atop of theirs. That stab at the back letter in a memoranda form reads:

Office of the Ambassador
U. S. embassy
Barbados, West Indies
April 22, 1992

To: the Hounorable Doug Berreuter
House of Representatives
2348 Rayburn House
Office building
Washington, D. C.

Dear Mr. Berreuter,
Thank you for your letter of April 2, 1992, concerning the non-immigrant visa application of Dr. Alhasan S. Ceesay, your constituent Rev. Mark Meyer contacted you on behalf of his friend.
Dr. Ceesay applied for a non-immigrant visa on March 31, 1992 and was found ineligible for the visa under section 214 (B) of the Immigration and Nationality Act.
This section of the law requires that all applicants for non-immigrant visa be able to determine to the satisfaction of the consular officer that they have social, economic or family ties that would compel them to return to their home after a temporary stay in the United States.
The officer who interviewed Dr. Ceesay was not convinced that Dr. Ceesay has sufficiently strong ties to the Gambia to compel him to return there after a medical internship in the United States. Dr. Ceesay has just finished two years of clinical training in England and was refused a non-immigrant visa in London under the same section of the law when he applied there before applying to Bridge town.

Dr. Ceesay may reapply for the visa and a different officer will review his case. His application will be given every consideration under United States Immigration law. Please do not hesitate to contact me again if I can be of further assistance in this or any matter.
Sincerely
G. Philip Hughes
Ambassador

This reply to congressman Berreuter reached me very late and as such left me dumfounded and angry at the unnecessary cost the strictness and red tape placed on my visa request by the Immigration officer at Barbados.

It would not be until August 1992 before the way was cleared for me to fly back to the UK and eventually the Gambia. Before then I lived on one can of sardine, which lasts three days before I dare open another.

And I stayed at a partly destroyed house with no running water or good toilet. Half of the building was without roofing, as it was among the casualties of hurricane Hugo in 1989.

I plaid hide and sick with rats, which wanted some of food and crumbs, I managed to bring from town. I have to stay awake almost all night for fear of being swept away into the Atlantic Ocean.

My former landlord once on a while would bring some fruits or yams for me to boil for food to keep me bone and skin together.

Simply, I lived by the skin of my teeth with no hope of help coming from any angle for me. My U. S. friends were discouraged and I became embarrassed to ask more than I have already done.

Mrs. Lois Leonard and Rev. Mark D. Meyer kept plugging in as much as they could humanly afford. It reached a point I could not walk to town because of lack of energy. I would stop every fifty meters to rest and did the same on my return from town, a distance of three miles from my shanty.

In fact I duped this half-roofed and blown windowless house, as Hotel Gambia and entered in my diary the snakes, various lizards and Iguanas that crises cross my bed room at night or come to take shade during the day. That I did not lose my mind or get bitten by some unknown wild rodent was pure luck.

The nightmare ended abruptly when Rudolf and Sophie Kurt, stepped in the second time and help me with an airfare back to the Gambia. I could not believe it when I boarded Liat flight 596 heading for Antigua and later BA flight to Heathrow International Airport, London.

These few words or phrases sounded musical to my ears. They spell freedom from being marooned and from the inhuman conditions I found myself after graduating from medical school. In the back of my mind was the Gambia political chasm but life I endured had made me inert to fear of dying any longer.

Normally, elation follows events like graduation, wedding or the arrival of the first and subsequent babies, but in my own case hell lost its head and metered the worst punishment it could throw onto a living being.

I never at any moment wished for death and had strong believe that God, who had this test for me, will pull me out safely when His time comes. I was vigilant in my prayers and seek that the Almighty come to my salvation sooner. I hope you have seen why it was necessary for me to prepare you for the curse I faced in Montserrat.

It looked unreal but I had endured worse than I am able to say to you. So faith, or devotion to God and kind people got me out of that mesh, just as happened when I was at the Mariner's Inn in Detroit, Michigan, USA. There too it was very challenging if not difficult and crazy living among former drug addicts, alcoholics, felons, gun turting teenagers and the downtrodden of Cass Corridor in Detroit.

At Heathrow I met a very kind Immigration Officer who was very sympathetic to me. The haggard sight and story he heard almost moved him to tears. He verified my passport and allowed me to proceed and actually my skeletal state and euphoria was so high that it was bound to carry anyone one I came across. I did not at this time cared whether or what the Gambia might say or do to me.

All I wanted to close that history and chapter of my life by either resting eternally with my maker or serving the Gambia. The officer and I joked and laughed through the time I was before him. It was big and stark difference between my experiences with my good U.S. visa officer at Bridge Town, Barbados, West Indies.

I contacted the Gambia Embassy and had the voice of a long time friend, Mr. Bai Ousman Secka, and he came to my rescue and lodged me for forty-eight hours I had before my next flight to the Gambia via Paris, France.

Secka took me to stay with him at 35 The Avenue, Kilburn, London NW6 7NR. Here all my hidden fears were wiped out for I met with lots of Gambians who assured me that tranquility and civility had returned to my beloved home, the Gambia.

There were no more witch hunting and that the Senegalese troops have disband and gone home for good. With my confidence rejuvenated about the Gambia, I was happy lad that boarded Air Sabina flight from Heathrow, via Brussels and to one of the best homes on earth, the smiling coast of the Gambia.

Flying over Senegal gave me so much lift and euphoria that made me very eager to meet my family. By the way my father died while I was in Montserrat. I had lost one of the dearest and best of all fathers.

Mother on the other hand was very poorly health wise. My arrival's dramatic effect on her gained extensive recovery even though her failing heart would not bounce to health. She was in her nineties and very frail.

Legend and luck had it that I landed in the Gambia August 9, 1992 not the least scared of anything going wrong. I was shocked by the dry state of affairs, especially the weather and dust that seem to envelope everything it comes across.

I later learnt it was the Desert that is causing such havoc. I encountered no problems at the Airport or with the security and two of best friends Latif Sanyand and Kering Marenah were there to pick me up from the Airport.

This gave me confidence that the political problems were then over for my friends and perhaps me.

All said and done my return surprised many except my sister Binta Ceesay who was expecting me more than a month ago. She joke saying, "I dreamt of meeting you at Njawara.

I was certain of your return in one piece." That is my lovely sister Binta Ceesay for you. She loves to lighten people's hearts. Everyone was eager to find out what happened to me and how everyone copped during the challenges. The next day it was agreed that that I stay at uncle Sherif A. Sey's place at Fagi Kunda until we know the direction and development that may follow my return. I stayed at uncle Sey's for six months.

While at Fagi Kunda alhaj Kebba Sanneh and his wife, Matida Sanneh, surpassed all friends in making sure that my resettlement was bearable. I met the rest of my family, relatives and friends at different villages in the Badibous.

I visited relatives at Njaba Kunda, mother's home village, Saba and finally Njawara, my home village. I found Njawara turned into a ghost town.

All the familiar shops and businesses were either closed or moved to either Banjul or Farafenye village, and other new trading centers which surfaced after independence.

The village was dead and in need of a socio-economic spark to rejuvenate it back to her golden good old days. I felt at lost and sad being in Njawara with out my father and to see my home village as dead as I found her. Most of the youth moved to where they can get jobs or hoped to pick up one. Some became teachers while others tried their luck at other vocations.

The population of a once thriving three thousand or more inhabitants has now dwindled to no more than 800 residents. The cattle and sheep looked hungrier than I ever known and again the dust seems relentless. Even the old colonial roads were abandoned for new dirty potholed once leading to dying hamlets.

Despite these horrors, I was very pleased being home once more in my life. Foe once there were familiar cheers and laughter I can relate to and not feel alienated.

My elder brother, Dudou Ceesay and I had a long chat about everything ranging from the last days of dad to current state of affairs of the family and our younger siblings who relocated to the Kombo area by the Gambia's Atlantic coast.

I was taken back and pretty ashamed of the way our compound had ran down through the years. It shadows our pride and for what resources existed if everyone cooperated. I was relived about how much he knew about my sufferings persistent determination to bring joy not only to the family but also to all those we can charitably touch. My poverty stricken life made me very depressed but I bounced back quickly and started implementing one my promises I made to myself and for my people.

I returned to Banjul to recuperate and plan my future in the Gambia.

My wife was at her home in Kindia, Guinea Conakry, at this juncture and was aware of my return but we had agreed to test the waters first before calling her to the Gambia and having to let her loose again.

It would be December before I ventured to the villages. This time, I went there with a mission in mind for them. I started at my village and later many others.

My message was simply to start doing something that will not only unite us but would be beneficial to generations to come. I made it very clear that the going would be worst than climbing a slippery mountain with bare hands and very little food to take along, but the summit holds a great reward for all concerned.

I suggested need to create some form of self-help village health organization to cater for our sick and needy. Even though I made sure it was known that projects like these take time and hard work and perseverance fro all of us and worse some of us may not live long to reap its fruits.

Even where that happens or turns out to be our fate we should be happy that we stood and did something for the next generation Gambians. The villagers were more than enthused and right away Torro Bahen village donated land between Torro and Njawara for the prospective medical center project.

This then was christened as Manding Medical Centre, to be located at Njawara, Lower Badibou, North Bank Division, the Gambia, West Africa. I followed this with monthly health field trips at which nearly 1500 sick villages attend the secessions.

We had our meeting at health centers were with help of volunteer doctors we treat the sick, give health education, talk about sexually transmitted diseases, Aids and guidance for family planning along with antenatal and postnatal advises to would be mother and mothers. I did this until September 1993 before taking up a job as a house officer at the Royal Victoria hospital (RVH) Banjul, the only referral hospital in the Gambia at the time. The RVH currently caters for 350 patients.

I was delighted resuming duty at the RVH as one of the physicians serving my motherland. Ninety percent of the nursing staff was new to me as most of my classmate and those that followed had either gone to higher paying jobs or retired and opened their own mini-pharmacies.

Colonial discipline I left in our nursing day had gone with its master and now the changes make one wonder whether that noble commitment we had in becoming nurses had not melted away because of salary interests and the political era.

Time has certainly changed. My wife and daughter rejoined me in the Gambia by May 1993 for the first time since they left me in London. We moved to a new rental apartment in Bundung Mauritania, a suburb of Sere Kunda.

I had to change my monthly trips to the villages to a bimonthly field trips because of my job commitment at the Royal Victoria Hospital and because the cost to me. My salary at the RVH was an insulting meager D1567 (One thousand five hundred and sixty seven dalasis) on integrated grade 8 scales. Whatever that meant, it was not sufficient to keep a dog alive more over the extended family that doctors encounter in the Gambia. I enjoyed my work at the RVH despite the ranges and insults that followed. I plan my travels to these field trips for the benefit of al Gambians.

Meanwhile, I was able to register the organization Manding Medical Centre and called attention of the International charities to the establishment of the center at Njawara village, the Gambia and our need for assistance to fulfill our dream of providing modern medical aid to the villagers.

Manding Medical Centre is now a registered charity in England and Wales at Colchester, Essex County, UK under the name of "Friends of Manding Charitable Trust" with charity number 1088136 effective since August 21, 2001.

Also Alpena City in Michigan, USA, under leadership of Dr. Avery Aten have spearheaded and established the Alpena Friends of Manding Charitable Trust, Michigan, USA; since May 2005 after the Alpena Community College's leadership class' visit of the center in same year.

Late Cousin Sainabou Jobe (RIP) and Husband Momadu Dukure, (RIP), Banjul, Gambia 1969

Chapter 32
Medical Officer Royal Victoria Hospital, The Gambia

There was no fanfare welcoming me back to the Royal Victoria Hospital (RVH) were I started putting into gear my medical dreams and ambition of providing much needed quality medical service to the villager.

I resigned from the Medical and Health Services, while a Dresser Dispenser, in 1967 to travel to the United States and study for a medical degree with which to serve the Gambia and man.

My re-entry to the Medical and Health Services, per say RVH, coincided with turbulence at the helm of the RVH. Dr. Hassan Jange had just tendered his resignation as chief executive of the hospital and the new tsar was one

Dr. Ogbaselasse, a WHO technical assistance to the Gambia for many years. My employment was left to him and like all new brooms Dr. Ogba Selaisse swept well and clean. He left no stones untouched regarding my qualifications and background.

Dr. Ogba Selaisse contacted my university and requested my transcripts sent directly to him.

It took two months of investigation before he called me in for an interview.

At the interview he made it clear that he could only start me as a House Officer for one year and that I most do a three months rotation in Pediatrics, surgery, medicine and Obstetrics and Gynecology under consultant supervision. My monthly salary was fixed at grade 8 level with a starting point of an insulting meager, if not measly D1567 per month on the integrated scale. This amounts to $156.70 us dollars or poultry seventy-five pounds sterling a month.

My colleagues started at grade 9 upward but Chief Executive Ogba Selaissse deemed it proper to set mine at grade 8 integrated scaling. Family and loyal friends begged me to take the offer for the time being and so this salary disparity continued on from September 1993 to October 1998.

I agreed to the rotation schedule but had to point out the fact that there existed a limited number of consultants at the RVH units that I am supposed to do my internship. Ogba was not happy with my observations.

All doctors of my level were sent to teaching hospital in Ghana, Nigeria or Sera Leone but I was made to do my internship at the RVH with scant consultants to supervise me. Ogba left my file pending because of I knew I was not treated right to start with.

I had to take the bull by the horns when my starting date dragged on and on beyond two calendar months by appealing the case directly to the Permanent Secretary and Minister of Health for a ruling on the matter.

In the interim the America University of the Caribbean faxed the following to Dr. Ogba Selaisse, Chef Executive of the Royal Victoria Hospital.

Dr. G. Ogbaselasse
Chief Executive, RVH
Banjul, The Gambia

Dr. Alhasan S. Ceesay is a graduate of the American university of the Caribbean School of Medicine.
Most of our graduates practice medicine in the United States.
Our graduates must earn the Education Commission for Foreign Medical Graduates (ECFMG) certification.
To earn ECFMG certification the graduate must pass step 1 and 2 of the United States Medical Licensing examination (USMLE) and an English language proficiency test.
Most states in addition would require additional postgraduate training in specific area (residency) for an unrestricted License. I hope this information is beneficial to you
Sincerely
Robert J. Chertok, PhD
Dean of Medical Sciences
This information helped to speed up the processing for it was also copied to the Ministry of Health. Hence an angry chief executive called me the following Monday and asked start rotations under

watchful eyes of Dr. Ayo Palmer, head of the Pediatrics unit.

Ogba added a stern warning to me while I was just on my way out of his office. He in an angry tone said, "You most not forget the protocol in the medical field. I am the head of this hospital and not some politician beyond the RVH fence."

With my letter in hand, I smiled at it all and asked if he dare make such remarks before the very politicians who have been his umbrella in the Gambia. We eventually developed mutual respect for each other but never turned to be, as the saying goes, one's beer drinking friends.

Ogba never liked his authority challenged and was one that had very little trust for power zealous folks. Hence my presence some time ruffles his feathers because of question I asked and seeking intervention where I felt some foot-dragging was going on in the matter.

Another branch assisting the chief executive was the Medical Advisory Committee (MAC). This comprised of heads of units of the hospital and it helped in the maintaining of proficiency, ethics, and standard of medical practice in the units.

I met with the MAC after chief executive Ogbaselaissse sent the following letter to me.

Hospital Management Board
Royal Victoria Hospital
Banjul, The Gambia

May 11, 1993

Ref: RVH/21/vol.v

Dr. A. S. Ceesay
5B Ingram Street
Banjul, The Gambia

I am pleased to inform you that the Hospital Management Board has, in principle, approved your appointment as House Officer in the Royal Victoria Hospital.
Please note that your appointment is subject to successful internship with the Hospital Advisory Committee (MAC) and the appointment Committee. You are advised to report to Dr. Oldfield, Chairman of MAC for further information and action.
Sincerely
Dr. C. Ogbaselaisse
Chief Executive, RVH
Cc: Permanent Secretary, MOH
Chairman: HMB, Chairman: MAC
File & R/file

Dr. Oldfield, Chairman of MAC sent this follow up after the committee reviewed my file forwarded to it by the CEO of the hospital.

Hospital Management Board
Royal Victoria Hospital

Banjul, The Gambia
June 15, 1993

Ref: RVH21/vol.v

Dr. A. S. Ceesay
5B Ingram Street
Banjul, The Gambia
Dear Dr. Ceesay,

RE: Provisional Registration with the Medical and Dental Council
Further to my letter Ref: RVH21/vol.v May 10, 1993 the Medical Advisory Committee has scrutinized your application for internship.
You are required to be provisionally registered with the Medical and Dental Council. Your internship will commence as soon as you present a certificate of provisional registration.
Sincerely
Dr. F. S. J. Oldfield
Ag. Chief executive
Cc: file & R/file
Chairman: MAC

A memo was released to the various heads of units, Registrars Gambia Medical and Dental Council (GMDC) and copied to me.

Hospital Management Board
RVH, Banjul
The Gambia
September 9, 1993

Ref: RVH21/vol.v

Registrar
GMDC, PMB 137
Banjul, The Gambia

Sir,

The above doctor will do a supervised rotating house job three months each in Pediatrics, surgery, medicine, Obstetrics, and Gynaecology.
Grateful if Council can consider him for provisional registration.
Yours Faithfully
Dr. G. Ogbaselaisse, FROG
Chief Executive
Cc: Permanent Secretary, MOH
Chairman, HMB
Dr. Alhasan Ceesay,
File & R/file

The Gambia Medical and Dental Council is an autonomous body of doctors who by act of Parliament is authorized to verify qualifications of new doctors wishing to practice in the Gambia.

The Accreditation Committee of the GMDC interviewed me and the following was sent in response to the chief executive's September 9, 1993 request.

The Gambia Medical and Dental Council
Kanifing
P. O. Box 137
Banjul, The Gambia
October 5, 1993
The Chief Executive
Hospital Management Board
Royal Victoria hospital
Banjul, The Gambia

Dear Sir,
Ref: Provisional registration for Dr. Alhasan Ceesay
Reference is invited to your letter RVH21/vol.v on the above subject. The provisional registration is granted on the terms of your letter.
Dr. Alhasan Ceesay had been requested to formally apply for provisional registration. This does not preclude his commencing the rotation house jobs.
Yours Faithfully
Mr. Mbye Faal (MBBS FROG, FWACS)
Registrar

My official appointment to the Medical and Health services of the Gambia would not surface until October 26, 1993, almost five months from the first day I applied for a job at the RVH. It takes less than a week to process application from other doctors but for me it dragged on endlessly for five solid months. Here is the full text of my reunification with the Royal Victoria Hospital visa avis the Medical and Health Services of the Gambia. It is dream come true indeed.

Hospital Management Board
Royal Victoria Hospital
Banjul, The Gambia
October 26, 1993

Ref: RVH/Board/3/vol.11

Dr. Alhasan S. Ceesay
Bundung, Serekunda
The Gambia, West Africa

Dear Dr. Ceesay,

APPOINTMENT

I am pleased to offer temporal appointment as House Officer with effect from the first of September 1993 for a period of one (1) year. Your Salary will be at the rate of D18, 768.00 (Eighteen thousand seven hundred and sixty-eight dalasis) per annum (i.e. D1564 per month) of the integrated pay scale. You will be required to conform to the General orders regulations, Financial Instructions and Public Service Commission regulations in so far as they are applicable to you. You will be entitled to 22 working days leave for every completed twelve months of service.

Please indicate in writing whether you will accept this appointment on the above terms. This appointment is terminable either by the Hospital Management Board or you upon giving a written notice of one month or payment of a month's salary in lieu of written notice.

Yours Sincerely
Dr. G. Ogbaselailesse
Chief Executive, RVH
Cc: Permanent Secretary MOH
 Permanent Secretary PMO
 Chairman: HMB
 Accountant General
  Auditor General
  Principal Accountant
  Personal file & R/file

As indicated earlier on in the chapter I reluctantly accepted the above insult duped as appointment because of pressure from family, close friends and my love for the Gambia.

The salary would not feed a rat much more help me get a compound to raise a family. Having made up my mind to serve my people I worked long and hard hours. I persevered more than any of my colleagues at the RVH; this earned me coveted respect within the administration and the staff. if nothing else. The MAC continued managing my Internship and sent the following:

Cousin Rohey Corr Sey, Faji Kunda, The Gambia

Medical advisory Committee
Royal Victoria Hospital
Banjul, The Gambia

Ref: HLS/MAC/1.94

Dr. Alhasan Ceesay

RE: Posting to Surgical Unit
As part of your rotation of duties in fulfillment of registration for full professional registration, you are being posted to the surgical unit for six months with effect from August 1, 1994. You will of course be assessed in the usual manner.

Sincerely
Dr. F. S. J. Oldfield
Chairman: MAC
Cc: Consultant Surgeon I/C
  Consultant Obstetrics & Gynecology
  Chief Executive, File

The Chief Executive wrote:

Hospital Management Board
Royal Victoria Hospital
Banjul, The Gambia
August 1, 1993

Dear Sir,

Re: Dr. Alhasan S. Ceesay

Further to our discussion (Ogba/AgbakwuruI on the above this is to confirm that Dr. A. Ceesay would be deployed to the surgical unit under your supervision for his house job with effect from 1/8/94 for a period of six months. You are kindly requested to submit progress report to this office at the end of three months.
Yours Sincerely
Dr. G. Ogbaselaisse, FROG
 Chief Executive, RVH
Cc: Dr. Azadeh, OBS & Gyne unit
Dr. Alhasan Ceesay, File & R/file

Dr. Agbakwuru left for Nigeria and was replaced by Dr. U. Jones who at the end of my surgical rotation sent the following report about my performance in the unit.

Hospital Management Board
Department of Surgery
Royal Victoria Hospital
Banjul, The Gambia

The Chairman
Medical Advisory Committee

Royal Victoria Hospital
Banjul, The Gambia
June 14, 1995

RE: Surgical Internship
Dr. Alhasan S. Ceesay

I write to affirm that Dr. Ceesay completed an internship in the General surgery between August 19994 and February 1995.
He was punctual to duty and his performance was satisfactory. He was a good colleague to have in this unit, with good relations with the staff and patients alike. His standard was satisfactory.
Sincerely
Dr. U. O. E. Jones
Head of Unit
Cc: Chief Executive, RVH
File, & R/file

Dr. G. Ogbaselasse resigned his CEO post early 1996 and was replaced by Ansuman Dampha, as Chief Executive of the RVH. Mr. Dampha got on my case immediately in an attempt or effort to restore the long and dragging affair about my being fully registered with the GMDC. He contacted the registrar Mr. Mbye Faal as follows.

Hospital Management Board
Royal Victoria Hospital

Banjul, The Gambia
May 3, 1996
Ref: HMB/PF

Dr. Mbye Faal, Registrar
Gambia Medical and Dental Council
2 Radio Gambia Road
PMB 137
Banjul, The Gambia

Dear Sir,
RE: Application for full Registration
I forward herewith for your consideration application from Dr. Alhasan Ceesay for full registration with the Gambia Medical and Dental Council (GMDC).
Supporting documents are also attached.
Yours Faithfully
Ousman Dampha
Chief Executive, RVH
Cc: Dr. Alhasan Ceesay
File & R/file

Dr. Mbye Faal, Registrar for the GMDC insisted on having more appraisal report sent before he would proceed. He did not like the format of the ones presented in my behalf. In a nutshell this was one of many ways this Registrar would forestall my registration for years to come.

Nonetheless we persevered and sent him different forms designed by his office.

Hospital Management Board
RVH, Banjul
The Gambia
June 11, 1996

Ref: RVH/21/vol.v

The Registrar Gambia Medical and Dental Council

RE: Submission of application report on Dr. Alhasan Ceesay's rotation

Please you will find copies of appraisal report from various heads of units of the Royal Victoria Hospital about Dr. Alhasan ceesay's performance during his rotation at these units.
We forward these for consideration by you for full registration with the GMDC.
Yours Faithfully
Ousman Dampha
Chief Executive, RVH
Cc: Dr. Alhasan Ceesay
File & R/file

The delays went on until September 1996 when I decided that enough was enough and I wrote the following reminder to Dr. Mbye Faal alias Jack Faal and copied it to various officials including the Director of Health Services.

Royal Victoria Hospital
Banjul, The Gambia
September 5, 1996

Dr. Mbye Faal, Registrar
GMDC, PMB 137
Kanifing, The Gambia

RE: reminder regarding my application for professional registration with the GMDC
Dear Dr. Mbye Faal,
This is to remind and call attention that my application remains pending despite my having completed the assigned rotations and having submitted all relevant documentation for you to kindly consider a year ago.
I would be most grateful if you would kindly deliberate on my application for professional registration.
I am anxiously awaiting your kind considerations. I now have waited for more than a year. Thanks
Yours Sincerely
Dr. Alhasan S. Ceesay, MD
Cc: Chief Executive RVH
Director of Health Services

Two weeks later Mr. Ousman Dampha, CEO of the RVH following reminder to the GMDC's registrar with his own. Mr. Mbye Faal's refusal to act on my application was frustrating both the administration and me.

The Chief Executive of RVH again sent the Council a reminder but instead he was replied by a Mrs. M.C. Jallow on behalf of the Director of Medical and Health Services.

Republic of the Gambia
Ministry of Health
The quadrangle
Banjul, The Gambia
September 16, 1996
HP/89/01/(77)

The Chief Executive
RVH, Banjul
The Gambia

RE: Reminder regarding my application for Professional Registration

Please find attached a photocopy reminder of an application for professional registration from Dr. Alhasan S. Ceesay, MD for your attention.

Kindly take appropriate action on this application as soon as possible.

Your Faithfully
Mrs. M. C. Jallow

For Director of Health Services

Again the CEO of hospital sent another reminder to Mr. Mbye Faal, alias Jack Faal, in other to seek appropriate action from Council on my behalf.
Hospital management Board
RVH, Independence Drive,
Banjul, The Gambia
September 8, 1996

Ref: RVH/21/vol.1

The Registrar
GMDC, Kanifing
PMB 137
The Gambia

RE: Reminder for the professional Registration of Dr. Alhasan Ceesay
I wrote series of letters with regards to the registration of DR. Alhasan Ceesay with photocopies of all relevant documents and appraisals reports from the various units in the Royal Victoria Hospital (RVH) but still no action has been taken.
The Hospital Management Board would like your office to kindly take the appropriate action as soon as possible.
Yours Faithfully
Ousman Dampha

Chief Executive, RVH
Cc: Director of Medical Services
Management Advisory committee
Hospital Administration
Chairman, HMB
Dr. Alhasan Ceesay

The CEO received, as usual, no response from Mr. Mbye Fall, alias Jack Faal, Registrar. It was now clear to me that my case was being bandied and deliberately left pending by none other than Mr. Mbye Faal, alias Jack Faal.

The delay and refusal to give any tangible reasons for the GMDC's indecision about my case left no doubts in my mind that Mr. Mbye Faal, alias Jack Faal would play God with me until when it suits him or until he discovers that he was far from being a deity and that he cannot break my spirit, will, and determination to serve the Gambia.

Nonetheless he was reminded about the need to act urgently on my request by Ousman Dampha, CEO at the Royal Victoria Hospital, Banjul.

RVH, Banjul
The Gambia
October 17, 1996

The Registrar
GMDC, PMB 137
Kanifing, The Gambia
RE: Registration of Dr. Alhasan Ceesay

I am sending a reminder for the registration of Dr. Alhasan Ceesay. If you can remember some time ago the Hospital Management Board had written to your office with copies of internship appraisal from unit heads to back up Dr. Ceesay's registration, which were submitted to your office. Thank you for your usual cooperation.
Yours Faithfully
Ousmab Dampha
Chief Executive, RVH
cc: Management Adviser
Hospital Administrator
Chairman: HMB
Dr. Alhasan Ceesay
File & R/file

Dr. Faal, alias Jack Faal, disregarded his previous appraisal forms and made new ones himself and asked that evaluations be submitted again on my behalf.

This was done, with everyone wondering if I had wronged the Registrar inadvertently. I told all concerned that I have no personal knowledge of having offended or said anything that should ruffle his feathers or turn him so callus towards me. I made it very clear that I shall continue to pursue what were my due, if not my rights, to whatever reasonable ends it may lead.

There were lots of sympathizers and people who believed that the Registrar was wrong in dragging my registration for as long as he did.

The new forms, I duped Mbye Faal registration forms, were dully signed and sent to Dr. Mbye faal along with a letter from Chief Executive Ousman Dampha, Ref: RVH/21/vol.v, dated November 8, 1996 in which he categorically stated, "Here are enclosed copies of comments for the full registration of Dr. Alhasan Ceesay.

I do support the recommendation from the heads of units." Well dear reader, I hope you can make sense out of the above nightmarish jigsaw or puzzle. Mr. Mbye Faal continued to wield his seal of power over poor fledgling medical doctor Alhasan Ceesay.

He refusal to act while hiding behind elusive authority is laid bare by the above sequence of event and exchange or the one way traffic of support correspondence from the Royal Victoria staff and it is Chief Executive.

It was slap on the face of the system and very discouraging as I later found out that all Banjul born returning doctors from Russia were sent to teaching hospital in Nigeria or Ghana and even Sera Leone while I was be subjected to the whims and caprices of the registrar of the GMDC.

Mr. Mbye may become the tsar of doctoring in the Gambia but with such exercise of power as he has taken in my case it was certain he would not be in the post forever and not for longer than he has. He will either retire or be forced out by lawful means in due course.

If I were in his shoe, I would write a letter of support for him and plead with the visa consular to reconsider issuing B2 prospective student status to allow my doing the internship and residency program as was scheduled.

No instead I was used to be pon for power tug of war that I had nothing to do. I doubt if he ever saw it that I was a Gambian like him needing his guidance. Why on earth was this man putting me through the grill and unnecessary roadblocks on my way?

Did he fail to realize that God is the only ultimate and ever lasting power in this life and after it? My measly salary of D1564, in other words an equivalence of seventy-five pounds sterling per month, was woefully inadequate and not able to sustain my family's need.

I have three daughters in school and poverty is depriving them the normal things and privileges their peer children are enjoying. Hence, I decided to try the big guns to bring relief to my situation and my family to allow me provides better footing for my children, if not my sanity. Here is a drowning man trying to cling onto straw floating towards him.

Bundung Mauritania
Serekunda
The Gambia
December 16, 1996

The Chief Executive
Royal Victoria Hospital
Banjul, The Gambia

Dear Chief Executive,
I would like to call attention that my House Officer job started September 9, 1993 and end September 1994.
However, I have since the completion of my house rotations been left on grade 8, receiving D1564 per month of the integrated pay scale.
The only other emoluments include transport fee or allowance of D150 per month and D100 per month call allowance. On the other hand my colleagues are paid a total of D5246.67 per month as follows.

Salary	D1979.00 per month
Responsibility allowance	D1250.00 per month
On call allowance	D100.00 per month
Car allowance	D400.00 per month
Residential allowance	D200.00 per month
None Practice allowance	D416.00 per month

Total payment per month to my colleagues equals D5246.76 (five thousand two hundred and forty-six

Dalasis and 67 Butus per month) While I earned a mare D2750.00 per month. I am hereby submitting this claim covering a period of two years, i.e. from 1994 to 1996 inclusive at which time I have been kept at grade 8 scale of D1564 per month.
Hence the difference in wages and allowances is D2492.67 per month which multiplied by 24 months will amount to D59, 624.04 (fifty-nine thousand six hundred and twenty-four Dalasis and 4 Butus) due me to date.
Again, banking on your good judgment and sense of fair play I look forward to a speedy, likewise a positive resolution of the above request. Thank you for being kind and for reviewing the above matter. I anxiously await your response.
Yours Sincerely
Dr. Alhasan S. Ceesay, MD
Cc: permanent secretary, MOH
Director of Health Services
Chairman, HMB
Accountant General
Auditor General
Secretary Public Service Commission
Management adviser

I was not sure what got to Chief Executive Mr. Ousman dampha of the RVH but his letter to me was no longer someone I had hoped would stand his grounds and do what was dully right for the Gambia.

Here, in his cold feet, is what he thought was appropriate to get my case off his back. I duped it my 1996 Christmas card.

Hospital Management Board
Royal Victoria Hospital
Banjul, The Gambia
December 24, 1996

Ref: HMB/PF/091

Dr. Alhasan S. Ceesay
House Officer
Thro, Head of Medical Unit
RVH, Banjul, The Gambia

Dear Dr. Ceesay,
I refer to your letter dated December 16, 1996 relating to the above-mentioned subject and to inform you with regret, that the Hospital Management Board cannot entertain your claim in view of the fact that you are still a House Officer on grade 8.
I am to inform you further that until such time that you obtained full registration with the Gambia Medical and Dental Council and promoted to the post of Medical Officer Grade 9, you will continue to receive your present salary and allowances.
Yours Faithfully
Ousman Dampha

Cc: Permanent Secretary, MOH
Permanent Secretary, PMO
Director of Health Services
Accountant General
Auditor General
Secretary, PSC
Management Adviser, HMB
Hospital Administrator
Personal file & R/file

Here is another in the saga to laugh, cry or wonder about. I would be until March 1997 when the Registrar of the GMDC, Mr. Mbye Faal, ventured to break his traditional silence in my case by finally breaking the lull from his end and throwing out the following insult, as usual of his attitude towards my registration request.
It is a shame that such cruel raw power would be exercised for no earthly dignified reasons. So here if is letter and vomit he sent to the chief executive, RVH.
The Gambia Medical and Dental Council
PMB 137
Banjul, The Gambia
March 4, 1997

Mr. Ousman Dampha
Chief Executive
Royal Victoria Hospital
Banjul, The Gambia

Dear Sir,

RE: Registration of Dr. Alhasan Ceesay

Reference is invited to your letter Ref. RVH/21/vol.v of November 8, 1996 on the above subject.

I am to draw your attention that the recommendations from the Heads of Units that have your support were incomplete in all cases as indicated on the certificate that are now being returned.

The certificates from Obstetrics & gynecology units, please note that there is no entry in the Registry of the Medical and Dental Practitioners in the name of Dr. B.S. Camara, consequently this individual cannot sign a pre-registration certificate.

Enclosed are new forms of certificate completion of apprenticeship, which you can now use in place of the old ones, which are no longer valid.

Yours faithfully

Kinay Drammeh

Administrative Secretary

As you by now noticed nothing new comes from Mbye Faal, alias Jack Faal. He is not the leader who encourages his juniors nor does he really care how much my innocent children and Gambia were affected by his foot dragging callous act.

Let me magnify this statement by just saying that a happy doctor is great asset to his patients as he or she would be able to give more of their time to the practice of medicine than groping for crumbs to keep their families fed. No wonder, most of our professionals, especially doctors are staying abroad. At times one tends to believe that self-interest kept them away from the downtrodden poor of their countries.

I now can see why some choose to stay rather than go through this shameless and doggy dog treatment day after day. In August 1997 we received another joke from the Administrative Secretary, GMDC; adding insult to injury. Notice that this one-man show tends to show its toothless dragonhead with definite loss of memory.

The Secretary's last letter was four months ago to a matter as urgent as had been my case. Again, I vowed to keep fighting for my rights no matter how long or how much foot dragging Mr. Faal may choose to do regarding my registration. Let me remind him that the darkest tunnel has light at the end of it.

I just wished him well and he can continue enjoying his folly. I will serve God and work for the Gambia. My family and country are my concern, not personalities.

The Gambia Medical Dental Council
PMB 137, Banjul, The Gambia
August 25, 1997

The acting Chief Executive
Royal Victoria Hospital

Banjul, The Gambia

Dear Sir,
RE: Registration of Dr. Alhasan Ceesay
Thank you for your letter Ref: HMB/PF/091 dated June 1997.
Please note that section 2b of the certificate of Apprenticeship in Internal medicine reads, Save with the limits herein specified work under supervision."
The Accreditation and Registration Committee (ARC) accordingly recommend that Dr. Alhasan Ceesay do extra four (4) calendar months at the RVH department of Internal Medicine with the current head of the said department.
Following the satisfactory completion of the full registration status may be granted to Dr. Ceesay. Kindly let us know the name of the current head of Internal Medicine, so as to address a letter directly to him.
Yours faithfully
Kinay Drammeh
Administrative Secretary

This sort of reply not only delayed my registration but tantamount to a stab on the backs of the head of units at the RVH, the MAC and the administration of the hospital.
Hence, the current head of unit at the Internal Medicine department RVH was urged by well-

intentioned members of the staff, to write letting the Registrar reconsider this unnecessary request imposed on me. It would now be complete three years since completing my apprenticeship and he still continues to spew out poison and disgust onto my face.

Anyhow, here is the letter from then head of Internal Medicine at the RVH.

Department of Internal Medicine
Royal Victoria hospital
Banjul, the Gambia
September 22, 1997

The Registrar
Gambia Medical and Dental council
Kanifding, The Gambia

Dear Registrar,

We are in receipt of your letter dated August 25, 1997 concerning Dr. Alhasan S. Ceesay's need to do another extra 4 months internship at the Department of internal medicine.

Having worked with Dr. Ceesay since May 1996 to the present time September 22, 1997 I came to know him and his abilities as a doctor. He is capable and a very confident doctor. I find him proficient and a hard worker.

I hence, recommend him to you for your kind consideration and for full registration.

I here by enclosed a completed form from May 1996, the time I met him at the Medical unit to September 22, 1997.
Thank you very much for any assistance given in behalf of this dedicated and capable Gambian doctor. Regards
Yours Sincerely
Dr. Jimenez Osvaldo
Consultant
Head of Medical Unit
Cc; Chief Executive, RVH
Chairman HMB
File & R/file

Again, this was met with the usual silence or refusal to respond to letters concerning me. At this juncture of my tenue at the RVH another Chief Executive, Dr. Mariatou Jallow, came to the helm of the RVH. I was urged to do the 4 extra months on internship at the department of internal medicine as recommended by the registrar to get him off my back and bring this ugly chapter of my life to close. We all held our breath and plied through the bitter four months of anguish and callous injustice to my children and family. So I did the rotation with malice but with much more zeal to work harder for the good of my patients and the Gambia.

I worked long hours and at times volunteered to take emergency night calls for a sick colleague or to make life easier for one that had an unexpected urgent need to take care of important family business in the interior or as far as in neighboring Senegal. The four months Apprenticeship that were supposed to be trying flew past so quickly by the time anyone noticed. We again filled evaluation appraisal form or certificate of completion of Apprenticeship form, as the registrar Mbye Faal calls his new invention.

I stopped anyone urging me or volunteering to have a face-to-face chat with the registrar in other to soften him. I felt that no human being of good intent would treat a beast or a dog in manner I already endured from the hands of this person that calls himself a Gambian. No, no! I will not demean myself for such a person.

He does not deserve the blessing of anyone trying to reason with him. Let him keep at his high pedestal and I will be with the common man who appreciates being human. Let me assure him that he has only waxwings and they do melt at unexpected heights and temperature making the fall very sudden and devastating if the person survives the encounter.

I am certain he will come down to us earthlings one fine day.

I use to tell my wife and family when their spirits seemed to be broken because of this senseless saga, to humbly submit to the Almighty God's will for me. The new Chief Executive, Dr. Mariatou Jallow, passed the completed appraisal forms from the heads of unit at the department Internal Medicine RVH, to the Registrar, as requested, on January 6,

1998. You bet your bottom dollar the registrar did not care to reply up to today. Dr. Mariatou Jallow sent the appraisal with the following covering letter.

Hospital Management Board
Royal Victoria Hospital
Banjul, The Gambia
January 6, 1998

Ref: HMB/PF/(091)

Att: kinnay Drammeh, Administrative secretary

The Registrar
Gambia Medical and Dental Council
2 Radio Gambia Road
Mile 7, Bakau, The Gambia

RE: registration of Dr. Alhasan Ceesay
Thank you for your letter dated August 25, 1997 in connection with the above caption.
Please find attached certificate of completion of apprenticeship in the medical unit covering period August to December (4 months).
Dr. Ceesay is currently still in the Medical Unit. The head of Medical unit is Dr. Jimenez Osvaldo.
Yours Sincerely
Dr. Mariatou Jallow
Chief Executive

It was not until November, 1999, five grueling years after completing my Internship, that a newly appointed revamped and dynamic Hospital Management board, lead by Mr. Kenneth Njie, that light started to shine at the end of the tunnel for me. These Gambian angels, being convinced that I was not properly treated during the past five years, decided to put their feet down and did the correct thing by promoting me to the post of Medical Officer to stop the starvation and pain inflicted upon my family by this long drawn inhumane saga Mbye Faal's refusal to register me imposed.

Words are aptly inadequate with which to thank and register profound gratitude to them for brining this phase of the saga to an end. Deep appreciation and sincere thanks to the new Hospital Management Board members and especially the Chairman, Mr. Kenneth Njie, the Director of Health Services, the Chief Executive, RVH, and last but not the least Dr. Alieu Gaye, an admirable and respectable man with whom I have worked with at the medical unit on and off for three years.

Though younger than me he had always shown courtesy, willingness to encourage his colleagues and is pleasant to team up with. Dr. Alieu Gaye, a million thanks for the interest you have in the Gambia and service you are so diligently rendering the Gambian people. I wished I were endowed with youthful energy you devote to the Gambia.

Yes, Dr. Alieu Gaye, any time you appear in the wards, it brings a spark of joy to my heart for I know you will give the day all you know and to the best of your abilities with due respect and concern for the patients.

Thank you for weathering so much for our people. Be happy that many noticed and are very grateful for your relentless service to our people. My dear reader, the coveted letter from the management board is thus reproduced for your perusal.

I hope, like me, you will be able to let a sigh of relief at the pinnacle of hell the above experience dragged my life.

Hospital Management Board
Royal Victoria Hospital
Banjul, The Gambia
November 22, 1999
Ref: HMB/PF/091/(41)

Dr. Alhasan Ceesay
Medical Officer
Thro Head of Medical Unit
Royal Victoria Hospital
The Gambia
Dear Sir,
RE: Appointment as MEDICAL OFFICER
I am directed by the Hospital Management Board to inform you that approval has affirm in appointing you as Medical Officer, grade 9.1, with effect from

October 1, 1999. You will be paid allowances commensurate to your grade in addition to your salary as Medical Officer accordingly.
By copy of this letter, I am informing the Principal accountant accordingly. Congratulations.
Yours Sincerely
Mrs. Corea: For Chief Executive
Cc: Permanent Secretary, MOH
Permanent Secretary, PMO
Accountant General
Auditor General
Chairman, HMB
Principal Accountant, RVH
File & R/file

It was a courageous act for which history will crown them as one of the highest dedicated board that ever served the RVH. Their stand to right wrong is an admirable yearning in many hearts and it dwarfs the high pedestal our registrar assumes his post. Needless to say everyone concerned was happy about this outcome and asked me to extend personal gratitude to the board and the entire administration at RVH for having the foresight, decency and moral courage to stand up and do justice to the Gambia and me in the face of the past ceaseless wrong that the refusal to register me inflicted upon me since the completion of my Internship five years ago at the RVH.

The appointment letter did not address the sticky point or business of compensating me for the five years in which I worked underpaid compared to my colleagues. I will pursue that avenue but for meantime let the elation ride its course until when things are sorted out.

I thanked God many times more than I ever did and now worked even hard for my people. My new income went into clearing old debts incurred over the years to pay for school fees and other necessities to allow my daughters attend school. I was not able to buy a compound or a car to take my children to school.

God has His mysterious ways of solving seemingly incomprehensible problems to human minds. At this juncture matters had gone too long and it would be foolish of me if I did not get my redress.

Now I decided to take the bull by horns by taking my case to the nation's second highest authority, vice president and Secretary of State for Health, Social welfare and Women affairs, H.E. Isatou Njie-Saidy. Doctors do not like being involved with politics but there comes a time and experience in one's life one must take a stand for what is just and rightfully ours.

I went before these officials because of sincere conviction that only they can move the registrar into recognizing that he has dragged my case unnecessarily for too long a time.

Having gone through all the expected authorities of the RVH, I sent the following appeal requesting arbitration to resolve my Professional registration saga with the GMDC.

Some friends were hesitant about the move believing that drawing politicians into the scenery might just be another cause to make the registrar feel big and further prolong my agony by stifling intervention any kind in the case.

I told them that it was Parliament that enacted such power as the registrar wheel and it may just be their onus to step into the arena to make sure that coming Gambian doctors would not have to undergo such experiences as I endured from the registrar's delaying tactics.

Armed with confidence of being on the right I told my wife and friends to believe in one God and His name was not "Almighty GMDC Registrar" Here is one of several appeals I made to higher ups.

Department of Medicine
Royal Victoria Hospital
Banjul, The Gambia
February 23, 1998

H. E. Isatou Njie-Saidy
Secretary of State for
Health, Social Welfare
& Women Affairs
The quadrangle
Banjul, The Gambia

Dear Vice President and Secretary of State,
RE: Request consideration of resolving Professional registration raw.
I write calling attention to a dilemma regarding my professional registration with the Gambia Medical and Dental Council that has been unsolved for the past four years.
I took up service with the Royal Victoria Hospital in September 1993 as House Officer and was asked to do three months Internship rotation in Pediatrics, Medicine, Surgery, gynecology and Obstetrics as stipulated by the enclosures in this letter.
My registration has been, since hitherto hindered by sequence of unnecessary delays and foot-dragging by the registrar Mbye Faal.
My colleagues receive a salary of D5246.67 while I remained on a salary of D2750 since 1994, under grade 8 integrated Scale. Various chief executives of the RVH sent a series of reminders to the Gambia Medical and Dental Council (GMDC) registrar but I am yet to be registered despite having completed my rotation and dully recommended by heads of units at the Royal Victoria hospital since 1994.

The last reminder was sent the GMDC registrar on January 8, 1998. To that reminder the administrative Secretary told us that I would not be registered unless a head of unit at the gynecology department, who signed one of the certificates, registers with the Gambia Medical and Dental Council.

Now Dr. Jimenez Osvaldo is the current head of unit at the department of Medicine and the only one authorized to sign such evaluations. He has done so as per enclosed. Let me reiterate that both the chairman of the board and chief executives have done all they could within their jurisdiction to resolve my case.

Hence, banking on your good judgment and sense of fair play and as a Gambian, I am appealing for redress of my case to allow me to be registered and as well be compensated for the four years I have been left on grade 8 at not fault of mine.

Thank you very much for your kindness as well as for taking time to resolve my case. I am anxiously awaiting your reply.

Yours Sincerely
Dr. Alhasan Ceesay
Cc: Permanent Secretary, MOH
Permanent Secretary, PMO
Director of Health Services
Secretary General. PSC
Chairman, HMB
Chief Executive, RVH
Chairman, MAC

Registrar, GMDC

A meeting with Vice President H.E. Isatou Njie-Saidy was arranged for me to discuss my problems her for she double as the Secretary of Health of the Nation. Sure enough she was the right authority to turn to for arbitrate the case when everyone else was unable to move Mbye Fall to unravel the dilemma. The Vice President listened to my woes for a good ten minutes and then told me that although she empathized with my unfortunate case, she was not familiar with the Medical and Dental Council's yard stick for registering doctors.

This discovery came to me as a surprise I expect persons appointed to head the health of the nation should be verse in how people are allowed or disallowed from practicing medicine in the Gambia. She did promise me to have a staff look into the affair she suggested my petitioning the president's Office to help since the Council was under that sector.

This to me seemed like throw the buck to another person to do one's dirty job. I thanked her for giving me audience and with laden heart I promised to press forward with the idea of meeting with H. E. President Jammeh to have my case solved.

I wrote to the president but protocol has it that as a civil servant, I need to bring my case before the Secretary General, president's office.

I passed it through the Secretary of State for presidential affairs who redirected me to the

Secretary General's Office were the matter should be handled. There I met, Mr. Tamsir Mbye, a colleague when we were students in America. Seeing him calmed me down and gave me confidence that perhaps the matter will soon be resolve.

Tamsir and got to business after a short reminiscence of the good old days in Washington, D.C. with this light or welcome atmosphere I thought things might not be as horrible as I had braced myself.

I gave him a complete rundown or trend of the case and he, in the normal politician's way, promised to do all he could to solve it to satisfaction of all concerned with the case.

Being an in-law to the registrar Tamsir Mbye assured me that there was no need to speak with the president about my case or fiasco he just heard and that he would do all he could to resolve sooner than later.

I left his office naively happy because I believed Tamsir Mbye does know how much I struggled in America to get my schooling done. He used to visit with me at my flat.

So there was doubt in my mind that someone like him would take my cause with alacrity and seriousness to bring it amicable resolution.

That much confidence and relaxation about him knowing was a costly mistake because Tamsir Mbye was about to go to China or some place with the president and the juniors he delegated my case only cared to talk to the registrar and communicated what they got from that office back to me.

I have no doubts that H. E. president Jammeh never heard a word about my plight with the GMDC.

A letter was written to me purporting to represent the president's views as stated in the following below.

Mr. Tamsir Mbye came back and took a retirement leave and so I was not able to meet with him because he traveled out of the Gambia.

First let me give you the reply that came from the state house. Brace yourselves.

Republic of the Gambia
Department of State for
Health, Social welfare &
Women Affairs
State House, Banjul
The Gambia
May 3, 1998

Ref: AD 543/01/(172)
Dear Sir,
RE: request for consideration of resolving Professional Registration row
I am directed to acknowledge on behalf of Her Excellency the Vice President and Secretary of State for health, Social welfare and women's Affairs

receipt of your letter of February 23, 1998 relating to the above mention subject. Such matters fall under the purview of the Gambia Medical and Dental Council. However, this office will approach the registrar of that body with a view to resolving this long drawn issue. Thank you.
Yours sincerely
Sukai Bojang
For Permanent Secretary

Two weeks later I heard from the Secretary General's Office as indicated below. Both letters threw mud at my face for they strengthened the noose the registrar had around my neck.
Both offices totally relied on wrong information supplied by the registrar instead of even checking with people on the ground and in the know about my case at the RVH. To put it mildly they agreed with everything the registrar spewed.
Whatever dossier the registrar may have on me was nothing other than his inventions or inventive creation. I would like to make it clear that this was just round one in a boxing bout between the GMDC registrar and I.
In the next round I will meet with H.E. President Jammeh and lay my complaints before him.
I will demand for just resolution and compensation for the four years I was under paid because of the aforesaid saga. The appropriate person(s) will make the compensation when God's time comes.

I was certain that someone out there cares and knows about my pains and deprivation this registration nightmare has done to my family and Children.

My gorgeous Princesses, at Brusubi, the Gambia 2017

The Republic of the Gambia
Office of the President
State House, The Gambia
May 17, 1999

Ref: OP277/14/01/1V (8-JP1)

Dr. Alhasan S. Ceesay
Department of Medicine
Royal Victoria Hospital
Independence Drive
Banjul, The Gambia

RE: Request for consideration and arbitration to resolve Professional Registration raw.
I am directed to acknowledge receipt on behalf of His Excellency The president of the Republic, your letter of July 8, 1998 in which you sought intervention and redress with regards to your bid to registrar with the General Medical and dental council.
Regrettably, this office is constrained by its inability, in the fact of the council's decisive position, to interfere in the registration process.
Yours Faithfully
Joseph P. Jassey, Capt. (RTD)
For Secretary General
These two heart wrenching letters left me much more ready to fight my case to the courts. The weak gives up easily but determined one does continue

and become heroes. I am not giving up because of this first volley of blows in the fight. This fight will go on to the final minutes no mater how long it takes to resolve.

The truth will make up for the pain my life endured and mistakes made in dealing with it. God will have me have the last laugh in this kaleidoscope. I am by the above poised to struggle against injustice and misuse of power in office.

Both fiend and foe warned me to accept that this was a fate accomplish for me from God and that any further act will only continue the agony my life has endured since my return to the Gambia.

Dr.Alhasan Ceesay graduating from the America University of the Caribbean School of Medicine 1992

I laughed at such suggestions and asked the person if he or she were present when God was planning my life or would they have stopped knowing that they right? I made it clear that this rift had to be dealt with squarely and there will be no cowardly surrender by me.

Letting matters end now would only set a very bad precedence for future doctors or civil servants as it will allow monsters to gnaw innocent souls like me that may come their way. No, no chance for that to happen in this case and this will be the last time a registrar of the Gambia Medical and Dental Council would toy with a Gambian doctor's bid for registration at will as if the registrar were dealing with powerless little children.

Some prayed for my success while others left bewildered at my determination. Of course my integrity and professional right were at stake plus my children's future relied heavily on the outcome of the stalemate.

I am not in any going to give up my entire life's investment lying down for all the wrong reason of the registrar. I know the truth is on my side and in the long run it will be so apparent that even Mbye Faal or some God fearing person will bring this Alice in wonderland Gambia tale to an abrupt and amicable end.

Meanwhile, I continued my daily work schedule at the Royal Victoria Hospital and the bimonthly health education activities I started in the provinces. This and my family became the only relief to me. All my plans of buying a compound and a car to take the children to school went over the window because my measly salary hardly feeds us to the end of the month.

My wife, who deserves the highest commendation through out the saga, never for one moment broke down. She had been fully supportive through out this ordeal and has helped me a lot with the children by selling tie-dye materials.

My friend, the going is rough if not very turbulent at present but its true that "laughs best he who laughs last." The struggle continues until the dawn of justice for all future doctors wishing to register with the Gambia Medical and Dental Council.

Roadblocks, roadblocks everywhere when will these treacherous immoral obstacles be removed out of my way? I will hop, skip and jump over every one of them if need be to bring medical service to villagers. Till then, meet you at the next appeal round of this elusive Jarkcle and Hyde saga of an entrant doctor.

By now you have heard me mentioned monthly health field trips to the provinces and I hinted at some point the formation of a village health organization at Njawara called Manding Medical Centre.

The next few pages will be devoted to the interesting part of my life instead of boring saga with the Gambia Medical and Dental Council (GMDC). First let us take a break and contemplate on how I chased elusive time since birth to now.

Mrs. and Mr. Kostas Meliotis, good UK friends

Chapter 33
Chasing Time to Catch a Dream

It is said that time and tides never wait for any one. For me I have been chasing elusive time from the day I came to planet Earth. It has been from time immemorial a challenge of my life.

The chase stared at birth when I stopped breathing in the first hour of my life. In those precious minutes and hence hours to follow time left me behind and I was declared none existent and was to be buried first thing in the morning.

Alas! I woke up before dawn and I have been chasing time since February 14th, 1942 to the present time. My peers in other villages started schooling at the age of 5 years and I started primary school when I was 12 years old.

I enrolled at college at the age of 22 years.

And I graduated from medical school at age 50. There has always been this huge gap between time and when things happen for me. Time, where are you?

Folks once on a while tease me for being the father of classes I attend. I wish there was a way I can reverse or stop time so that all delays in my life would level up with elapsed time.

All my peers have grown gray or have complete white hairs or totally bald but I look like some 28 year old lad and as fit as a 16 years old athletic kid, even though I never ceased chasing after time.

Time for that precious priceless record of history has not arrived for me. Imagine at my raw age of 68 I am still struggling to get my postgraduate courses for the MRCP level in medicine while my comrades have retired long time ago.

William Shakespeare said of time thus: "Come what comes May. Time and the hour runs through the roughest day." For me it kept flying and irreversibly so. Friends console me by telling me; "Your time will come." In desperation I ask when? Time cares less for it will tick with or without us.

Hence, it is my duty to catch up and do so well and early to live footprints on the sand of time worth following when my time comes.

Navigating through the valleys and gorges strewn at us on life's path is a nightmare. I came to England for two reasons they are to do the MRCP degree and to bring international awareness to my self-help village health NGO, Manding Medical Centre at Njawara in the Gambia, and return to my homeland in the shortest possible time.

This time would not allow as I unknowingly fell into the deepest darkest gorge of visa and job problems. The Home Office's refusal to change my status to that of student left me in limbo and a destitute. Returning home without at least completing the plab exam would be disastrous as experience had taught me while doing my internship in the Gambia. This made it difficult to pass my exams because of being torn between hunger and struggling to find help to send money to feed my equally beleaguered wife and children back in the Gambia. I became catechetic and weak that even the archangels of death and hell would feel sad and sorry upon meeting me. It got so bad that I collapsed at the Central Library in Manchester by because of hypoglycemia.

Again time and tide refuse to wait for poor Dr. Alhasan S. Ceesay. All my compatriots got through the PLAB because most of them had monetary help enabling them to pay for expensive PLAB review courses.

For me I had to feed from the surface of my teeth while I chase time to take my exams under very difficult circumstances that would drown most people. Time was far ahead of me and I needed to catch up before my dream becomes too late for the Gambia and me.

Let me reiterate that the greatest of all faults is to be conscious of none. Hence, time would have not slipped from my fingers had I taken a moment or two to seek for a student visa while at the British Embassy in Gambia.

Anyhow hindsight is always too wise as I later learnt from bitter experience. Despite this long and hard experience, I never gave up and things happened at a surprising and lightening speed for the arrival of a new dawn in my life and goal for the Gambia.

I passed the PLAB exam and started winding down and preparing for my return to the Gambia, the smiling coast of Africa. These were not not only ten painful and trying years but also the most challenging years of my life on planet earth I will never forget nor will I ever wish the worst of my enemies to endure such torturous experience. Thank God to good Brits and Yankee friends and my steely will that I was able to sail through for my villagers and country. I remain deeply grateful and eternally indebted to all who stood by me from the year 2000 to the present.

My three gorgeous Princesses, Brusubi, Gambia 2017

Chapter 34

Creation of Manding Medical centre, Njawara, NBR, The Gambia

When God wants to destroy someone, He first made him an unusual dreamer. So Gandhi had his dream of people solving social deference none violently and Martin Luther king, jr. held onto his admirable dream of children of Jews and Gentile, black and whites holding hands and living in harmony spearheading peaceful cause for mankind.

There are the Albert Schweitzer's and mother Theresa's of the world dreamers who spent their lives believing in their dreams for mankind. My dream, since 1956, was the simple goal of providing medical aid to those far and in remote villages. The villager, who is forced to walk miles on end to seek medical aid for his already dying child, wife or friend, deserves a better health system.

Something I saw in 1956 left an indelible mark in my mind and I have since then asked and prayed that God help me bring part if not full solution to the kind of tragedy that was passing right before me. I was hopelessly unable to give relief except to comfort those involved.

In 1956, while on my way to Saba village, I met an anxious father carrying his son and his almost dead pregnant wife on the back of donkey heading for the health center at Kerewan village, another three or more miles from where I met him.

The child was vomiting yellow stuff, he was sweaty, his eyes were reverted backwards and the pregnant lady groaning every time the mule moves. There was some greenish fluid dripping off her lapper. She could barely hold the ropes controlling the donkey.

I went to Kerewan later that evening and asked about the status of that family, only to be told that the boy passed away half a mile to the dispensary and the lady was referred to the central hospital in Banjul but the family had no money to pay for her transportation nor was the River ambulance available as it was undergoing maintenance at the Dockyard.

To cut a long story short, both child and mother died because of lack of medical facilities or modern medical aid to the villager. One or all of those lives could have been saved and remain beneficial to the country than the fate that befell them. I prayed and grieved with the family for months and redoubled my efforts at school in other to solve such development in future.

I committed myself to medicine from that day on and never regretted making such a challenging decision in my life. Hence, when on the day I was taking the Hippocratic Oath, I not only swore to uphold all therein but to make sure that God help me not to ever deviate from my commitment and promise to be part of the solution in the health services of the Gambia, to foster health education for the villager, and to complement the existing medical facilities in the Gambia as well as ease the shortage of medical service personnel.

To many, except the dreamer, such Erewhons leads to failure as they turn to be white elephants.

Some friends tease me by flatly promising to rise from their graves on the opening day of such an Alice in wonderland project.

Let me make it crystal clear that I had no elusions about what was needed, or to be done and that the building of the hospital would indeed be a lifetime challenge I am fully ready to grapple with.

There would be a lot of well-wishers but very few will ever want to join until the opening day ceremonies.

So first things first, I met an attorney friend Mr. Ousainou Darboe, a villager like me, on September 24, 1992, and pleaded for his assistance with the legal aspects of setting up a charitable foundation, Manding Medical center at Njawara village in the provinces for the sole purpose of providing much needed medical aid to the villager.

He was very obliging and requested no payment in return for his services. In the mean time I got a board of governors elected while he prepared the memorandum and articles of association of Manding Medical Centre at Njawara village.
Also, I met with the Lower Badibou district chief, Kitabou Singateh, who by the way was my primary school class mate at Kinte Kunda from 1953 to 1957, the District Authority, Commissioner and the kerewan Area Council.

Dr. Alhasan Ceesay holding Africa

All of whom were more than delighted and did all they could under the law to help me set up a grassroots local advisory committee, which was headed by the commissioner, to assist the board and also let the villagers feel being part of the ongoing project.

At my home village, Njawara, a group organized itself and formed a pioneering committee to formally ask the Alkalo (village head/mayor) and the people of Toro Bahen village to donate the earmarked land between it and Njawara for the sole purpose of establishing the Manding Medical Centre on it.

The land issue was partially cleared by the first week of the appeal. In October 1992 Alkalo Alh Omar Koi Bah of Toro Bahen, along with alhaj. Musa (Njabi) Bah and Sirimang Bah called my brother, Doudu Ceesay, the elders of Toro Bahen and I to officially inform us that the earmarked land of two plots have been donated to me for the sole purpose of erecting a medical center and hospital facility for the villagers of the region and Gambia. We thanked him for his foresight and kindness towards future generations.

I went back to my lawyer, Ousainu Darbor who by then had finished all work needed for the registration of Manding Medical Centre. We are forever indebted to Alkalo Omar Koi, residents Arfang Bah, Musa (Nyambi) Bah and Sirimang Bah, and the people of Toro village.

Lastly but not the least our venerable able lawyer Mr. Ousainou Darboe, without whose kindness and legal mind the registration of Manding Medical Centre would have taken longer that it did assisted me.

I also express profound gratitude to the Hon. Chief of Lower Badibou district, Kitabou Singateh, the commissioner, and the local district authority for their understanding and willingness to contribute positively towards our goal and growth.

I submitted the registration application material to the Attorney General's Chambers at the Justice Department, Banjul, on October 22, 1992 and Manding Medical Centre was officially registered as an incorporated charitable organization under the companies Act, 1959 by the 27th of October 1992. Manding Medical Centre' certificate of incorporation is number: 224/1992.

With the completion of the paper work and registration of the center, I embarked on a blitz of letter writing informing philanthropists and organizations world wide about Manding Medical Centre and the need for assistance or donations of medications, equipments, medical videos with which to teach our cadre and villagers to become health worker or evangelist, or nurses and to help us build the center.

To complete the establishment process, after the land was officially ours, I wrote to the following letter to the Ministry of Health informing them of the formation of Manding Medical Centre, a self-help health organization at Njawara, Lower Badibou, North Bank Division, The Gambia. Our temporal address was at 5B Ingram Street in Banjul, capital of the Gambia.

Manding Medical Centre
5B Ingram Street
Banjul, The Gambia
March 2, 1993

Permanent Secretary
Ministry of Health
The Quadrangle
Banjul, The Gambia
West Africa

Dear Permanent Secretary
Re: Application for the establishment of a Medical Centre at Njawara in the North Bank.
We are pleased to bring to attention the setting up of a self-help Health organization in the North Bank Division at Njawara village.
The directorates and members of the organization would be more than grateful if the Ministry of Health would allow us establish Manding Medical Centre at Njawara village, Lower Badibou District of the Gambia.
Manding Medical Centre, when fully operational, will provide medical, surgical, gynecological and obstetrics; Pediatrics and other facilities to the

villagers. It will also help ease the shortage of medical facilities in that region. Manding Medical Centre will have health education secessions in the villages as an effort to enlighten our youths.

Again, thank you for taking time to consider our application and we certainly look forward to a positive recognition of the need for such a center in the rural sector of the Gambia.

I am anxiously waiting to hear from your office at your convenience. Regards
Yours sincerely
Dr. Alhasan S. Ceesay, MD
Director and Coordinator

Meanwhile the villagers grew more enthused and throngs of them attended our monthly health field trips or clinics. The attendance grew so large that we ended up listing the villages to attend in turn of nine villages per trip. This usually totals to a bit above 1,000 patients at a given visit.

I normally go on weekends with three doctors and at times four volunteer doctors along with Nurses aid Mrs. Mbee Sonko and Ida Njie to assist us do the job. The field trips/clinics start with an announcement by Radio Gambia giving the names of villages expected to attend and at which village health center.

The clinic day starts with an early morning breakfast by the team and then a ride to the village health center where we would find the villagers and their sick ones assembled. Every occasion starts with the offering of prayers and then the various village heads, in attendance help us in organizing the flow of people wanting to be see by one of our team doctors. In most cases the day goes trouble free but at certain localities the political tension does make it very difficult to have such large groups of people without little arguments.

Thanks to the Commissioner (s) for deploying the police or making them available to quell trouble and help us maintain order during these clinics. Commissioner Lamin Koma can tell you how rough things can be at some of these clinic centers. He was trapped in one of these bad moments of people rushing to be in the front line of the queue to see one our doctors.

The Ministry of Health finally sent us the following affirmative reply as thus: -
Ministry of Health & Social services
The Quadrangle
Banjul, The Gambia
Ref.P510/289/01(95)

Dr. Alhasan Ceesay
Manding Medical Centre
5B Ingram Street
Banjul, The Gambia

RE: Application to establish a Medical Centre at Njawara

I acknowledge receipt of your letter of the 2nd March 1993 on the above-mentioned subject. I wish to inform you that this Ministry has no objection to your application to establish Manding Medical Centre at Njawara.

This initiative is in line with our national health policies and we would render our support in our joint efforts to improve the health of the people.

Signed: N. Ceesay

For Permanent Secretary

After several more field trips it was suggested we apply for a None Governmental Organization (NGO) status. It was believed that if we become and NGO, help would come our way quicker.

I went to work on this suggestion and arranged for Tango Secretariat Centre to send one of the United Nations voluntary program officers to come and evaluate our performance relative to the objectives of Manding Medical Centre.

This was accepted and a field trip was set up for September 12 to 22, 1995. Radio Gambia made the announcement well ahead of the time for our arrival and the following was the outcome of that august gathering of September 21 &22, 1995.

Chapter 35
Tango Secretariat Trip Report
Manding Medical Centre
September 21 – 22, 1995

A field trip to Kerewan at the North Bank Division was organized by the Manding Medical Centre Executive Director Dr. Alhasan S. Ceesay in conjunction with Tango Secretariat Centre to see the organization's activities and meet the members before recommending the organization as a member of Tango.

On September 21, 1995, two meetings were organized in two big centers where members gather to air their views and experience from the organization. Alkalos, chiefs, imams, women, men and youths attended these meetings. The key leadership from five villages in their speeches showed interest and support for the project and organization.

Alkalo of Toro Bahen Omar Koi and chiefs donated the land for the constructing of Manding Medical Centre, the hospital and its ancillaries. The two meeting were highly attended and successful. The Tango (UNV) program officer Mr. Muloshi on behalf of Tango gave a keynote speech on Tango's operations and activities as an umbrella organization and urged members to work hand in hand with the organization in their efforts to develop their villages and North Bank area.

The three meetings with the commissioner during the field trip on our courtesy call were successful and encouraged the executive Director of Manding Medical Centre, Dr. Alhasan Ceesay, to cooperate with the strict, especially the commissioner who is one of the advisors in the local committee.
The commissioner thanked Tango for making the purpose of the mission clear to him and promised that he will try by all means to cooperate with Tango in the area of Technical advise and institution capacity building. Clinic day was organized on September 22, 1995 at Njawara and 150 people attended and got treatments.

RECOMMENDATION

Looking at the caliber of the leadership and developmental activities compared to some NGO tango members in comparison to Manding Medical Centre, the organization need consideration since they have already activities with a promising future. Looking at the composition of the Board, they have people with a great vision.
They have strong membership and backup at the grassroots levels. The organization has chosen to do what is right at the right time and their concentration in one area is vital and a good starting point. Any success achieved by any organization depended on good leadership and discipline.

Manding Medical Centre has quality leadership and deserves NGO status.
Signed: M. Muloshi
UNV Program Officer

We were delighted by the recommendation made by the United Nations voluntary Program Officer in the Gambia. We redoubled our efforts to contact organizations seeking help worldwide.

In between letters and monthly field trips to different select health centers we were blessed with visits from interested friends and groups or representatives of similar organizations in the globe. I had several telephone calls to Dr. Edward Brown, an official of the World Bank in Washington, D. C. responsible of the bank's health affairs at the time. He was very receptive and had several added discussions with Dentist Melvin George, then Director of Medical and Health Service for the Gambia, on how the bank could help in the financing of the building of Manding Medical Centre.

These talks went on well and Dr. Edward brown gave me his promise and personal commitment to helping the project and that we have to start in a small scale and the building will have to be done in several well planned phases.

Dr. Sidi C. Jammeh, a former Armitage School colleague, promised to help me keep the momentum at the bank alive by consulting and constantly reminding Dr. Brown of the need to help us with the

project. Among our guest were a couple from Colchester, Essex, UK, Lorna V. Robinson and husband Keith Robinson were very impressed by our project and enthusiasm of the ordinary villagers about Manding Medical Centre.
They fell in love with the idea and objectives of the self-help health organization and promised to help as much as they could. We had by this time submitted application for NGO status and ACCNO Secretary replied thus:

ACCNO Secretariat
Dept. of Community Development
13 Mariner Parade
Babjul, The Gambia
September 12, 1994

Ref.CD/ACCNO/Vol3/(183)

Dr. Alhasan S. Ceesay
Director/Coordinator
Manding Medical Centre
P. O. Box 640
Banjul, The Gambia

Dear Sir,
RE: application for an NGO status within the ACCNO framework
Please find enclosed a self-explanatory letter from the Ministry for local government and lands

concerning the approval of your application for NGO status.

ACCNO Secretariat congratulates your organization for successfully completing the registration process and wishes you a fruitful relationship in the field of development.

Thank you for your cooperation
Yours Faithfully
Musu Ngujo
For: ACCNO desk Officer
Cc: file & R/File

Replies from our worldwide appeal letters did not pour in money nor did these materialized beyond promises to help in due course. Hence, I decided to open up a pharmacy at my expense at my residence in the Bundung area of Serekunda using the proceeds from its sales to finance the health field trips and activities of the organization.

This meant spending an extra three to fours at the pharmacy daily after eight hours at the RVH before rejoining my family. All drugs used for the treatment of patients at our field trip clinics were purchased from sales I made at the Bundung Pharmacy.

A local agency, known as IBAS, lent me D8000, interest free, which was used in buying drugs and paying for transportation for the project's activities. The loan was completely repaid well ahead of the allowed sixteen months period given by IBAS.

We are obliged and grateful to Aja Ndey Oley Jobe and management of IBAS for their kindness to assist us at the time. Just when things were about to be financially complete for us to start the first phase of building the various sections of the hospital, came the unexpected coup d'etat of July 22, 1994.
The reaction from would be our donors and supporters or sponsors were swift and equally unexpected.
All those who were considering giving the project a chance sited likelihood of sudden national unrest and instability as reasons for their withdrawal of promised aid and participation while some suggested my waiting until after the transition phase of the coup d'etat before they would reconsider reopening our files with them. Again it resorted to case of the chicken the egg, which came first as no one, knew when the transition will end and we kept our fingers crossed hoping that daylight will be ours in not far distance.
It was a severe blow to our hope and for getting the type of interest and support that was engendered for Manding Medical Centre would be difficult to match after such crisis that occurred in the Gambia. Many were acting in conjunction with their governments, which were not sure of what the future under military rule would be for the Gambia.
All prospective and possible international sources earmarked for Manding Medical Centre were either frozen or evaporated into thin air with the coup

leaving me floating in the middle of the ocean of despair without a life jacket except God's merciful hands. I knew the villagers would grow restless if nothing happens in the direction of building the center.

I called an emergency general meeting with members from most of the villages and told them of the new challenge and development and this information not only fell on deaf ears but left their spirits dampened.

Interest waxed and waned at some quarters but I kept on trying my best not to be despondent like the others have shown. I kept the organization alive under very limited funds raised from the pharmacy at Bundung until my trip to the UK in January 2000.

Before leaving the Gambia, the Commissioner for north Bank Division and chairman of the local advisory committee for Manding Medical Centre, Mr. Lamin Koma, gave me the following letter to assist me in my fund raising drive while in England and possible other European countries. It read thus:

The Commissioner
Kerewan Village
North Bank Division
The Gambia, West Africa
June 15, 1998

TO WHOM IT MAY CONCERN
I hereby write to testify and confirm that Manding Medical Centre is a self-help health project situated at Njawara village, North Bank Division. As the Commissioner of this division I was elected as the Chairman of the local advisory Committee of the Manding Medical Centre.
As I am concerned, I am aware of this self-help project since it took off the ground, by the able hands of Dr. Alhasan S. Ceesay, a born citizen of Njawara village. The purpose of the establishing of such a medical centre is to provide medical attention/care to all Gambians irrespective of religion, tribe, nationality or gender and age within the country and sub-region.
It is in these regards that this office writes to seek for your assistance in providing support in cash/kind to make this medical center a reality. I look forward to your continued support and cooperation.
Signed: V. Baldeh
For Commissioner
North Bank Division
The new millennium started with good omen for Manding Medical Centre. I have been invited to go to Europe and America on a found raising trip for the center but could not because of my commitment with the Royal Victoria Hospital (RVH). I needed a longer vacation period to be able to travel and keep my job at the sane time. Above all my family

needed the monetary support, which would fade away if I lost the post at the RVH.

Hence, to my delight and greatest timely occurrence I heard from my long-standing friend in Colchester, Mrs. Lorna V. Robinson, inviting my wife and I to come to the UK to attend the wedding of their younger daughter on January 9th, 2000.

Coincidentally, I had just started my annual leave, which was to finish on the 26th of January 2000. The excitement mounted when we received a fax from the visa officer at the British High Commission in the Gambia requesting that we report to the visa processing office with our passports on Tuesday 8.30 am January 4th, 2000 for processing of our visas for our pending travels to the UK.

This took me by surprise because of the casual way we had discussed the possibility of such a trip. So when we got the telephone call followed by the said fax from the visa section I was caught off guard and had to rush through all the preparations for my wife and I to travel to UK without a second thought on whether adequate arrangements were being made for my eventual pursuit of a postgraduate degree (MRCP) in internal medicine.

Hind side has it that I needed to discuss this aspect with the visa councilor and request for eventual student visa status or leave to remain until my completion of the post graduate degree I wanted to pursue. God's ways and timing are best for every occasion. I was yearning to get a way out of the

financial limbo the center ran into since the change of government in the Gambia.
Now that opportunity was suddenly thrown on my laps by Lorna Robinson's open-ended invitation for my wife and to attend their daughter's wedding ceremony in the UK.
Interested donors started being weary about Military rule and possible restlessness that may ensue.
Hence, Manding Medical Centre literally lost all it's prospective over seases support as well as sponsors most of who had cold feet after the July coup d'etat of 2004.
I ended up running the center from my meager salary of D1500 or seventy-five pounds sterling per month and of literally hard labour with long hours at a time. The other source was from what little I could make from sales at the Bundung pharmacy.
To cut a long story short we were granted visas to travel to the UK. We left the Gambia on the 6th of January 2000 on a new footing and challenge to bring back some life into Manding Medical center while in England. I got on the ball as soon as the wedding ceremony was over.
I obtained a three–year study leave from the Management Board of the Royal Victoria Hospital in Banjul. This gave me all the time I needed to try to rekindle interest in the center and thereby inject into Manding Medical center cash flow it needed to help us meet or our targeted goal and objective for the farming community in the North Bank Division

of the Gambia. It was more like a miracle entering this new concrete and direct ways. Help from my host Lorna Robinson of Colchester, Essex, UK further anointed my hands.

Lorna and I wrote several letters to various places, including celebrities and organizations, most of who replied in the negative because of perception they had about the political climate in Gambia since the coup d'etat of July 22nd 1994.

Nonetheless some hinted being interested at a later date, meaning when the solders return to camp. A few donated small amounts plus hospital items. By now it became clear that we have to counter the perception most, on this side of the isles feel or had about the Gambia at the time.

This dreadful start did not alarm me much for I am fully aware of the wrong information about the average African in the village, who like most, is just a descent human being trying to earn an honest living for himself, family and community.

Villagers are least interested in all the political gimmickry shrouding and clothing their lives.

I do not at all blame the rest of world for getting sick and tired of helping and not seeing any tangible good come out of it and worse some African politicians and regimes show no interest in helping move the African people onto better and modern rewarding modalities of life.

They offer more lip service than opening avenues for progress. How many knew that the Ethiopian starvation was politically orchestrated by the then Mangestu regime? Genocide regime and the heartlessness of some African politicians made me feel sick.

To remove any possible skeptics regarding Manding Medical Centre and its objectives we decided to have it registered as a charitable organization in the UK under the name of Colchester Friends of Manding charitable trust.

The Robinson knew a solicitor who would be so kind to help us with the legal aspect of the registration process with UK charity Commission. They spoke to Mr. Bruce Ballard of the Birkett long Solicitors to come to our aid.

This kind gentleman, like my lawyer friend, Mr. Ousainou Darboe, gladly agreed to help and sent us a draft of the Trust deed. After a series of changes were made on the draft he forwarded our request to be registered in the UK as a charitable organization helping its twin partner or parent group, Manding Medical Centre at Njawara village in the Gambia, West Africa.

Meanwhile, we concentrated our activities through media campaign effort to call attention to existence of Friends of Manding and their desire in building a hospital for Manding Medical Centre at Njawara, the Gambia.

Again we ran into a very gentle heart in the person of Miss Helen Anderson of Colchester who was the Community website editor for Essex County.

She went head over heels regarding the idea of helping others so far away when approached by Lorna Robinson.

Helen thought the idea wonderful and at the same time helped us have our own website and also had an article published by the Evening Gazette which had a large reader circulation.

In the same vein I got the interest of Dr. Linda Mahon-Daly, Dr. Peter Wilson, Dr. Laurel Spooner, Dr. Richard Spooner, Dr. Philip Murray, Dr. Barbara Murray, Dr. Fredric Payne, who by the way was our Medical superintendent under who I worked at the RVH during the later part of colonial Gambia, along with many surgeries in the Colchester area.

These were my Good Samaritans of the day who worked acidulously to make Manding Medical Centre become a reality for the villagers in the Gambia.

Dr. Linda Mahon-Daly helped distribute letters about Manding Medical Centre to nearly all her colleagues in the Colchester Borough and so did Dr. Laurel Spooner. Bless their hearts for kindness and job well done. The news article published by the Evening Gazette brought us another very helpful and kind person, Mr. Malkait singh who is an ophthalmologist and had made several trips to the Gambia before knowing about the Friends of

Manding. He was delighted to join Neville Thompson, Connie Thompson, Lorna Robinson, Keith Robinson, Loenard Thompson, Mark Naylor, Barbara Philips and others as pioneering members of Friends of Manding.

Mr. Malkait Singh and I grew to be very good friends and he had since given me lots of personal monetary help to cater for my exams and family back in the Gambia.

I am very grateful for interest and kindness, and concern he showed about my family. A few months after the formation of Friends of Manding, Dr. Laurel Spooner spent a week in the Gambia vacationing and doing some fact finding about the center.

During which time she visited Manding Medical Centre at Njawara in the North Bank Division. The villagers were happy to meet her and thanked her about good work being done in Colchester regarding Manding Medical Centre.

Everyone was happy about the news that people in the UK were poised to assist Manding Medical Centre go forward in its drive to provide medical aid to villagers. A meeting of member of the Friends of Manding was scheduled for the first week of February 2001.

Mean while our solicitor continued pressing for registration of Friends of Manding, which is the arm and Manding Medical Centre's Colchester branch support group, as charity in the UK.

Dr. Laurel Spooner suggested we start with small-scale form of the center and then gradually expand as funds become available. This consideration would be studied in full and deliberated upon by the committee during the forth-coming February meeting.

My elder sister Binta Ceesay and her name-sake

Chapter 36
What is Manding Medical Centre?

Manding Medical Centre is a self-help village health organization founded by Dr. Alhasan S. Ceesay, located at Njawara village in the North Bank Region of the Gambia, West Africa.
Its objective is to provide medical service to the villagers by providing efficient and affordable medical aid to all people in and around the Gambia, especially the rural sector.
We are dedicated to relieving suffering and ensure effective treatment for villagers and all attending Manding Medical Centre at Njawara, NBR.

ESTABLISHED

The Manding Medical Centre is founded by Dr. Alhasan Sisawo Ceesay, a native of Njawara village in 1992, because of sheer shortage of medical service to the region and the preponderance of premature deaths by children from Malaria, malnutrition, diarrhea, and worm infestations. These childhood maladies account for almost 25% of Gambian children's death before the ripeful age of five years.
The Gambia Ministry of Health officially recognized the Centre in 1995 and prior to which it became a None Governmental Organization (NGO) on September 12th, 1994.

In addition, the Manding Medical Centre now has Friends of Manding Charitable Trust, Colchester, Essex, UK as its arm and liaison in the UK and the European Union countries. The Friends of Manding is a registered charity in England and Wales. Its registration number is 1088136 since August 21, 2001.

In similar development and purpose, Dr. Avery Aten heads the Friends of Manding Alpena Charitable Trust, Alpena, Michigan, UAS since May 2005.

MISSION STATEMENT

Suffering in another human being is a call to the rest of us to stand in fellowship. It requires us to be there and it is a mystery, which demands the spirit of caring, sharing and our presence.

Our duty as healthcare professionals is providing medical care, which is a fundamental right of all human beings.

This village health organization is dedicated to providing medical aid to the rural sector and farming community in the Gambia. It will compliment the health service in the Gambia in addition it will promote preventive medicine in the hinterland of the Gambia.

L – R: Dr. Alhasan Ceesay, Prof. Sulayman Nyang
Mr. Cloyd Ramsey and Prof. Francis Conti

MEMBERSHIP

Well over twenty thousand villagers, comprising of farmers, village heads, and chiefs, the Kerewan Area Council, Commissioners and local District Authority are now fully active enthusiastic members of Manding Medical Centre.

All are welcomed to join the endeavors of the center. People from the rest of the globe are more than welcomed to participate or share with us our dream in bring much needed medical service to people in desperate state because of lack of medical facilities.

ACTIVITIES

Manding Medical Centre tries to alleviate some of the above mentioned health problems and situations by having bimonthly health field trips/clinics to villages teaching them about health, preventive medicine and hygiene that would help reduce the number infected and the vectors responsible for these diseases.

We encourage antenatal and postnatal attendance of clinics by mothers and we treat the sick amongst them with minimum charge to not so elderly and pregnant young ladies.

The service is free to children, the very elderly, and the indigent needing emergency treatment. The rest pay amounts well below tat in private practice.

Money accrued is subsequently used to buy drugs with which to treat the patients and for other projects of the center. When in cession the center treats well more than 1000 patients per field trip to the villages.

We provide free information and advisory service on aids and sexually transmitted diseases (stds) to the young, all patients, their relatives and friends. We also plan to have a Nursing School in due course to augment not only staff but also the government health centers when the need arises.

IMMEDIATE GOAL AND APPEAL

The villagers are very enthused about the center and Toro Bahen village, next to Njawara village, has donated two plots of land for the building of the center and its ancillary units, which is now leased to manding medical center for ninety-nine years.

More than 2000 children die tragically from malaria and other childhood ailments stated above for shortage of health services.

We are eager to start building the children' and maternity wings of the proposed Gambia General Hospital at Manding Medical Centre and do need raise the required £900,000 pounds sterling to accomplish our goal. Ten bags of cement cost thirty pounds sterling or $60 (sixty us dollars).

Also we would be most grateful if we could be assisted with medicines and equipment to facilitate our work. Hence we implore you to kindly support our yearning to build the children' and maternity wings of Manding Medical Centre. We are dedicated to providing medical aid to the villager, especially children.

We are investors in people and you are invited to join the endeavors of Manding Medical Centre at Njawara village, the Gambia, West Africa.

Help us make a difference and beacon of hope for the villagers. Please give generously. Today's hope can be tomorrow's reality.

We want to contribute positively towards the health services of the Gambia, and with this center in place it will create greater health awareness and privation by the villagers.

Cash contributions of any amount should be sent in the name of Manding Medical Centre, to the Friends of Manding charitable Trust, 82 Finchingfield Way, Blackheath, Colchester, Essex, CO2 OAU, and England.

It is vital to be certain that Dr. Alhasan S. Ceesay is informed of your contribution via email thus: **alhasanceesay@hotmail.co**.uk

Your kindness and humane consideration to help save lives will always be deeply appreciated and grateful for by the villagers, the Gambia and I.

OVERSEASES LINKS

The Friends of Manding in Colchester, Essex County, UK, is a local group of residents, doctors, and nurses who regularly visited the Gambia and is in support of Manding Medical Centre. Manding medical center through the auspices of the Friends of Manding recently received recognition and registration by the UK Charity Commission. They serve as support and our liaison in the Europe Union. The Friends of Manding in behalf of Manding Medical Centre at Njawara has been entered in the central Register of charities with effect from August 21, 2001; the registration number is 1088136 for England and Wales. Also, a similar charitable trust, the Alpena Friends of Manding Charitable Trust of Michigan, USA, has been established in Alpena, Michigan in June 2006. It's headed by Dr. Avery Aten a resident physician chairman of the Women and newborn of the Alpena region Community Health along with the medical community of Alpena.

My grandson: Alasan Mballow Jr, Swedenb 2017

Chapter 37
Manding Medical Centre Milestones

Manding Medical Centre has been in my mind's drawing board since the early 1950s but it took off in earnest when I returned to the Gambia, after graduating from medical school in 1992. The Centre is registered as a charity with the Attorney general's Office, Department of Justice, Banjul, The Gambia, since 1993. The Gambia Ministry of Health also recognized it in the same year.

Toro Bahen village, Lower Badibou, NBD, Gambia, donated two huge plots of land for the location of the center in 1993.

Our none governmental (NGO) status was approved in 1994. On September 21, 1995 Tango Secretariat sent a United Nations voluntary program Officer, Mr. Muloshi on field trip to evaluate the organizational and extent of support for Manding Medical Centre at Njawara village.

Mr. Muloshi's recommendation after two days field trip to the region stated thus; "Looking at the caliber of leadership and development activities to some NGO Tango members in comparison to Manding Medical Centre, the organization need consideration since they have already activities with a promising future. Looking at composition of the Board, they have people with a vision.

They have strong membership and backup at grass root levels. The organization has chosen to what is right at the right time and their concentration in one area is vital and good starting point.
Any success achieved by any group or organization depends on good leadership and discipline. Manding Medical Centre has high quality leadership and deserves NGO status".
It was not until my travels to the UK in 2000 that the Friends of Manding Charitable Trust was formed and registered as charity in England and Wales by the UK Charity Commission.
Friends of Manding is the extended arm of Manding Medical Centre at Njawara, The Gambia. They serve as our liaison in the UK and the European Union. Please browse on our website thus: friendsofmandinggambimed.btck.co.uk, to learn more or for further information about our work and organization.
We are still on fund raising activities to earn enough to enable us build the children' and maternity units of the hospital at Manding Medical Centre at Njawara.
In May 2005, 11 American students and their instructor Mr. Thomas Ray visited Manding Medical Centre at Njawara.
Additionally, input from has now resulted in Alpena City, Michigan, USA, twining by proclamation with Njawara and Kinte kunda villages in Gambia respectively on the 5th of December 2005.

In June 2006, Dr. Avery Aten, Chairman of the Women and Newborn of Alpena Region Health Community along with the medical community of Alpena commenced processing application for a charitable Trust to be named Alpena friends of Manding Charitable Trust, Michigan, USA.
This will soon be finalized and up and running to help Dr. Alhasan Ceesay in the provision of medicine and educational assistance to schools in the Lower Badibou district, the Gambia, West Africa.
In August 2008, Dr. Alhasan Ceesay and the Badibou Cultural Dance Troupe will visit Alpena and other cities in Michigan for fund raising drive to enable the building of the Manding Medical Centre children and maternity units at Njawara village.
Dr. Richard Bates, an Obynge, and a number of medical professionals involved in obstetrics and gynecology at Alpena, Michigan joined Manding Medical Centre's crusade on 17/08/07.

Chapter 38
Template for Regional Development

Manding Medical Centre became a template for districts elsewhere and villagers to nurture, develop further and handover to the next generation. This None Governmental Health Organization epitomizes a developmental watchtower for the region.

Manding medical center at Njawara village is now a pulsating source of hope, jobs, training and superb medical service to the region.

Every one knows that government alone does not move things fast enough. Society must be radical and pragmatic to pitch into its development.

We know all too well that the developed world got where its because private efforts were self prophetic and projects like Manding Medical Centre goes long ways to initiate and stimulate community to work together for a positive agenda for its people.

Manding Medical Centre is a positive good that help our regions to cross the road.

We thank every one for making it possible that our center became a platform and guide in rejuvenating our regions. We now provide medical service to all Gambians and none Gambians domiciled in the Gambia. We will create more jobs as need arises. This was the reason why I gave my life's comfort for reward that will benefit most needy villagers. It came through determination and kindness of many people worldwide.

There are some things only governments can do but together communities through collective initiatives can achieve at least fifty percent of their developmental needs in addition to government effort.

Fatou Koma-Ceesay and Isatou Ceesay, Birmingham UK

Chapter 39

Appeal to the International Community

Dear Readers,
The above information about Manding Medical Centre is included in this work only hoping that it will help spread the word more extensively and draw awareness to a greater community of people and readers of my work.
It is my beliefe that lots of good people out there may want to participate or give to the cause and goal of the Center should they be aware of its existents for the villagers.
Hence, I am appealing for help and participatory support from all able to extend their hearts to make this much needed medical endeavor to come to fruition for the rural sector of the Gambia.
Who knows you might even end up coming to bask in our beautiful seasides and relish Gambian generosity. Music for me is reaching out to help others and my patients are yearning for your kind participation and donation in cash/kind.
Thanks a million for considering our appeal. God blesses your heart(s). I write with believe that by it money can be generated to provide a much needed medical service to the rural sector.
Writing about the Manding Medical Centre may course some Good Samaritan and any wanting to leave foot prints on the sand of time for a good

cause to come to our assistance to help us meet the goals of the center at Njawara village, the Gambia, West Africa. My head, heart and soul are devoted to my family, the Gambia and Manding Medical Centre.

It is not a God given calling but a mere conviction that our rural folks deserve better health service than currently available and hence human calling to want to contribute positively to bring resolution of some of our rural health service inadequacies.

I never had an angel come down to me nor have I ever heard the voices of God saying, "Ceesay, you must do so and so" as many mocked Manding Medical Centre emanated from sheer conviction that it is a dutiful way of doing the right thing for curbing premature deaths of children before reaching 5 years of life from malaria, water born diseases, and warm infestations; and in the same vein providing both pre and postnatal care to the pregnant.

Hence, portions of proceeds of sales in all my work go to help meet the center's operational costs and in providing scholarship to indigent indigenous rural candidates due course return to serve rural Gambia wishing to read for a medical degree or agriculture and Medicine.

Chapter 40
American Guests Visit Manding Medical Centre, Njawara, Gambia, May 2005

The telephone call of the 5/01/05 and following fours later from Mr. Thomas P. Ray (Tom) opened the Pandora's box that became harbingers to a remarkable trip to Manding Medical Centre at Njawara village in the Gambia West Africa by the Alpena Community College's Leadership class headed by none other than Mr. Thomas P. Ray.

I contacted Mr. Ray as soon as it was brought to my attention that some ACC students were contemplating visiting Manding Medical Centre at Njawara in May 2005. My message sent on the 6/01/05 to Mr. Thomas Ray ran thus:
An old friend, Mr. Mathew Dunnkel, staff of Alpena Community College, had a long chat with me last night and he brought to my attention of a possibility that the leadership class plants to travel to the Gambia as guest of the Manding Medical Centre at Njawara.
I am more than willing to and happy to pave the way for those that would venture the trip. I do need an e-mail or fax from you indicating desire to go to the Gambia on a mission for Manding Medical Centre. I will speak to both the district authority and the schools about your most welcomed trip to the Gambia.

Manding Medical Centre is a self-help village health organization I setup in Njawara upon returning to the Gambia in 1992. We provide medical service to villagers. Torro Bahen in Lower Badibou District has donated Land for location of the medical center and its ancillaries. We only have a corrugated shed as a clinic at present.

We are now on the verge of building the first phase, being the children and Maternity units of the center, and do need monetary assistance. I am delighted to know of your intentions. Please contact me, as soon as get this I want to speak with the class.

Mr. Thomas P. Ray replied the next day 7/01/05 thus, "I was thrilled when Mathew discussed the possibility of a trip to the Gambia for our leadership students. I will meet with whole class next week to discuss the possibility.

As I am sure you are aware of the cost of airfares from Alpena to the Gambia is high. So I will need to be certain the students are committed to raising the money needed before we begin making plans.

I have traveled to many locations, but never to Africa.

So I am also very excited about the prospects for myself. After I meet with the students on Tuesday next week I will e-mail you with further information. I wish to commend you for your personal achievements. I plan to purchase a copy of your recent book to share with my students and for my personal reading.

Thank you for your help and enthusiasm." I replied advising that he bargain for insured group tickets. And on the 12/01/05 Thomas ray emailed that he had spoken to the students who had agreed to take on a service trip as part of the course.

They would only be able to travel in a group and stay from 10 to 14 day at Njawara in May 2005. Thomas wanted to know if there was an existing program at Njawara that would be able to accommodate the students.

He further assured me that the students would be comfortable in a dormitory housing or make shit dormitories. In addition I let Ray know on the 14/01/05 that I have spoken to the Commissioner, north Bank Division and the local District Authority in the lower Badibou District regarding their pending trip to Njawara as guest of Manding Medical Centre and the region.

I assured him these authorities would be more than happy to have his class visit with them. I requested that he e-mail me stating specifically y what they would want to do while in the Gambia. I suggested that they could help teach in some schools. I assured them that even though business and some residents have moved out of Njawara there is still some activity at the village.

Thomas replied sending the following on 15/01/05, "Thank you for the great news. I am very excited about the prospect and have begun search for group airfares with special student rates.

I will inform the students on Tuesday and contact you immediately afterwards via email. I have a few questions. What costs do we need to expect in the Gambia and in your village? How will we travel from Banjul to the village?

We need to be certain we have both for ourselves and for the foundation from which we hope to receive grants. When I write the other email, are there tasks other than tutoring that I should include? Are there other ways we can help while we are there?

I am more excited about the prospect of this service trip everyday and the students are quite enthused.

In another email dated 15/02/05. Thomas Ray wrote, "The students in the leadership class are so committed to this project that they voted to contribute their own money toward the travel to Njawara in May.

I have begun drafting the letter to the commissioner many times, but I have some questions. Am I asking the commissioner to help organize local housing for us? Do I want his permission to visit Njawara/ Should I tell him what we would like to do there?

What subjects might they tutor? Are there any construction projects for the center or the village with which we could help? I would also like to know if there are any material supplies we could bring with us to donate to the center or the village?

One possible way for us to save money would be to fly into Dakar Senegal and travel from there overland to Njawara." All the above concerns and questions were answered but a small hiccup in fundraising occurred leaving a distinct possibility that the students will not be able to raise enough to make the trip, the reason being that the majority source for funding for the trip fell through.
This left all of us jittery but Thomas Ray and his leadership class were in no mood to change their plans to travel to the Gambia in May 2005.
On the same day 15/02/05 I received another email from Jay Walterriet, Director of Public Information for Alpena Community College. It stated that he was asked to contact me for more photos of myself and those of the clinic at Njawara.
He wanted more information regarding the leadership-planned trip to the Gambia. I was told that the local television station would like to do a segment on the leadership class and their trip.
As part of the segment photos I sent as much relevant photos as I had at the time to enable the reporter to do his TV-segment on the planned leadership trip to Njawara the Gambia.
Mr. Jay on the 17/02/05 emailed thanking me for providing the photos and also assured me that the Alpena Community College students have received good deal of interest from the local media regarding the Leadership trip and both he and Penney Boldrey were trying to provide all of the information they

could. My email was given to reporters who might want to contact me for more information. The entire twenty students could not enlist for the final take off to Africa. Hence, Thomas P. Ray and 11 students took on the venture of their lives to the Gambia as guest of Manding Medical Centre at Njawara village.

On 17/02/05 Thomas P. Ray, instructor of the leadership class, sent me the following email copy of the final letter he sent to the commissioner and the local district authority at the Lower Badibou District spelling out their intentions and wish while guest of Manding Medical Centre for a two weeks duration. Here is the letter.

Thomas P. Ray
Alpena Community College
666 Johnson Street
Alpena, Michigan 49707
17 February 2005

The commissioner,
North Bank Division
Kerewan Headquarters
Lower Badibou
The Gambia, West Africa
17/02/05

Dear Commissioner,

I am pleased to inform you that our plans to visit Njawara on behalf of the Manding Medical Centre. I am the Advisor and instructor for a group of college students from Alpena Community College in Michigan in the USA.
We plan to visit Njawara in May and hope you will help us find lodgings with the local families during our two weeks stay. Our plan as of now is to fly out of the US on May 6th to Banjul via London and return on May 19th 2005.
During our stay in the Gambia, our hope is to provide any assistance we can to the community on behalf of Manding Medical Centre. We would like to visit the schools in Njawara and tutor the children and share stories and activities with them.
I also hope that we will have the opportunity to visit the important centers of the community and learn as much as we can in our short stay about the people and life at Njawara and Gambia.
I have communicated our plans with Dr. Alhasan S. Ceesay, who has kindly extended the invitation to us on behalf of Manding Medical Centre.
Sincerely
Thomas P. Ray
English Instructor
The Regional Commissioner and the district authority of Lower Badibou in the Gambia acknowledged this letter. Now being certain of the

trip I set to inform my Board members about the trip even though it was widely known affair leaving everyone expectant. The certainty of the trip was concretized by Thomas's March 10, 2005 email. It simply updated me on the progress made regarding the trip and that the students have raised half the amount of money needed to travel to the Gambia.

He further reaffirmed the fact that everyone concerned is working hard on the remaining sum. They arranged inoculations and are preparing to apply for visas to the Gambia. Ray said they were all enthused and had used my address in Gambia for the visa information requirements.

Again, I was delighted for things were now heading the right direction for the historic and unique trip to Njawara. I am now certain that more doors boost ours and the centre's goal for the Gambia will be opened by this simple friendly act of the Alpena Community College.

Here is finally my dispatch to board members of manding Medical Centre at Njawara village.

Manding Medical Centre
United Kingdom Contact
245 Great Western Street
Manchester, M14 4LQ
England
25/03/05

Dear Board Member,

I am pleased to bring to your attention about American guests to Manding Medical Centre at Njawara. Mr. Thomas P. Ray along with 11 Alpena Community College students will be visiting the Gambia as our guest in May2005.
They will be leaving the USA for the Gambia on May 6th, 2005 and depart for the United States on the 19th, May 2005. I would be most grateful if you give some of your time to meet them and make their visit memorable. There are many benefits to be accrued for the center and the Gambia.
I am at present arranging the form of placement and possible scholarships in various fields of study at my previous colleges in Michigan USA. I have been in constant contact with Commissioner Batala Juwara at Kerewan and I would like all of you to brain storm and make this an ongoing link between us and Alpena Community College and other Michigan cities I am now in negotiation with. Alpena city has developed interest in our project.
I am also happy to report that my former college, Alpena Community College, has awarded me, "Distinguished 2005 graduate."
Find enclosed correspondence from Mr. Thomas Ray, in behalf of the leadership class of Alpena Community College to the Commissioner Batala juwara and Sefo fafanding Kinteh.

I look forward to your understanding and participation to help open up the Pandora's box of goodwill for the Gambia. This is a onetime opportunity for the Gambia that would make out two people linked for good goals and noble cause for generations to come.

My regards and keep in touch.

Yours Sincerely

Dr. Alhasan s. Ceesay, MD

Founder/coordinator

Cc; Ousainou Darboe

Fafa Mbye

Dr. Dawda Ceesay

Dr. Ayo Palmer

Mr. Saim Kinteh

Mr. Sambou Kinteh

Mr. Mustapha Njie

Elh. Maja Sonko

Dodou Ceesay

Siswao Ceesay

Mbee Sonko

On April 7, 2005 Thomas Ray updated me stating that the visa applications were going well and that most of the students have received their visas. In addition let me privilege readers to some of the emails to me about the pending trip by students and what it would mean to them.

Alison Jane Smolinski said, "Hello Dr. Ceesay. I am really excited about the service trip, only a couple more weeks. Right now we are trying to prepare for the trip, just getting the basic necessities and what we should be packing.
I just read about you are trying to build a bakery at Njawara. Even though our resources are limited, is there any or something we could do to help out? I thought we could help in some way.
I also want to say thank you for the wonderful experience you giving to us. I realize it will be truly an eye opener. I feel as if I could be able to repay you for these two weeks that you about to give us. Thank you Dr. Ceesay."
Another email from Brittany Posthumous simply said, "I am one of the students from Alpena Community College that will be coming this May 2005 to help. After learning all the things that you have done I must say you are an inspiration and the world can use more people who care as much as you do. I can't wait to come to Njawara.
I am very excited to be able too help and thank you for the invitation." Lastly, Ms. Grace Schmitz sent in the following before leaving for the Gambia. "I am a member of the Alpena Community that will be assisting you this May at Njawara. I am greatly looking forward to my visit to the Gambia. Thank you so much for the invitation."

The Friends of Manding, a charitable Trust at Colchester, had the following in its website about the pending trip to Njawara, the Gambia. It read, "News flash 12 Americans visiting:
A class of 11 students and their instructor Mr. Thomas P. Ray from Alpena Community College, Alpena, Michigan will be visiting the Gambia as guest of Manding Medical Centre from the 6th of May to the 19th of May 2005.
They will be visiting communities and tutor at local schools. Alpena has developed interest in project Manding Medical Centre at Njawara. We are negotiating are negotiating to have this exchange as an going affair between Alpena and Njawara."
As time drew near to the flight to Gambia Thomas Ray contacted the Commissioner on several occasions to clear last possible huddles that may surface.
Nonetheless preparations went smoothly and Mr. Thomas P. Ray and his Alpena Community College leadership class left America on May 10th, 2005 via Madrid and then Dakar, Senegal before embarking at Banjul, the Gambia.
As fate would have the team instead hired a bus from Dakar to Hamdali village in the North Bank, which was nearer to Njawara village. I later learnt that they were given a VIP escort from Hamdali via Kerewan to their final destination Njawara village.

As expected, I called the mayor /village Alkalo of Njawara, Aja Hadi Panneh and enquired about tour American visitors. She told me they were fine and housed at the semi motel used for foreign guest at Njawara village.

Mr. Thomas Ray and I spoke at length with Sefo fafanding Kinteh who reassured me that everything possible will be done to help make, "Our guests comfortable and like wise a memorable visit in due course."

I spoke briefly to the Commissioner the next day to get feed back from him. He was elated and concord that good can emanate from such interaction between diverse people. The two weeks flew fast for the students most of whom did not want to leave at the time for kindness rendered them by the villagers. It is said that good thing do not last long and this was the experience of the students who went to Njawara in May 2005.

Here are the reactions of the American students after their trip to Njawara, the Gambia. The Alpena Community College started sending report and appraisals of their experience as guest of Manding Medical Centre at Njawara. Alison Jane Smolinski was first to submit a commentary.

She wrote,

"Hello Dr. Ceesay, the trip to Njawara was incredible! I did not want to leave. It was an experience of a lifetime that I will never forget. Everyone in the village was very kind and helpful.

I have never met such kind people in my entire life. I found the villagers doing everything possible to make their lives better. I realized that many people work together to get a job done or finished. This is absolutely wonderful.

Everyone was helpful in the village. The people of Njawara gave us such wonderful hospitality. The food and shelter was more than we deserved.

Also your wife, Mrs. Fatou Koma-Ceesay, was all too good to us.

We had a remarkable time with her at Bundung/Serekunda. Her cooking was excellent. And the gifts she gave all of us, we did not deserve. Your family is wonderful and was too kind to us. I would like to thank you for the incredible experience you have given me.

I could not asked for anything more. I immensely enjoyed myself. I want to go back one day. I also want you to know I will do my best to help in whatever way I can.

I realize that actions are louder than words and hope I can prove that to everyone. Thank you." Another missive came from Grace Schiimtz. It read, "I really enjoyed my time at Njawara. The people treated us very well and it was a pleasure to spend two weeks with them. Your wife is a wonderful person and was very hospitable to us. I will always be grateful to her kind treatment. I hope to make another visit to Njawara in the future. It is a wonderful place.

It was an eye-opening experience. The people were absolutely marvelous. They treated us as their own family and welcomed us with open hands. I had no idea that they would be that hospitable.

I really miss walking to the river and spending time with the children. It was my first experience in Gambia and hopefully it will not be my last.

I hope I can return their kindness. Would love to see how the kids have grown."

The last but not the least came from Mr. Thomas P. Ray, English instructor and leadership advisor at the Alpena Community College, Alpena, Michigan, USA. It read: "I want to thank you for the opportunity you provided my students on this trip to Njawara, Gambia.

The entire experience was enjoyable and valuable as a means of teaching my students something about the responsibility that comes with the privileges they enjoy here. Everyone was kind to us on the trip and the students came away with many great souvenirs and memories.

I have many digital photos and am working on producing a CD of them to send out. I also plan to type up a version of my journal for posting on the Internet and I will send parts of that to you.

I plan to call the village this weekend to extend my appreciation to everyone.

Do you know anything about the proposed potential sister city relationship between Alpena and Njawara? I would like to start making some local contacts here to help that process. I am also hopeful that future trips will be possible for my student." As you know very well man proposes but God disposes things.

Thomas Ray took over the running of the Department and with that came a hand full of challenging responsibilities.

He was not able to provide CD until the 11th of October 2005 after several reminders from me and those visiting my website: (www.friendsofmandinggambimed.btck.co.uk) or www.publishkunsa.com to learn more about us.

Finally, Mr. Thomas P. Ray contacted me on 4/11/05 to let me know he had the college mailing office send the CD and other materials registered delivery to me.

Then he made a donation of $1000 (One thousand us dollars) in the name of Friends of Manding, a charitable trust at Colchester Essex County that organizes fundraising for Manding Medical Centre at Njawara village.

With regards to the state of the sister city status in the pipeline, I was the proponent of it. It was one of my goals for inviting the Americans to my village in the Gambia. I just believed that unveiling the false masks and stigmata others had about Africa would create harmony in its unique way. People need to accept difference in the cultures. I transmitted all reactions presented by our American visitors to the Commissioner, the chief and village heads especially Aja Hadi Panneh of Njawara village. Sadly, Mr. Ray left Alpena Community College for another lucrative post in one of the universities in New York.

I am still trying to trace but was not making head way at the time this book was being printed. Friends and his former students are trying to trace him out and hope to do so in due course.

89 year old Mrs. Binta Ceesay, elder sister, Banjul, The Gambia West Africa 2016

Chapter 42
Distinguished 2005 Graduate Award

I attended Alpena Community College (ACC) in Michigan from September 1967 to December 1969. My contacts with friends at Alpena never waned. Hence, the wheels of profound recognition by the institute started rolling when Mathew Dunckle called me to let me know he read my book, "The legend against all odds."

He was very impressed and intrigued by my experience and fortitude since my leaving Alpena Community College in 1969. I met Mathew Dunckel when he was twelve years old. His father Dr. Elbridge Dunckle was my academic advisor while I was at the Alpena Community College.

I will without any hesitation or reservation still recommend Dr. Dunckel for academic advisor to any foreign student attending the college.

It was during one of our telephone conversation (02/0i/05) that Mathew Duckel told me of the possibility of Alpena Community College recommending me for the Distinguished 2005 Graduate Award offered annually by the college to outstanding Alumni.

Alpena Community College recognizes its graduates annually for their academic and their career accomplishment for their communities. It simply recognizes the aspirations of Alumni for their people.

The Pandora's box was opened by an innocuous telephone conversation in recognizing my aspiration and goal for providing medical aid to Gambian villagers. Mathew asked me to fax him any and all possible documentation about work and me I do in the Gambia.

He would then speak to the relevant authorities regarding my being nominated for the Distinguished 2005 Graduate of Alpena Community College coming May 5th, 2005 spring/summer commencement.

Mathew did just as promised.

In a nutshell, here is the letter from Mrs. Penny Boldrey, Executive Director Alpena Community College Foundation. It read:

Alpena Community College
666 Johnson Street
Alpena, Michigan 49707
January 6, 2005

Alhasan S. Ceesay, MD
245 Great Western Street
Moss Side
Manchester, M14 4LQ
England

Dear Dr. Ceesay,

Mathew Dunckel shared the information that you recently provided to him regarding your professional achievements since your early years at Alpena Community College.

I am extremely pleased to share with you that your many outstanding accomplishments have earned you the distinction of Distinguished Graduate of Alpena Community College (ACC) for 2005.

We commend you for your humanitarian efforts in founding and developing the Manding Medical Centre in the Gambia, West Africa. I am anxious to read your book, "The legend against all odds" once Mathew has finished with it.

Without a doubt, you serve as an example of how a solid educational foundation from Alpena Community College can launch a lifetime of achievements.

You will be honoured at our spring commencement Exercises on Thursday May 5, 2005; which begins at 7:00 pm in the Park Arena at Alpena Community College.

We invite you to join us on that evening. However, we certainly understand that making a trip to the United States, on so short a notice, may not be feasible.

During the commencement program, I will share a synopsis of your extraordinary career that has earned you the honour of Distinguished Graduate.

If you are able to join us, you will be invited to join me at the podium to receive your award and to address the audience if you wish.

Would you be willing to provide us with the following: (1) a copy of your professional resume, (2) a paragraph on your memories of Alpena Community College and how your experience helped you achieve your goals and (3) a professional photo for use in our alumni newsletter as well as an ad that will appear in the Alpena News paper. Please feel free to call me or e-mail me with any additional questions you may have.

Again, congratulations! We look forward to hearing from you in the future.

Sincerely

Penny Boldrey

Executive Director

My response to this honour and invitation to my second home America was swift and obvious as penned below. I emailed Penny forth with as my heart was overwhelmed with joy for being recognized by my Alma Mata Alpena community College.

It simply read:

245 Great Western Street
Manchester, M14 4LQ
England
13/01/05

Mrs. Penny Boldrey
Executive Director
Alpena Community College
Foundation
666 Johnson Street
Alpena, Michigan 49707

Dear Penny Boldrey,

I am overwhelmed and do not know where to begin this note of thanks to Alpena Community College. In my mind it is the American people who deserve such honour and distinction for I am only recipient of the goodness of the Americans.

I am humbled and further rejuvenated by the thought and recognition of my goals and work for the Gambia. I remember in the 60s when people used to tell me, "You will end up just like all foreign student who came to America. They end up getting trapped by the greener pasture syndrome of America."

To such challenges my response had always been, I for one will disappoint a lot of you for I will never rest until I bring to my people the American know how and willingness to share with others.

This stance has never changed and will not ever change because the only I can, in small measure compared to what you did for us poor ones, pay back is to able to show what the USA is all about and her stand for the little guy anywhere on this planet. I will look into my schedule to see if I can afford to be in Alpena May 2005. I will let you know by the end of February 2005. Meanwhile I am faxing a resume and will try to send my photos via email or surface mail.

Where it is not possible for me to attend in May 2005, would it be okay for my first American family friend, Mrs. Rita Riggs, to represent me at the ACC spring commencement? She was the first people in Alpena that opened their homes to me. She and her family will certainly appreciate recognition of their help to this simple Gambian.

None toeless rest assured that I have not yet slammed the door to my seeing Alpena once more. Timing and visa problems might make it unattainable. Again, please accept profound gratitude to all of you and to Alpena Community College. God blesses you and rain peace on earth in 2005. Cheers and regards.

Sincerely
Dr. Alhasan S. Ceesay, MD

Mrs. Penny Boldrey wasted no time in replying thus:

Alpena Community College
Alpena, Michigan 49707
13/01/05

Hi Dr. Ceesay,

Yes, I did receive your curriculum vitae and thank you for forwarding that to me. We are extremely proud of you and your accomplishments.

Once I get my hand on your book, I will pay special notice to the ACC chapter. The best part of my job is the opportunity to meet former alumni and learn of the impact ACC had in their lives.

Please believe me that we understand if you are unable to join us at commencement on May 5, 2005. Indeed we would be pleased to have Rita Riggs accept this honour on your behalf. Rita is a remarkable and kind woman.

My husband speaks fondly of her and has stayed in close contact with her. I look forward to getting to know you better through our correspondence. And meet you in person someday. Regards

Mrs. Penny Boldrey

Executive Director

As tine drew near to May commencement and at the end it was not possible for me to travel and attend the ceremony in person. So Mrs. Rita Riggs and her family stepped in for me.

Her elder son Robert Riggs was designated to receive the award in my behalf as representative of the Rita who was in her 80s at the time. I emailed the following remarks to be read by Robert Riggs at the time the award is given. It is titled:

A FUTURE FOR ALL

Mr. President, staff, graduates, Ladies and gentlemen. I am deeply moved and humbled being chosen Alpena Community College's Distinguished Alumni for 2005.

This recognition belongs to America. Without the good will and foresight of the staff, students and the community of Alpena in 1967, I might never have had the chance to earn education with which to help my people move forward in life,

Hence, allow me reiterate profound gratitude to Alpena Community College, my fellow student, people of Alpena and America at large.

My life after Alpena Community College has been full of trials and tribulations detailed in my first book, "The legend against all odds". One relief in it is the robust blessing and peace of mind I have knowing that I am right in what I am doing for my people.

There are those who claim heaven in being rich but for me it is reaching out to help others that matter in life. Upon graduating from medical school, I returned to the Gambia and setup a self-help village health organization (Manding Medical Centre) at Njawara in an effort to provide a much-needed medical service to the rural sector.

I am happy to report that membership has grown beyond twenty thousand villagers. Please join me to catch a dream for my villagers. Manding Medical Centre will help portray the America we all dream and yearn to be part.

We are on the verge of building the children and maternity units and do need monetary, equipment and medicines assistance in our drive to provide this unique service to villagers. To the graduates, I would like to remind you that, the great tide of history flows and as if flows it carries to the shores of reality what binds us as one human race.

Be aware of the extent, depth and gravity of the challenges ahead as you set out to transform, reconstruct and integrate America into a global icon. Sincere congratulations for your march towards success and fulfillment.

Alpena Community College has given you the first footprints. Walk your way with head held high and determination to succeed in the world. Confucius said, "Our greatest glory is never failing, but in rising every time we fail" Stockpiles of Atomic bombs or weapons of mass destruction and dictators do not measure greatness.

I believe strongly and sincerely that with deep-rooted wisdom and dignity, innate respect for human rights and lives, the intense humanity will make us more cherished and better leaders.

This will make us able to contribute towards the future and progress of mankind. I am happy for you and hope that you will fly the American flag for it is the great American constitution.

Finally, I would like to pay tribute to pas and present staff, students and Alpena community for having given me the opportunity to forge for my people. Allow me make special mention and express thanks to the remarkable and noble friends I met in Alpena. Sincere thanks from my family, villagers and I to Howard and Rita Riggs, Judge Philip and Viola Glennie, Mr. Henry Valli, Dr. Eldridge Dunckel, Dr. Strom, Bill and Magnet cruise, Dr. Charles T. Egli, Mr. Cloyd and Norata Ramsey and the Medical Arts Clinic, the Jesse Baser Foundation and all who helped make my sojourn to Alpena a remarkable success.

If I have a million friends, I would like many more to be like you. I hope you will believe in, as well as join me, in my dream of providing modern medical aid to the Gambian villagers. Thanks a million and bless America!

BY: DR. ALHASAN S. CEESAY, MD

Mrs. Penny Boldrey called to let me know she confirmed the details with Robert Riggs, who was selected by the family to deliver the speech. She assured me that Bob was all set with my remarks and had been practicing many times.

Rita and Donna will also attend with other friends. To make it official she sent this note to Robert Riggs (Bob).

Alpena Community college
666 Johnson Street
Alpena, Michigan 49707
April 21, 2005

Robert Riggs
312 Liberty Street
Alpena, Michigan 49707

Dear bob,

Dr. Alhasan Ceesay has informed me that you will be representing him at our commencement ceremony and accepting the distinguished Graduate award on his behalf.
Our spring commencement exercises will be held on Thursday, May 5, at 7 pm. There will be VIP seating near the front left section of the Park arena for you and your family. During the commencement program, I will share a brief synopsis of Dr. Ceesay's career.
I will invite you to join me at the podium to receive Dr. Ceesay's Distinguished Graduate Award. Following the presentation, you will have the opportunity to share Dr. Ceesay's remarks.
I shared with Dr. Ceesay that his comments must be kept brief (2-3 minutes) because our program consists of many individuals who will also be addressing the graduating class.
After the ceremony we would like to take some photographs, so if you could remain near your seats, I will come to you. A reception at the Jesse Besser Museum follows commencement and you are also invited to join.

Enclosed you will find a copy of Dr. Ceesay's remarks. I look forward to hearing from you. Please call me to confirm your participation.
Sincerely
Penny Boldrey
Executive Director.

Two weeks prior to the ceremony I received an email from Karen Eller, administrative assistant in the president's ACC office of public information, letting me know that she intend to write about me in the College's newspaper, the Lumberjack Link issue of the spring/summer Alumni news letter publication.
Penny Boldrey also informed me that Kerrie Miller, news writer for the Alpena News would like to feature me in the local paper. I immediately emailed the following to Kerrie Miller at the Alpena news.
Hi Kerrie,
I just received Penny's email with the good news that you want to feature me in the Alpena news. For me this would be a dream come true.
Yes! By all means go ahead and feel free to contact me should you want more information about work or me I am doing in the Gambia. I am a simple person that loves helping others get on with life the best way they can during their short sojourn on mother earth.
I strongly believed that those of us privileged to learn from America have responsibility to share

American goodwill with our people. That would be the only way our people can experience the real America that stands for the downtrodden and the innovative. I still feel very happy when I come across an American.

If your paper is able to help me get Manding Medical Centre at Njawara out of its current limbo, then you would have participated in the most noble and worthy cause that will outlive us and will be a spring board of hope and medical service for generations we can ever dream of.

We are still on fundraising stage to build the first phase, the children and maternity units, which according to estimates will cost around #250,000 or about $500,000 I committed a portion of proceeds of my books, "The legend against all odds, Medicine for the villager and When hearts melt in love" to the Manding Medical Centre but they are not selling enough to get things in fast gear.

I need help to bring relief to my villagers. Well, this is enough introductions until I hear from you. God bless you and thanks a million for being kind towards us.

Sincerely

Dr. Alhasan S. Ceesay, MD

Kerri replied requesting a synopsis of how I found out about Alpena in the 60s. So I sent her the following summary.

I came to Alpena City by simply going to the then American consulate in Banjul, the Gambia and asked for a catalogue with information on American colleges.
As a beggar normally has no choice, I started from the top alphabets. Well, Alpena Community College was there and was the first that accepted my application among the schools that replied to my desire to pursue further education in America.
This part is well documented in chapter in my book, "The legend against all odds" highlighting my experience at ACC from 1967 t0 1969.
I was born and bread in abject poverty and I am only fighting for my villagers to have a chance to proper medical care nothing more and nothing less. I hope you will help me get your readers interested in Manding Medical Centre and its objective for the villagers.
Thank you for taking upon the task of writing about my work and me in the Gambia. Manding Medical center is at present in limbo and we yearn for a boost or a short in the ram to get things moving faster. Please visit our wed site: beehive.totalessex.co.uk/gambimed.
Signed: Dr. Alhasan S. Ceesay
I will reproduce both articles by Karen Eller of the Alpena Community College News letter, the Lumberjack Link and that by Kerrie Miller of the Alpena News respectively.

For now let us head to spring commencement podium to hear or listen to what Mrs. Penny Boldrey had in mind about this simple village doctor. Robert Riggs and family attended the ceremony in time but is now Penny's turn to deliver her remarks about my achievements from the day of Alpena Community College to the present. It is simple and movingly states:

"Good evening and congratulations graduates!
The Alpena Community College Foundation created the Distinguished Graduate award not only to recognize, but to honour our graduates who have gone on to contribute to society through successful careers.

Our recipient tonight serves as an example of how a solid education foundation from ACC can launch a lifetime achievements. I am pleased to share with you that our 2005 Distinguished Graduate is Dr. Alhasan S. Ceesay from the Gambia, West Africa. Dr. Ceesay received his Associates of Arts Degree in 1969, exactly two years after leaving the Gambia. He credits many individuals, and the generosity of others, as the driving force behind his success. Following his graduation from ACC, Dr. Ceesay transferred to Olivet College, on full-tuition scholarship provided to him by the Besser Foundation.

In 1971, he earned a Bachelor of Arts Degree in Biology from Olivet, and in 1973 completed his Master of Science degree from Michigan

Technological University at Houghton, Michigan, USA. Dr. Ceesay taught biology for several years in the Gambia before entering University of Liberia Medical School in 1979 and years later completed his medical education at the American University of the Caribbean at Plymouth, Montserrat, West Indies where he was awarded his Doctor of Medicine Degree in 1992.

Dr. Ceesay again returned to the Gambia and provided free medical assistance to the villagers for an entire year before he took a position as House Officer at the Royal Victoria Hospital, Banjul, the Gambia, and was eventually promoted to the post of Medical Officer in 1999.

He is the proud founder of the Manding Medical Centre; a self-help village health organization located in the Gambia, which has provided much, needed medical care to over 8000 villagers.

In his autobiography, "The legend against all odds", Dr. Ceesay shares his struggles to survive in his quest for an education. All the proceeds from his book go to supporting the Manding Medical Centre. Dr. Ceesay and his wife have three beautiful daughters, ages 14, 11, and 7.

In my correspondence with Dr. Ceesay over the past few months, he shared his profound gratitude for his American education. He said, "In my mind, it is the American who deserved such honour and distinction, for I am the recipient of the goodness of the American."

Due to travel difficulties, Dr. Ceesay is unable to be here tonight to accept this ward. However he has asked his first American family, the Howard Riggs family to represent him.

At this time I will ask Robert Riggs (Bob) to join me at the podium to accept the ward for Dr. Ceesay. Indeed, it is truly an honour to recognize Dr. Ceesay for his many accomplishments and humanitarian efforts. We congratulate him on earning the Distinction of Distinguished Graduate of Alpena Community College.

-Penny Boldrey-

I am told that Robert Riggs eloquently delivered my remarks aimed at the ACC graduates and residents of Alpena City. It was most welcomed as was later reported by those who emailed me after the ceremony.

This distinguished Graduate award came thirty-six years after I left Alpena, Michigan. Mathew Dunckel sent me the following comments about the events of the award. It read:

"Alhasan, your address was given at the commencement. It was the portion of the evening that was enjoyed by most. Partly because it was delivered well and partly because of my father was mentioned. I think what you said was inspirational for our students and brought home the need for them to think internationally.

Tom Ray is making final preparation to depart for the Gambia with the leadership class early next week. What a great adventure for the students. I am looking forward to hearing about it on their return. Thank you for helping make it possible.
Your Friend
Matt.
A month later I emailed penny Boldrey the following, "I received both the award and enclosures. Accept my deepest appreciation for the kind words spoken about me in your presentation speech during the spring graduation ceremony. Thank you very much for your kindness."
Thereafter, I suggested we pursue the possibility of twining Alpena with two villages in the Gambia. Dear Reader, I hope your patience is not running out as you are eagerly looking forward to the publication from the Alumni and friends of Alpena Community College.
Karen Eller wrote to let me know that she was assigned to write an article about me for the local paper announcing my receiving the Distinguished Graduate 2005 award. She reported having read my book, "The legend against all odds" to garner more information about me to help her on the matter at hand.
She let me know that she found my story very interesting and she intend to do a good job of bringing me to public attention in the article. Here then, without further ado is Karen Eller's promised

article about me. This idea unfolded, exploded and led to the chapter on sister city proclamation.

THE LUMBERJACK LINK: ALPENA, MICHIGAN
DR. CEESAY NAMED DISTINGUISHED GRADUATE

Dr. Alhasan sisawo Ceesay of the Gambia, West Africa, was recognized with the Distinguished Graduate Award at the ACC spring commencement ceremony in May 5, 2005. On hand to receive the ward for Dr. Ceesay was members of the Howard Riggs family, his first host family when he came to Alpena in 1967.
According to Dr. Ceesay, "The Riggs were the ideal American, an average working class who readily shared the little bit God gave them with others less fortunate."

Dr. Ceesay earned his Associate of Arts degree from ACC in 1969 and went to Olivet College to earn his Bachelor's degree in Biology with help of a full-tuition scholarship from the Besser Foundation.
He earned his Masters degree in biological sciences from Michigan Technological University in 1973.

In 1979, Dr. Ceesay returned to Africa and entered the University of Liberia Medical School in Monrovia. Because of political unrest in the Gambia in 1981, Dr. Ceesay escaped to the United States in the hope of completing his life long dream, "to

provide much needed medical relief to the villager who is forced to work miles on end to seek medical aid for his already dying child, wife or friend."
During the time he was seeking political asylum in the United States, Dr. Ceesay, never gave up his quest for education, and he continued under very strenuous conditions to take classes at Michigan State University and Wayne State University.
He was finally accepted at the American university of the Caribbean School of Medicine in the West Indies, and he began the final segment of his journey to becoming a doctor.
In 1992, after 25 years of educational struggles, Dr. Ceesay was awarded his Doctor of Medicine Degree from the American University of the Caribbean. He returned to the Gambia where he provided free medical assistance to the villagers for an entire year before taking a position at the Royal Victoria Hospital, Banjul, the Gambia, West Africa.
Dr. Ceesay founded the Manding Medical Centre in 1993. This self-help village health organization provides much needed medical aid to the villagers of the Gambia.
His autobiography: "The legend against all odds" chronicles his struggles to survive in his quest for Western education. Proceeds of his book go to support Manding Medical Centre at Njawara village and provide scholarships in medicine and agriculture for indigent rural candidates in the Gambia.

To learn more about Dr. Ceesay's ambitions, you can e-mail him at: alhasanceesay@hotmail.com.
Dr. Ceesay was honoured to receive this distinction from ACC and would like to "express thanks to the remarkable and noble friends" he met in Alpena. He credits the goodwill and foresight of the staff and students at ACC for giving him the chance to earn an education and help move his people forward in life.
Karen Eller

I thanked Karen Eller for work well done for the revealing commendable article. Here now is that featured by the Alpena News written by staff Kerrie Miller. Enjoy Miller's version about me and my goal.

ALPENA NEWS, MICHIGAN, USA 2005
A LONG ROAD FROM GAMBIA TO ALPENA

When he was 14, Dr. Alhasan S. Ceesay saw a family tragedy unfold that would change his life forever. As he was walking to school, he saw a woman, pregnancy full-term, who was obviously ill. Her husband was carrying their young son who was nearly comatose from illness.
Ceesay later found out the pregnant woman's baby died in her uterus and she died from toxins built up in her body as a result.

The young boy also died three quarters of a mile before his family was able to reach the Health Centre at Kerewan village. "That day I said, "If God will help me none will ever have to go through that again." That picture is what made up my mind for me'" Ceesay said.

Ceesay, a native of Njawara, the Gambia, is a graduate of Alpena Community College, class of 1969. He earned his Associates of arts degree from ACC before attending Olivet College, Michigan Technological University and Howard University, earning his doctor of medicine degree from the American University of the Caribbean in 1992. But how does a young man from a village in the Gambia get to Alpena to attend its community college?

Dr. Ceesay in warm handshake with good friend Abdinisir Hassan, at Liverpool, UK 2010

In an e-mail message, he stated that after reaching the American Consulate, and asking for a listing of American Colleges, Alpena Community College was at the top of the alphabetical list. And ACC was the first to respond to his application. Once here, life was not without challenges.

In a telephone conversation, he said it was first time he had left his country, and when he got here no one spoke his language. "But I do not give up", he said. Another goal Ceesay never gave upon was making it possible for the village families, such as those like the one who affected him as deeply as a young man, to have access to health care services.

With the creation of the Manding Medical Centre, which has helped over 8000 patients free of charge, he is doing that though progress has been slow in coming to the center.

Ceesay said officially he employed by the central government and is only able to help the villagers on the weekends. He is able to man the center along with the help of three or more doctors who volunteer their time. Ceesay say the center sees no fewer than 500 patients and as many as 1500 patient in a weekend.

He said currently the center is in limbo and is a little more that a shed. He has been working on fundraising to get the first phase the children and maternity units built. It is expected to cost approximately $500,000.

Members of the ACC Leadership class are currently conducting fund-raising to go to the Gambia and help with the children and volunteering at the center. The trip will last two weeks. Ceesay is the author of a book chronicling his life's experiences called "The legend against all odds" (available at Amazon.com) and he has committed all proceeds from its sale to the center.

He said he is never regretted the decision he made to become a doctor. "Sometimes I feel like I have oil on my feet and I am climbing a very steep hill." Ceesay said. "I have always believed I will reach my goal… you have to be crazy like me and you have to ignore lots of things that take you away from your goals."

A typical day in Ceesay's life begins at 5 am with prayer, before boarding public transportation to the hospital where he works, 7miles from his home. From 7 ---11 a.m. he does morning ward rounds, followed by clinics, then evening round.

Days can last up to 10 0r 11 pm before he heads back home. "In between, I try to please my wife and children. It is a very simple life really." He said. He and his wife have three daughters, the oldest of which has dreams of attending Alpena High School and ACC before going onto medical school like her father.

Ceesay's long-term goal revolves around the Mading Medical Centre at Njawara village, which he hopes will continue to grow for generations helping mare patients. "I plan to stay at the center until the day they bury me. That and having my children educated, that is it." He said.

Kerrie Miller

Kerrie dispatched a copy of the above as soon as it got out of the printers of Alpena News. And in return I sent her the following appreciation note of the good work she did.

Kerrie, I just received the copy of the article in the Alpena News featuring me. It was a job well done. I hope it help move my dream of providing medical aid to villagers a notch higher for Manding Medical Centre and the Gambia villagers.

The Gambia and I are most grateful for enlightening your readers about us and our need for a medical facility. Extend our thanks and deep appreciation to the staff and management of Alpena News. We shall effeminately be in Gambia in due course.

We look forward to your crew attending the ground-breaking ceremonies in Gambia soon. I have started a collection of documentations about me to be placed in Dr. Alhasan S. Ceesay's Archives.

Kerrie replied stating that they missed me at the ceremony but she look forward to attending the grand opening of the center.

Penny Boldrey simply said, "I will certainly make sure you receive a copy of our alumni newsletter once it is completed. Indeed, we are very proud of your accomplishments and humanitarian efforts."

Chapter 43
Twined: Alpena-Njawara-Kinte Kunda

Having been now recognized as Distinguished 2005 Graduate by Alpena Community College I made a proposal for a sister-city or twining relationship status between Alpena City and select villages in the Gambia, West Africa.
I, you guessed right, contacted Mathew (Matt) Dunckel as a soundboard or trial balloon for the above idea. Mathew replied that it was sound idea and suggested my contacting the Alpena City Council members on the subject as soon as possible. He gave their web site,http://www.alpena.mi.us/council/members. In addition he supplied names of Councilman Dave Karschnik and Councilwoman Carol Shafto for me to initiate direct contact with the Alpena City Council.
Mathew told me that the Mayor was John Gimlet and the City Manager was Alan Bakalarski. Armed with this vital information I made my first push for the twining through Mrs. Penny Boldrey, Executive Director at the Alpena Community College, Alpena, Michigan.
I had doubts that getting her interested in this unique wish of the villagers she would do all she could within her power to not only contact the right people in authority to make it eventually happen but would open up more doors for my villagers and our health

project at Njawara. Mrs. Penny Boldrey upon hearing from me linked with Councilwoman Carol Shafto on June 14, 2005 thus: "Hi Carol, from one Distinguished graduate to another…..I received the enclosed message from our 2005 Distinguished graduate, Dr. Alhasan Ceesay.

I am wondering if perhaps you can help me with his inquiry regarding the possibility of twining between Alpena City and two villages in the Gambia, West Africa."

Mrs. Penny in-turn informed me that she had contacted a good friend Carol Shafto, who is a member of the Alpena City Council and also an Alpena Community College Distinguished 2003 Graduate recipient, regarding my request for twining between the above communities.

She enclosed Councilwoman Shafto's response to the twining idea with Gambian villages. My reaction was swift and I contacted Councilwoman Shafto thus: "Hello Councilwoman Carol.

Mrs. Penny Boldrey sent me correspondence she had with you regarding a proposal I made to the Alpena City. My initial email kick starting a twining proposal between the city of Alpena, Njawara and Kinte Kunda villages in the Gambia, West Africa, was sent to Mayor John F. Gimlet, Dave R. Karsctunick, Mike Polluch, Sam Eller and Carol Shato.

It read:

I am pleased to write and inform you that I am deputized by village heads of Njawara and Kinte Kunda to contact you and initiate a twining/sister city status proposal between Alpena and the above two villages. Njawara is my home village and Kinte Kunda is where I attended school in the early fifties. Thomas Ray and the leadership class students visited both places during their two weeks stay in the Gambia.

They met the chief of the District Sefo Fafanding Kinte at Kinte Kunda. Kinte Kunda village has been the seat of many chiefs of the region and Fafanding is the most recent of several from this village. Njawara is historically a trading center connecting Gambia and northern Senegal.

Today she has become a tourist Mecca and destination. One can easily log onto information about Njawara on the Internet It boasts of lot female education oriented projects. In addition it has an agricultural training center.

The contact was made on behalf of the heads of two villages and the district authority in the North Bank Division of the Gambia. This twining would be a very rewarding interaction and educational for both your and the villagers. The people are eager to make worthwhile friendship with America.

The chiefs and village heads have urged me to initiate their wish for the twining between them and Alpena City or any city willing to go into such relationship with the villagers.

You can link with Thomas Ray and his students for feed back on their personal experience as guests of Manding Medical Centre at Njawara village, the Gambia. The villagers and I would be most grateful if given the chance to link up with Alpena City."
Councilwoman, Carol Shafto sent in this hiccup: Dr. Ceesay, I cannot proceed with any more discussion with the City council of Alpena until I am much clearer about what a Twining proposal entails. Could you describe to me what you have in mind? Although we may be supportive of your work at Njawara and Kitne Kunda in the Gambia, we cannot really act on your request until we know what we are agreeing to.
Could you send me a brief outline of what you are seeking from the City of Alpena? I will be happy to act as a liaison between you and the City, but cannot do so until I have a clear idea of what I am advocating for. Thank you most sincerely."
Carol-
On July 13, 2005 I sent the following required clarification to Councilwoman Carol Shafto.
"Hello Carol, I am glad to hear from you. To be simplistically clear, twining means a sisterhood relationship between Alpena and the villages for mutual rewards of those involved.
Hence, it is a friendship like affair where people from Alpena can be part of and like wise the villagers involved but at no cost to either party.

For example Councilwoman Carol Shafto choose to spend two weeks in the Gambia helping reorganize or create a more functional administrative system or even learn from the villagers. In brief it is a two-way international relationship. Call it cultural bonanza where cultural dance troupes from the Gambian villages can be coming to entertain Alpena and other cities during the summers.

This will help raise funds for the city, the villages, likewise our health project Manding Medical Centre at Njawara. It will provide much awareness and understanding of the two people merged in friendship. It is like adopting each other and opening up rewarding human adventures at no cost involved. In a nutshell, it means ratified friendship between Alpena and the two above villages.

I hope this makes it palatable for Alpena to want to be part of such endearing relationship. I thank you in behalf of the Kerewan local authority, the villagers and the Commissioner for North Bank Division, the Gambia. God bless all of you." –Dr. Alhasan S. Ceesay-

Needless to say Councilwoman Carol Shafto was very pleased with the above clarification and appealed to Alpena City Council to consider the idea of twining on behalf of the Gambian villages. Hence, Carol on the 13/7/05 sent me this email after reviewing the above message of clarification of what it means to twin with an African village. It said,

"Hello Dr. Ceesay, I have forwarded your information to the Mayor and City Manager and offered to be the liaison if the City should consent to comply with this request. I will keep you posted with any development."
Carol-
I updated the Commissioner and all concern at the LowerBadibou district authority along with the two village heads involved in the sister-city state regarding progress of my initiative with Alpena City a few weeks after hearing from councilwoman Carol Shafto he Commissioner and local authority sent the below covering letter in support of my push a twining Relationship with Alpena City in Michigan, USA.

Njawara/Kinte Kunda
Lower Badibou District
North Bank Division
The Gambia, West Africa
E-mail: **njawaranato@yahoo.co.uk**
November 5, 2005

Dr. Alhasan S. Ceesay
Manchester, M14 4LQ
England

Subject: Twining of Njawara, Kinte Kunda & Alpena City, Michigan, USA

Dear Dr. Ceesay,

Your first letter dated September 23, 2005 has been received and the cont of which is understood, both the Commissioner, the Chief and the Alkalolu (village heads/ mayors) of Njawara and Kinte Kunda are very pleased and much interested in having Njawara, Kinte Kunda and Alpena City twined.
The Communities of both villages met and discussed the issue and they are very much happy about the lofty ideas. Njwarara and Kinte Kunda are located in the North Bank of the Gambia. They are just about 90 kilometers away from Banjul, the capital of the Gambia.
Kinte Kunda is just two kilometers away from our administrative headquarters, Kerewan where both the Commissioner and Area Council stay. Where as Njawara is located nine kilometers away from Kerewan. Regards
Sincerely
Aja. Hadi Panneh (Alkalo)
Alh. Fafanding Kinte (Chief of Lower Badibou)
Cc: Batala Juwara (Commissioner, NBD)

I replied to the above with this short note dispatched immediately to the village Alkalolu, the chief and Commissioner, North Bank Division at Kerewan village.

245 Great Western Street
Manchester, M14 4LQ
England
16/11/05

A BIG THANK YOU

Dear Commissioner, Chief/Alkalolu,

I am profoundly grateful to you. Sefo Fafanding, the local authority, Kerewan Are Council and especially Alkalo Arfang Bah of Torro Bahen, lastly but not the least a big thank you goes to the people of Badibou, Njawara and my sister Hadi Panneh alkalo of Njawara Village.

I am very happy for support and understanding given to Manding Medical Centre. I am pleased to inform you that I have initiated a twining process between Alpena and the villages of Njawara and Kinte Kunda.

I have forwarded your note of the 5/11/05 to the Alpena City Council. Copies were also sent to Mr. Thomas P. Ray at the College.

Again, thanks you for making our American friends happy and welcomed to our beloved country. God bless all of you. I will continue working for our development.

Sincerely
Dr. Alhasan S. Ceesay, MD

Director/Founder/coordinator
Manding Medical Centre.

I forwarded the letter from the district to Councilwoman Carol Shafto to reinforce my stance and wish of the villagers to be friends to Alpena City. I urged her to kindly take action on behalf of the villagers.

Mrs. Carol Shafto
Council Woman
Alpena city council
208 North First Avenue
Alpena, Michigan 49707

Dear Mrs. Carol Shafto,

The enclosed is reply to your last email dated 25/9/05 regarding the twining proposal made to the Alpena City council earlier on by me on behalf of Njawara and Kinte Kunda villages in the Gambia, West Africa, respectively.
The enthusiasm about having this relationship with Alpena is immeasurable. The villagers are looking forward to a warm and fruitful relationship between the two people. They all pray that you would be as eager to consummate it as they have already done in their wishes and hearts.

Finally, may friendship and human kindness be an everlasting link between all humans. God bless you and we look forward for a positive reply soon. My personal regards and thanks to the City Council and all of Alpena.
Yours Sincerely
Dr. Alhasan S. Ceesay, MD

On September 21, 2005 I sent a reminder to Carol Shafto regard the lofty idea of twining Alpena with Njawara and Kinte Kunda villages in the Gambia. I enquired if Mayor Gimlet had taken any action at the time.
I assured her that all hopes of bring this entity into reality wholly and solely relied on her good work. We bank on her efforts. The next day God smiled onto our dream to befriend America.
Councilwoman Carol Shafto sent me the following reply to my inquiries about the status of my dream for America and the Gambia. It rang in the most melodious and cherished news I ever had for a long, long time after my being admitted into medical school and upon treating my first patient in the villages.
Here is Carol Shafto's historical e-mail.
"Good morning Dr. Ceesay. I appreciate your persistence in accomplishing this goal. Without that it surely would have failed. I do apologize for this delay. I have just returned this week from a wonderful month long tour of the UK and Ireland.

My last communication, before I left, with the City Manager was that this was a good idea, will be good for public relations, and that we should go forward with the proposal. The Mayor is also in favour. So there is absolutely nothing standing in the way of this happening.

I am willing to do the work of it, but I honestly have no idea what to do. Do you know procedures or paperwork or any such thing from your end? Is it as simple as a proclamation?

I would like to have more information about your village, your people, and why you are interested in twining with Alpena. What connection there is with the city?

I would then put together a presentation for the City Council and ask them to decide that we are sister-cities (the term used here, although I know the UK and Europe use "twining") with the villages of Njawara and Kinte Kunda. We could erect a sign at the City entrance, etc.

If you have any idea or directions for me, please let me know. Also any information you can provide on your village would be helpful. I will continue to work with you on this until it is accomplished. Your friend in Alpena"

Carol Shafto—

I followed this letter with an addendum to what already were at hand with the councilwoman's desk. Being the architect of this friendly union much was expected of me.

And so I never relented supplying as much information as many times as I can afford. My phone bill sprouted to a warping six hundred plus. Most important addendum was the one below.

SYNOPSIS OF NJAWARA AND KINTE KUNDA VILLAGES

Njawara is a 350 years old market village situated on the bank of the Miniminiyang bolong, a creek of the River Gambia, in the Lower Badibou District of the North Bank Division of the Gambia.
Njawara has a population of a thousand residents and is 95 kilometers from Banjul, Gambia's capital city. The village lies close to the fringes of Senegalese border and has been the trade hub or link between Gambia and Senegal during the colonial era.
Njawara was established and founded by the Panneh family of the Wolof tribe and initially called "Mpanneh Village" the elderly still refer to it as Mpaneeh.
Among the residents of now Njawara are Mandinkas, Fulas, Serere, Jolas, Koyaginkas, and Bambara tribes' men. All of who are farmers, with a few serving as petty traders, growing Peanuts, rice, coos, millet and a variety of vegetables. The nearest government administrative post is nine kilometers away at Kerewan village.

Njawara lacked modern luxuries of electricity, proper telephone, sewer system, pave roads but water is now pumped from a nearby borehole. The village has a thriving school and a dynamic citizenry working hard to improve their lot and the future of the younger generation.

Kinte Kunda village has been the political base of Lower Badibou District for decades. It has provided us with several chiefs in the past and sefo Fafanding Kinte is the most resent contribution.

Kinte Kunda village comprises of mostly Mandinka tribes men and women. It is the home of venerable late Sefo Njanko Kinte who, in the 30s ruled the district with an iron fist. It was he who imposed one of his brothers, Almami Kinte, to take over the administration or village headship of Njawara (Mpanneh).

Nonetheless he was a respected chief. Kinte Kunda was the first village that had a school in the entire Lower Badibou district and I am told that the chief insisted that the school be built in his home village leaving a row that lasted through his rein.

Kinte Kunda has now smaller population than Njawara and the current appointed chief of the district, Sefo Fafanding Kinte resides there. Residents of Kinte Kunda are all farmers eager to improve their lives and those of their children. They are friendly, peaceful, charming descent hard working people who contributed a lot to growth of the Lower Badibou District in the North Bank

Division. Today Kinte Kunda is highlighted by the movie 'Roots' of Kunta Kinte' ancestral home. The villagers and I are interested in the twining with Alpena, Michigan in an effort to open up the Pandora's box of friendship, goodwill and more understanding of people and cultures that would allow us relate in this shrinking globe we all share.

There is a lot we can do for each other once the ugly veil of ignorance, misunderstandings and fear is removed. And this can be done only through learning and interacting with one another. I am sure the students, who went to the villages, can tell how much warmth and friendship they received from the villagers they met at the Lower Badibuo District, the Gambia.
Exchange visits and whole host of beneficial programs to both parties can be organized within the framework of this twining. Once again, I personally appeal to the Mayor and Alpena City Council to give this desire of the villagers a chance of fruition for Alpena City and the above villages in the Gambia.
BY DR. ALHASAN S. CEESAY, MD

In sort while, I received the following reply from Councilwoman Mrs. Carol Shafto of Alpena City Council letting me know the final details, date of the proclamation for the sister-city relation between our villages and Alpena, Michigan.

Without further ado I present the message as sent on November 17, 2005.

"Good morning Dr. Ceesay.

After many months of communication with you, I can finally announce a DATE for our twining/sister-city Relation! The Alpena City Council will adopt a resolution to establish a Sister-city Program with Njawara/Kinte Kunda villages on December 5, 2005.
I am going to be personally preparing the resolution since it will be a part of a permanent record for both the villagers and the City of Alpena.
I would like to be sure all of the information is accurate. Penny Boldrey suggested that I email the text to you after completing it. If you are willing, you could read it for any factual errors or omissions before I send it on to the City. If you are willing I will send it via email when it is ready some time next week.
Finally, I have invited several people to the City Council meeting to provide testimony and support for this proposal. Both Penny Boldrey and Thomas P. Ray will be there. Also they are inviting some of the students who went to the villages to also be present and speak to the issue. So it would be a very nice presentation and will be more than just a formality.

Also if you would like, I can arrange to have a tape of the meeting sent to you. Our meetings are videotaped and played for the public on the public access television channel several times a week between meetings. I can make a copy of the tape of the meeting and have it sent to you or to the village officials or both if you would like.

Late Mrs. Huja Sarr, (RIP). We will miss you forever

Also, the resolution will have an official seal of the City of Alpena and the signature of the Mayor.
I will have as many copies as you need made and will laminate them so they will be preserved. I will send you those to you and whomever you designate. I will get several if necessary.
I am so pleased to finally be able to bring this completion. I know it must have been frustrating to you to have to have this take so long and to have us seen to be so unresponsive. I hope this totally enthusiastic ending make up for all of that!
Your Friend in Alpena"
Carol Shafto---
On the day of ratification or passing of the resolution for the sister-city status/relationship between Alpena City and Njawara/ Kinte Kunda villages several speakers were heard. These included, among many others, Penny Boldrey, Mr. Thomas Ray, two student representatives of the leadership class that visited Njawara in May 2005 and Dr. Avery Aten.
This was buffered by a loop of fifty photo slides of the villages taken by the students while in the Gambia. At the end of the presentation Mayor John F. gimlet read into the record the above proclamation and vote was tabled to pass it.
The sister-city proclamation between Alpena City with Njawara and Kinte Kunda villages, Lower Badibou District, the Gambia was moved by Councilwoman Carol Shafto, Seconded by

Councilman Karscnick, that the proclamation to establish a sister City program was carried by unanimous vote. A copy of the sister-city Resolution passed by Alpena City Council on December 5, 2005 is reproved for your pleasure to read.

PROCLAMATION TO ESTABLISH A "SISTER-CITY" PROGRAM WITH NJAWARA AND KINTE KUNDA, LOWER BADIBOU DISTRICT, THE GAMBIA, WEST AFRICA

WHEREAS, the City of Alpena recognizes and supports the concept of global cooperation and community, and

WHEREAS, the villages of Njawara and Kinte Kunda through their leaders and Dr. Alhasan S. Ceesay, have reached out their hand in friendship and goodwill, and

WHEREAS, relationships were established by students and faculty of Alpena Community College when they were warmly welcomed to the villages for a service project earlier this year, and

WHEREAS, mutual understanding of our diversities as well as our similarities and the cultural exchanges that will result, will be beneficial to the citizens of both areas, and

WHEREAS, true global community is often established one person at a time, and one city and village at a time, leading to beneficial relations and programs for all,

NOW, THEREFORE, I John F. Gilmet, by virtue of the authority vested in me as Mayor, DO HEREBY PROCLAMIM a sister-city program with the villages of

    NJAWARA AND KINTE KUNDA
    LOWER BADIBOU DISTRICT
    THE GAMBIA, WSET AFRICA

And urge all area citizens to extend the hand of friendship and an embrace of genuine fraternity to their friends in NJAWARA/KINTE KUNDA and pledge support and loyalty as these communities of two great nations join together as "Sister-Cities" Signed at Alpena: Michigan, United States of America on this 5th day of December 2005.

Councilwoman Mrs. Carol Shafto read my reply into the record for Council and Alpena City residents. It states:

ALPENA, THANKS FOR TWINING WITH US

Lord Mayor John F. gimlet, Alpena City Council and resident of Alpena, please allow me convey heartfelt thanks as well as greetings from the

Commissioner, NBD, Kerewan Area Council, the chief of Lower Badibou, the Alkalos (village heads) of Njawara and Kinte Kunda.

I am today full of joy and gratitude for twining resolution ratified by the Alpena City Council. I am speechless as one of my dreams for the villager and America has now materialized in this twining resolution passed by Alpena.

We are two good people now merged in goodwill for humanity and friendship. This coming together will achieve a lot for both of us. There is a lot for us to gain as well as learn from each other and generations to come will thank us for having taken the first footsteps of bringing people of diverse cultures and understandings together.

Enclosed is message from the Gambia in response to the most welcomed news in your last email. This is the top of the iceberg for there are lot more benefits in this act. In addition, as long as I live Alpena and the Gambia will not only benefit from this unique venture but will smile yearly for having dreamt along with me.

Let me, in passing; mention with thanks the first harbingers of this day. They are Mr. Thomas P. Ray and his leadership class of students from Alpena Community College, who visited Njawara village in May 2005. Thomas Ray and the students laid the marvelous foundation we today concretize.

Mrs. Penny Boldrey and Mathew Dunckel deserve our appreciation for remaining interested and in constant contact with me. The Gambia, the Lower Badibou District Authority, village heads and villagers remain eternally grateful for giving us the chance of twining with you. Huge thanks to Alpena City, the Mayor of Alpena, John F. Gilmet, and Alpena City Council for work well done. Councilwoman Mrs. Carol Shafto who relentlessly steered the twining proposal to completion also deserves our profound gratitude. The villagers and I are eternally indebted to all at Alpena. In addition, we look forward to working hand in hand for the reward of all parties.

Finally, I would like to pay tribute to past and present friends at Alpena who helped me reach this pedestal. All of you helped make my sojourn to America a remarkable success. I would like many more of my friends to be like you at Alpena.

I hope you will believe, as well as join, in my dream of providing modern medical aid to the Gambian villagers. Thanks a million and God bless America!

Your Friend

DR. ALHASAN S. CEESAY, MD
FOUNDER/COORDINATOR
MANDING MEDICAL CENTER
NJAWARA, THE GAMBIA.

Two weeks later I received three copies of the "Sister-City" proclamation along with a videotape of the Alpena City Council meeting of December 5, 2005.

Also enclosed were the Alpena News and a copy of the Alpena Public notices showing minutes of the City Council meeting, which carried ratification of the sister-city proclamation by a unanimous vote.

I must confess exhilaration in my heart for Alpena City Council having done so much for my villagers without reservation and accomplished with great speed.

I contacted the current US Ambassador in the Gambia, Ambassador Joseph D. Stafford alerting them on the arrival a package from Alpena City Council for them to kindly deputize in ceremony of handing the proclamation copy marking sister-city status between Alpena City, Njawara and Kinte Kunda villages in the Lower Badibou, District, North Bank Division.

Manding Medical Centre
UK Contact Address
245 Great Western Street
Manchester, M14 4LQ
E-mail: **alhasanceesay@hotmail.com**
October 10, 2005

Joseph D. Stafford
Ambassador
Embassy of the USA
Kairaba Avenue
P. M. Box 19
Banjul, the Gambia

West Africa

Dear Ambassador Stafford,

RE: Alpena, USA -Njawara-Kinte Kunda twining/Mamding Medical Centre

I am Dr. Alhasan S. Ceesay from Njawara village and currently on studies in the UK. This is to introduce the above self-help health organization at Njwawara as well as kindly request favour of your good office's service in behalf of Alpena City, Michigan and the villagers of Njawara and Kinte Kunda, the Gambia.
I pioneered the above center, after graduating as a doctor and upon returning to the Gambia in 1992. It became an NGO in 1994 after being fully registered by the Justice Department and recognized by the Ministry of Health in 1993.
In addition, we are now a registered Charitable Trust, as Friends of Manding, in England and Wales by the Charity Commission of the UK. Our charity number is 1088136 since August 21, 2001. One can learn more by browsing our web site thus: beehive.thisisessex.co.uk/gambimed. It will show our home page, "Friends of Manding". Alternatively one can use a short cut by typing in "Mandingmedicalcentre.Njawara" and Google search. The same home page will show.

I have also written two books and hefty portion of sales from these books is earmarked to help support Manding Medical Centre at Njawara and our goal of providing medical aid to the villager, especially children.

More information about my work and commitment to providing much needed medical service to the region in conjunction with the Gambia Ministry of health can be seen in our web site as above.

Finally, I am more than delighted to report that Alpena City in Michigan, USA has just ratified a Sister-City program with my home village Njawara and Kinte Kunda village respectively in the Lower Badibou District, North Bank Division, the Gambia. Hence, I have asked the Alpena City Mayor's Office to send five copies of the final proclamation declaring the Sister City status between Alpena and the above two villages in the Badibou to you for your office to kindly deliver the documents to the Commissioner North Bank Division at Kerewan. Thank you for taking time to assist us in the above matter.

Please feel free to contact me any time convenient to you. Best washes for good health and achievement in the coming year. Regards to your family

Yours Sincerely

Dr. Alhasan S. Ceesay

Founder/Coordinator

Manding Medical Centre

Njawara, NBD, The Gambia

I followed this letter with two telephone calls to the United States Embassy in the Gambia to verify receipt of the package sent from Alpena to Ambassador Joseph D. Stafford. The secretary told it normally takes a month or more before none official mail arrives at their desk.

I was assured that the office would do as requested whenever the package reaches the Embassy. I called Sefo Fafanding Kinte and Alkalo Hadi Panneh and told them to be checking with either Ambassador Joseph Stafford directly or one of the officers in the know for their copies of the Sister city proclamation of which the villagers are unsung heroes for having received the Alpena Community College students who visited Njawara in May 2005 with open hearts, hospitality, generosity and warmth.

It was not until Thursday, February 16, 2006 that Ambassador Joseph D. Stafford and team where able to deliver, in person amid tumultuous reception and celebration, the sister-city proclamation between Alpena City, Njawara and Kinte Kunda villages in the North Bank of the Gambia.

I made it clear that the brief ceremony at Njawara on the 16/02/06 marked the end of phase one of the sister city relationship between Alpena, Michigan, and us. I suggested the following four areas for food for thought by all concern. They are:

EDUCATION: This already started in earnest as some in Alpena express desire to sponsor worthy candidates at the Njawara Primary School for an experimental period of one year. Higher levels such as College, nurse training or other relevant skill areas will in due course be included.

HEALTH: A lot is planed for health oriented programs and Manding Medical Centre will be enhanced to a much functional status. Already Dr. Avery Aten and other colleagues in Alpena Health care delivery are working on program to assist us in our services and health care delivery. There will be training programs for health personnel etc.

TOURISM: With building of a 66 bed ultra-modern hotel I have in mind and finding ways to create tourist attraction to the region will in due course make Badibou the Tourist Mecca of the North Bank Division.

CULTURAL EXCHANGES

This will enable exchanges entailing having cultural dance troupes from the Lower Badibou District travel to Alpena Michigan and other American cities during summers to display our artistic fabric of entertainment, history, and arts.
These are a few ideas in the pipeline.
Feel free to add yours to enrich the program. This is by no means binding or final but seeking more suggestions on how to benefit both parties in this

unique twining program just approved by Alpena City. Let me make it crystal clear that there is no financial commitment from Alpena City. However, the cultural show can net us or raise a lot of money upon performing in America.

I thanked the Commissioner, NBD, Sefo Lower Badibou, Kerewan Area Council and the district authority for having worked so hard with me to provide this excellent opportunity to our people. I promise more was on the pipeline.

Three weeks later I received from Councilwoman Mrs. Carol Shafto announcing good news of her efforts. "Dr. Ceesay, we have sent five copies of the proclamation to the American Embassy in the Gambia, which you provided the address. I also have three copies of the proclamation for you as well as a copy of the tape of the meeting, a copy of the Newspaper where the action appeared, and a copy of the newspaper with the official minutes of the meeting.

I will get these out today. It was a most wonderful evening, as you will see on the tape. Five people, your friends old and new, spoke in favour of the proclamation. This included Dr. Avery Aten who I have now spoken t with and who is very enthusiastic about working with you by phone he said.

But you will be able to see him and hear what he had to say during City Council meeting of December 5, 2005.

Also peaking were two students who have visited the Gambia, Thomas P. Ray, Penny Boldrey, and me of course. I read your wonderful letter for the record. We also had a loop of over fifty slides showing on screen during the presentation.

It was the nicest Sister-city ceremony we have ever had-by far! Usually we just read the proclamation and that is it. I think this ends my part in all of this – except for one thing my son and I were going to "adopt" a family through Save the Children.

This involves sending a letter each month and with an amount of money. We would be happy to adopt some children from your village instead if there is an easy way to do this.

We would need a name and address and what form we could make our donation in (money order?). We are not really wealthy but could send $20 - $25 a month for at least a year to a deserving child. Of course, we would hope that they might send a note now and then but this all up to you.

I hope you are pleased with all that has happened.
I remain your friend
Carol Shafto.

In reply I sent my friend Carol Shafto the following:

245 Greatwestern Street
Manchester, UK
November 20, 2005

Hello Carol,

Now I am able to respond to your email. First, please accept our eternal indebt ness for having worked so hard to bring the twining into reality. Only God can reward your efforts. Please kindly extend our heartfelt gratitude to the Mayor and your fellow councilors at Alpena City.

Kindly send me the Mayor's telephone. I need to convey our appreciation to him. I had a long chat with the villager and they were in cloud nine about the approval of the sister city program.

I will be forwarding the names of deserving school children you might want to sponsor/adopt. I will call you before forwarding the names, about it when I get the list that the parents and headmaster promised to send me.

Again, thanks a million and God blesses you and yours. Best wishes for good health and successful 2006. I look forward to our traveling to the Gambia soon. Regards

Your Friend

Dr. Alhasan S. Ceesay, MD

In the interim Mrs. Penny Boldrey was also busy doing a story for the Alpena Community College Alumni News. In addition Carol Shafto had a feature about the approved sister-city program done by a local newspaper. She was very happy about it as the below email from her shows.

"Good Morning Alhasan Ceesay, "Our Story" is headline, above the fold, in the Alpena News today! It is wonderful publicity for your project.
I will send you copies but you can read it on-line today only at
http://www.thealpenanews.com. It reads, "Alpena's sister city ACC graduate initiates partnership with the Gambian villages." And there is a wonderful colour picture of one of the ACC students with village children. I hope you enjoyed the story and you are pleased with my efforts for publicity.
The news reporter, Sue Lutuszek, will do a follow up story about people "adopting children for education purposes", like I am doing with my son. It is a good day for celebration checks the Web Site.
Your Friend
Carol Shafto

The first hatchling of this merging of diverse hearts is as follows.

Njawara Basic School
Lower Badibou District
North Bank Division
The Gambia, West Africa
January19, 2006

Dear Sir/Madam

RE: To whom it may concern

These students are promising student whose parents are not able to fully support their educational needs. As a result, we would be very grateful if a concern person(s) can assist the students and their parents in taking care of some of the financial difficulties they are encountering to earn an education.
These include school fees, uniforms, books, bills and other school needs. Thank you and in anticipation, I remain
Yours Faithfully
Lamin K. Juwara
Principal

The initial list of needy students was sent to Councilwoman Carol Shalto on 23/02/06 for what is now dubbed Manding medical center scholarship grants. The fax read:
Manchester, UK
23/02/06

Hi Carol,

Hope you are okay and back at work. I hereby forward a list of school children from Njawara Basic School needing sponsorship. Feel free to contact those you think would like to participate in sponsoring a child for this educational project.

The first three candidates in the list are earmarked for you and your son(s). See name 1 – 3 in the accompanying list. Send all monies via Western Union in the name of Aja. Hadi Panneh, Alkalo/village head of Njawara, to any Gambian bank that Western Union deals with in the Gambia. Then email me stating the amount(s), date sent, and for who.

I will follow up by contacting Hadi Panneh, the Principal of Njawara Basic School about and the child's parents about it. I will also let the chief of the district know about such benevolent acts from America to the Gambia. This ascertains prompt disbursement.

In addition, I will have Aja Hadi Panneh (Alkalo), the parents, the Headmaster and where possible the recipient student(s) to write acknowledging the amounts received.

Please feel free to contact me if you have any questions or ideas to promote the above noble educational commitment. Once again, thanks and we remain grateful for your stand.

Your Friend

Dr. Alhasan S. Ceesay, MD

Chapter 44
Grandpa Bajoja Ceesay on Traditions

Children and elders look forward to the old wise sage's stories and lectures. Hence, we gathered beneath the shades of the spreading Mango tree to listen to the wise of the wisest at the village talk to us about marriage, christening, even circumcision, about leadership, and a whole host of compendium on Mandinka culture as practiced in the Gambia. Everyone listens, learns, and try to understand the importance of the message.

He started, after offering prayer for the gathering, saying that it becomes his duty to speak to us about tradition. The shifting sands of time may make his thoughts to appear a sphinx arising from the ashes of the old ways. He said, "It's my pleasure to do my best bit at it," evoking broad smiles from the audience for we knew something interesting was about unfolding to us.

He started the discussion by simply letting us know that every living thing one-way or the other procreates. He said only man, through moral and judgmental powers enacted an elaborate form.

The form being marriage following certain prescribed norms by society.

In general, nearly all humans practice marriage by the union or wedding of adult male and female into sanctioned and sanctified couples. There are monogamous, polygamous and even group marriages in some societies. He emphasized that theses relationships between men and women are a blessing from God who chooses continuance of his wonderful creation in this fashion.

The old sage stressed that the marriage was knoll and void and meaningless without blessing of the involved parents of both to be couples and priest of their faith.

He said, being unmarried at certain adult age, unless sickness and natural deformities prevails, was a taboo and culprits will and are severely chastised by their communities.

He told us that marriages were the couples are spoken for before they were born was in line. "How wise man?"; Enquired his listeners eager for a much more concise and concrete reason for such unfair sealing of unborn lives, especially in today's generation and life styles.

He replied by telling us that such marriages were outcome desire on the part of the deciding parents not only to perpetuate long-standing friendships between proponents but also to reduce the possibilities of going for unwanted clowns.

This was followed by thunderous roar of loud laughter for it delighted the listeners. Usually parents of both sides had or most likely experienced such offers to them or want to maintain loyal connection through to the next generation.

There is no trade value in these arrangements made out of pure good and rewarding intention for the would be future couples and their parents.
Above all he emphasized, the proposals are not binding to the involved children to be couples. A well-meaning explanation is give to them when in their early adolescence as well as their twentieth year.
If the would be couple express no doubt or have reasonable objections that would be the last chance before the intention of the involved parents is announced to the village and surrounding hamlets. Baring any objection the date of the marriage is set and the marriage is consummated at the Mosque on a chosen Friday afternoon.
He said there is no objection in marriages between tribes; in tribal and even Caucasian for they are God's children. What bad marriage is, being unfaithful, argumentative, unfulfilling partnerships, intolerance, and being lazy. Time, tides and season waits for no man. Some marriages do come to an unfortunate end, called devoice.
This tragedy happens when irreconcilable state persists between couples for long even after advisory intervention by parents, priest and community. Devoice is granted to couples with understanding that children will not suffer its aftermath.
Devoices are rare and far in between in rural areas as its outcome destroys and sets centuries of

relationships between the parents of both parties in turmoil. Grand Pa counselled us to do all we could never to allow that to happen by first making certain our own side of the affair was immaculate and impeccable. He said the Pot cannot and should not call the Kettle black.

One cannot be demanding, deviant and intolerant and expect their partner to be overly receptive if not tolerant to them. The world is never always favouring to our way.

No children like seeing their parents separated and the psychological effect on their lives cannot be measured and pain and loneliness can only be told by those unfortunate to have devoiced parents. Living through such an experience is hellish indeed. In the event of death a husband, the wife, if she chooses, is normally adopted by the brothers of the deceased for her to stay along her children in the compound or village.

Most young ladies of child bearing age opts to move and marry to another man within the village or elsewhere, preferably not too far from the children of the previous marriage. In most cases the children of devoice mothers stay at their father's home and are taken care of by the family of the previous deceased husband.

Having said this much about marriage the sage turned onto the outcome of marriage, procreation and childbearing. He said in a happy marriage between healthy couples children soon emanate.

This brought in another roar of laughter while men peeked at the ladies pretending to be shy but most interested in this aspect of the lecture. This was another occasion for paying homage to God, gratification, festivities and a host of pleasant responsibilities demanding more of us than we will ever imagine.

Parenthood teaches us different lessons of life, loving and caring way and managing of the upbringing of another tender human being is the most rewarding as well as challenging.

The changing phase of the newborn, toddler, teenager and eventually fully-grown adult/person is a marvel and unbeatable art only parents can experience.

GrandPa then rhetorically asked, "What is the naming or usefulness of christening one's child?" A Few brave ones hazard an answer. Some said that we do so to give names and in illustrating one of the audience said, "I am Jato, the strongest and king of the forest."

The old man laughed at the simplicity of the later answer and pointed to the next eager to cash into the discussion who said, "I am Mansane Manneh and my father is well known warrior." At that juncture the old thanked them for their answers.

He accepted their version but added that there are a lot more to why we humans have this tradition in the animal kingdom. "Christening," he began by saying that "Since mankind came up with the spoken word, he developed ability to communicate and differentiate things. We all cannot be called Jato for it will be meaningless and confusing when one wants to call to a particular person in a group." Heads nodded in agreement with the sage.

Hence, he gave a few tangible reasons why christening came to be a modus opera die in human societies. Naming ceremonies serves as way of paying homage and expressing gratitude to God for letting us continue in this new comer and the other reason given for christening was to express joy that our loved one not only survived the challenges of pregnancy but scaled that risk in the last hour of child birth.

He said there was no greater sin than that of not appreciating, respecting, loving and protecting one's wife or mother. Mothers take risk and are the first in our coming to this world who risked their lives in other for us to join this earthly Garden of Eden. He jokingly asked if there was any father who went through the nine months pregnant.

An old friend laughed and the wise sage retorted and said not you Mr. Potbelly, drawing another laugher but more from the ladies who where delighted to note the impartiality of the sage.

Grand Pa admonished us to be always kind to both our parents, especially our mothers and wives. He then told us the third reason for christening, which was to provide a name for that innocent individual with which society will identify them.

A name can be colourful, historical and even off superstitious nature. It is a name for that individual and is echoed in his life unless changed or his or her death. Someone in the crowd asked what is in a name? The old man replied they all sound sweet as a rose.

The forth and last reason for christening was it gives the chance to couple or new parents an opportunity to share their joy and celebrate along with family, friends and the communities far and wide. Christening brings people together and creates cohesion and bondage between villages. He warned us to note that no one is an island for we all need the other and it is always good to share our lives for what ever worth it may be.

We might just lift somebody's life by so doing. It will be good we open our hearts and share life than succumb to fear and innuendoes. Grand Pa concluded the christening subject by telling us that those were the times when women accept and appreciate gift, meaning babies, we gave them. It cements our loyalty to them.

A bust of laughter from the men's corner reverberated under the spreading Mango tree while the ladies applauded him. Among the last topics of the day the sage dwelt on relates with circumcision and why men do it.

He said in ancient days or times some disease occurred in the genitals of men and also it was noticed that some men experience serve pain when erective because of the foreskin tightening around the penis. His blunt and frank talk about private parts of men was entertaining to the young ladies while embarrassing the old menopausal ones. All of which were drastically or dramatically eradicated when a wise butcher thought that removing a portion of the foreskin may just alleviate the agonies of these poor men.

The butcher tried it on few chronically affected men who after three months came with gifts to express gratitude for the blucher's coming to their rescue. Some even told of how they would not let their wives sleep the rest of the nights when they regained their manhood.

Again, laughter and peeking at some old men went on for a while before the sage proceeded with his lecture. He made it clear that such was not the case nor needed by women. He said it was mere stupidity that led to the current mutilation and circumcision of women.

This was not welcomed by the ladies and most elderly women protested for being castigated as stupid to recklessly cause harm to themselves in competition with men. The old man pointed that pregnant women in ancient times might have had small pelvis for the exit of their babies to cause the village attendant to try to cut flesh out, similar to modern day's episiotomies, to widen the way to enable the baby's head pass through without much risk of death to mother and child.

This having brought relief to most ladies led to today's rampant female genital mutilation and an uncalled for circumcision. He said aside this error we must respect women even when we know it was a mistaken fashion.

Let us now devote the rest of the discussion on male circumcision. We have history telling us its origins as above but there are lot more Mandinka added aspects of male circumcisions.

We do it for the above reasons plus it is used to school or induct would be adult males into manhood and to prepare them for their responsibilities to themselves and community they came from. It engraves loyalty and team spirit in these men.

It is a challenging 90 days crash course in sociology, responsibility and problem solving that would become memorable events in every male at the circumcision camp.

They are taught how to meet challenges of the seasons, fire, wind and storm, find solution and unselfishly relate these to the safety of all involved. Here African Pharmacopoeia becomes a miracle for as the green concoction prepared from leaves and tree barks are applied or plastered on to cut skin it stops bleeding instantly and allows rapid healing. No one ever suffers from tetanus infection.

Only a very few ever suffer from pneumonia for lying on cold floors. Local voodoo men and local herbalist handle the treatments of sick circumcised ones.

Deaths from pneumonia or tetanus are far and rare in occurrence for herbalist had good medicines for it, which modern day African lost for lack of written recordings. Today's so called civilized African allowed all these knowledge to disappear, in reliance on colourful pills and creams from lands beyond, right before their noses out of ignorance and the shunning of their traditions.

The old sage lamented about the error and Africans depending too much on the easy way out but failing to realize it might not be the best way out of having to use their brains to manufacture or modernize known local medicaments.

He worried that the young are drifting too fast towards colourful life while failing to know more about their own traditions and cultures. The end of the encampment moulds the boys into fully-grown mentally mature males according our world.

They return home ready to take reign from their parents, elders and become husbands as soon as possible. Yes the village is reborn again and certain of its continuity with its traditions upheld by incoming generation of adults.

The villagers and fathers of the newly returning adults gleefully server the occasion knowing that they too have done what was expected of them in the Mandinka context and will now continue to give guidance when and where needed but not enforcing it.

The handing over of Mandinka beliefs and customs from one generation to another along established customs or methods of procedure of the tribe is complete and the young now holds the baton. He said what he told us was based on style of the Mandinka traditions passed upon from centuries of creations.

With a stern face, literally pleading to us, admonished the gathering to be serious custodians of the Mandinka traditions and pass it on to our children so that they can disseminate it to their own. The sage then digressed and talks in great length about leadership as understood by Africans, especially the Mandinka.

Leadership starts with the head of house whole, heads of families, priests, village heads and chiefs, governors and the very head of state of the country. They all have one thing in common; first they are voluntary servants of the people they govern or guide.

Secondly, their roles are akin to that of the umbrella, which when opened shades all and everything beneath it shades. It does not discriminate, that is engage in differentiation of tribe, advent colonialist, tribalism and foreigner phobia or encouragement of AK47 trigger-happy nuts and rebels.

Leaders must be humane, competent honest servants and not disguised mafia to their subjects. They should be kind, considerate as they themselves need love, and support until their time to die.

He reminded us that man has limited time on earth and should strife to leave footprints and examples that the next generation can follow and replicate for generations to come. We wholeheartedly agreed with all he told and promised to be good leaders to family and state. In modern terms one can say comfortably those stockpiles of atomic bombs or weapons of mass destruction and dictators do not measure greatness.

It is deep-rooted wisdom and dignity innate respect for human rights and lives, the intense humanity will make us more cherished and better leaders.

Africa would advance had the above stance been kept by our current leaders. It will make us able to contribute towards the future and progress of mankind.

The events of the day always end with a prayer and handshake with the old sage smiling up to his big ears. I would come last and say well done Grand Pa but you miss one point and he would smile knowing that I enjoyed the talk in good spirit.

Abdoulie Ceesay boarding train from Germany to Holland, Spring 2018

Chapter 45
Return of an Ambitous Village Son

In the 50s, no one envisioned that a poor village boy, like me, would venture to leave his round hut home or village and fly thousands of miles across the vast Atlantic Ocean to the great apple city skyscraper New York, USA.

No, the big apple was never a day-to-day conversational topic among villagers. The talk of the village reverberated on the good or bad yield of the crops farmed for that season and who married whose daughter or the pending circumcision due in a couple of months time. It was bad dream and foolhardy for any villager to think of such a perilous venture as was my plan.

America, Europe or even famous Hong Kong became topics of conversation among a few due to the advent and arrival of radios and later television to our regions in the early 1960s. There was no national radio in my country until 1963. We used to glue ourselves literally to Radio Senegal for International news and drama and theater entertainments.

Television only surfaced in the Gambia in 1995. There was only one government biweekly news bulletin, the Gambia News Bulletin, which served only government interest. It never said much about other places, not even America.

Colonials kept us in the dark. Hence, it was suicidal thought to carry the idea of traveling to unknown continents. It was recon as unfeasible because neither government nor family was in position to support such an ambitious mission. The challenging task or phenomena of carrying out a dream became my fate and I left the Gambia for New York in August 1967.

I was to engage in adventure that continued to today. Yes, dear reader, after many, many years of endless struggles and hard work I am now able to say I have the Golden Flees for the Gambia. In addition, I am finally on my way home, sweet home. I feel like I am heading for paradise.

Forgive me, for pinching myself to be certain that I lived to witness such a day in my life and to carry out this last leg of my sojourn. Allow me to be very elated and sentimental about today. It is history in the making for me and I feel like being in cloud ninety-nine today.

Dr. Alhasan Sisawo Ceesay of Njawara, Lower Badibou District, is finally heading back to the smiling coast of Africa. What a fit! Preparing to return home carries enormous challenges and responsibilities.

Family and friends back in the Gambia were equally elated by the good news that I am finally returning for good after ten grueling years in the UK. Yes, I was returning to Njawara village and Manding Medical Centre for good.

However couched within this elation is a great expectation from all camps. Everyone would want to know what have I brought from yonder land where milk pours out spontaneously from street pipes and money grows on trees waiting for able bodies to plug them off for keeps. This golden mythical Europe and USA still exists in minds of yonder land.

There would be speculations on the number of cars I brought with me, the quality of those cars, mobiles, yes, we too have been infected with the modern electronic bug and virus, televisions, cosmetics and clothing gifts etc, etc I am bringing along with me. Was the rumored container mine and was it full of gifts for the villagers?

Some even breathe a shy of relief hoping that I will employ their child or kin at the Manding Medical Centre. There was rumour that I bought a small car for each of my daughters. The speculations, expectations and hope for salvation generated by the news of my pending return home became feverishly high that I felt inundated as to what to take besides personal necessities and the little humble possessions I had with me.

I know I cannot go home empty handed as during my student days. I am very happy to be heading home and I am determined to meet the challenges head on. As the saying goes, charity begins at home. Therefore, I bought dresses, shoes, Jewels, mobiles, and cosmetics for my wife and daughters.

I bought quality long Shari dresses for all eight brothers at a cost of an arm and a leg each. No, I did not forget my sisters, Binta Ceesay, Fatou Isata Ceesay, Jainaba Ceesay, Mariam Ceesay, Hawa Ceesay and Roheyata Corr-Sey. No forgetting boys and daughters of my brothers. This is a family affair indeed.

As for Njawara, Toro Bahen, and Kinte Kunda villages, I had a few hundred pounds for the elders to share appropriately among themselves or do whatever they wish with the gift. I bought sofas, office furniture and, computers for personal use. I got lots of pens and even watches to present to friends.

Not all of the above dwarfed the magnanimous welcoming ceremony planned for my return. I fought cold feet when I went to tell my landlord my decision to go home to Gambia for good. His face flushed with admiration mingled with misty eyes and expression of well wishes for my family and me.

His last sentences were, "We are sorry that you are leaving the UK doctor. Do not worry, we will, by God's grace keep in touch. Bon voyage my friend." I bagged all my humble possessions and gifts and then embarked on paying my last farewell visit to friends in Manchester, Colchester and London where I bought a one-way air ticket to paradise Banjul, the Gambia.

Friends in Manchester poured their hearts out in prayer and gave abundantly gift to take along to my family and friends. I remain grateful to each and every one of them.

At Colchester, it was very moving. Mrs. Lorna V. Robinson and I have been friends since my medical student days in the 1990s when I was a trainee doctor at the Essex County and Colchester General hospitals, where she worked as a general nurse. Lorna and I turn out to be good friends who worked tirelessly to bring Manding Medical Centre into fruition.

She in the latter days of my sojourn to the United Kingdom stay was lifeline for both my family and I. She and her husband Keith Robinson went to great lengths to ascertain that I was comfortable during my stay at their home in Colchester, Essex County. Recall that it was these kind angels who were instrumental in the setting up of the Colchester Friends of Manding Charitable Trust.

God blesses them and rain happiness in their golden hearts. Above all they opened up their hearts and pocket to support me and prevent from my starving to death while facing unfortunate circumstances that marred most of my stay in the UK.

They were magnificent and magnanimously generous to me and I remain eternally grateful to them for being so kind and considerate towards my family and I.

George Eliot say it best about Lorna V. Robinson when he said, "Perhaps the most delightful friendships are those which there is much agreement, much disputation, and yes more personal liking." Mrs. Lorna Robinson used to quote the great Albert Schweitzer's timeless saying to buoy me when my spirit gets low.

It went like this, "Anyone who proposes to do good must not expect people to roll stones out of his way, must accept his lot calmly if they even roll a few more upon it."

There was mist in our eyes and uncontrollable drop of a tear or two dripping from our eyes down our cheeks as we bit the final goodbyes and urging each other to visit sooner than later.

Other members of the Friends of Manding Charitable Trust were equally touched but happy that I could finally go home and be with my wife and children who missed me more than can be imagined.

Those last moments remained eked in my brain because Mrs. Lorna Robinson's mould was a rare breed of good friends I ever had. One hardly comes across folks like her. They are few and swallowed by greater England.

Above all we are advancing in age. I look forward to not only seeing Keith and Lorna Robinson at the opening ceremony of Manding Medical Centre but to serenade them at Njawara village, the Gambia.

London, the world's historic nerve for power and regal pump beckoned as the train from Colchester snaked its way to this grand ancient city of Europe on the moat on the silver seas. Here I met numerous Gambians who were helpful to me in my early days at the city.

Among them was Aja jojo Cham-Ceesay. She is the adopted grand mother to nearly all Gambians in London and she doubles as the woman sage and matriarch of the London Gambian Community.

I lodged briefly at her flat in Mill Hill, London when I left Colchester in 2002.

Again, the goodbyes and well wishes amidst misty eyes came from those present at the flat. Some even envied me for being able to disentangle myself from mythical greener pastures attraction and opportunities to go home and be with family and friends for good.

Yes, England is a big trap of mythical greener pasture that many find it difficult to part from once they found themselves entrenched in its net of false security and comfort. Going home made me feel like a hero serenaded by admirers.

I had mixed feelings of joy and sadness for I was leaving good friends. Most of who are or were getting old and we might never meet again in this life. Prayers and gifts rained in adding excess poundage to my luggage.

Some walked with me to the ticket office, where I smilingly purchased a one-way ticket to paradise

Gambia. Other disbelievers walked with me to the bus heading to the Airport while others drove to see me off at terminal four at Heathrow Airport London. Soon our bus came to creaking stop and we disembarked, picked up our luggages and three of the fellows escorted and or walked with me into the terminal, as usual, full to the brim of travelers to the rest of the world.

I was eager to find my boarding queue and gleeful joined the good old Brit fashion, the long queue to the checking in counter. The flight to Banjul departs in three hours time. The boys hugged me and left and I looked at them until their disappearances in misty cloudy space of England.

Yes, it was pungent moment for me. Alas, I was alone in a crowded terminal and finding it hard to believe that I survived all the mayhem my life endured in these past ten years in Great Britain. The hall sounded like being among homing bees. However, soon it was my turn to hand in my tickets and have my luggage checked for the Sabena flight to Banjul, via Paris and Brussels enrooted to Africa. All said and done I had a big suitcase for which I paid a hefty sum of money for the 16kg beyond the allowed 50kg weight permitted for flights to Africa. It was worth it and leaving a few pounds sterling behind was a charitable act.

Checking in and tags all done we were asked to follow the line leading to the boarding lounge for our flight due to take off in an hour barring unforeseen delays.

On my way to the boarding station Lorna and Keith in misty tears and half Brits smiles but stiff lipped bade me farewell with hugs and wishes for safe flight back home.

They too have become part of me as I theirs. Lorna yelled I would come to visit soon. Huge the little girls for me and tell them auntie loves them. I remain eternally indebted and will carry this family's love with me till my last days in life.

Walking happily ten meters further down I came across another queue.

This one dealt with departure formalities, where security, custom and immigration worked acidulously to clear the queue in time for boarding. The security and customs searched my handbags and marked then ok for boarding.

I met a very nice young fellow at the immigration post. He was all-smiles and upon seeing the last date of visa renewal looked at me and I told him my last renewal was in another expired passport already in the Gambia.

He looked at my face, as if saying, "Please go on. We have heard many twisted truths than this simple one". He even jokingly asked if he was invited to my home in the Gambia.

Guess what he was a regular visitor to Gambia and had spent nearly most of his holidays in the Gambia. Our brief chat let me know he knew the Gambia well. So I told him he is more than welcome to share bread with my family and I in the Gambia if he would not enter any unasked for recording.
We shook hands and he stamped my passport. I gave him my card and he in turn gave me his e-mail address to link with him when in the Gambia.
All is well that ends well.
He is proof that some youngsters are not bureaucratic and do have insight as to why people come to the UK. They know we come either to learn or make money to send to our beleaguered families back in Africa or other developing country,
I will certainly e-mail him an invitation to come to my home as soon as I am reposed. Shortly after the last passenger got through boarding formalities a door was open to allow us start boarding our flight out of the UK.
The big Sabena Air was flying via France, Belgium enrooted to Africa. At the door of the big plane was a gorgeous lady who gave broad smiles and welcomed us onboard the flight destined to Rabat Morocco, Dakar, Banjul, Free Town and Conakry.
I took my seat at a window in the non-smoking area and applied my seat belt before take off time.
The Airhostesses did their routine demonstration of usage of oxygen masks, safety gear under the seats and exit windows and what to do in serious air

turbulent. Very soon the metal bird took off away from England's gray and almost cloudy skies heading to much yearned brilliant bright and warm African blue skies.

Meals and refreshment followed but I could not eat much for eagerness to meet my family, especially the youngest of my daughter, Roheyata Ceesay, who I left at the tender age of two years. She looked grown and taller than me. I can't wait to huge her and the other girls.

A minute after take off I took a last pip at the UK bellow it and me cold cloudy weather I was happy to leave behind for good. Three hours after the flight from Brussels the seat belt sign came on and I looked through my window. And "vous a la!" it was the Roget rocky mountain and Sahara Desert of Marrakech in Morocco.

Yes, the heat bellow was harbingering to temperature of the desert bellow us. We taxied and at last! I was once more on African soil not far from my own homeland, Gambia, the smiling coast of Africa.

We viewed exquisitely beautiful embroidery and tapestry by none other than Arabian weavers. I did not buy any but servo their beauty and intricacy of the display and carvings of both stone and wood. Forty-five minutes latter we were in our seats with seat belts fastened and ready for take off to the last leg of our flight to the Gambia.

The big jet engines rowed louder and louder until we swerved into the sky as if to challenge the African falcon or Eagle. Off we went far away from gray cloudy English weather into the blue skies over the mountains and desert sand leaving dust bellow. The desert became an empty void full of glistening sand dunes.

It was sand dunes until above 15, 000 feet before I lost sight of the desert amid clouds and longed for blue African skies. As I ruminated after take off, it became clear that things do not just happen people make them happen and that the villagers would be more than happy I took this painful venture in their behalf. With it also life taught me how to look after myself and that I can only give what I have and have learnt not to rest on my oars else I fall into very deep and turbulent sea of troubles.

The trip thought me to have to keep on running to remain with the best or be where I am. It sharpened my desire to learn and perform and work hard for what I believe possible even if at the time most may not want do or see things the way I saw or perceived. I have learned to control my irritability and sensitive but remain very sensitive to the needs of others. This may be intriguing but this is the simple me appealing for you to join me to bring more medical aid to the villagers by making Manding Medical Centre at Njawara, in the North bank Region more viable and valuable to all living in the Gambia.

Chapter 46
A pride of the Villager

Ideas are good but must be believed, acted upon and allowed to grown into reality. Surely, God changes not the condition of a people until they seek to usher change.

Today there is a tint of pride in our hearts and for which the glory belongs to God and every one who directly or other wise encouraged the fruition of Manding Medical Centre.

To my international friends, I find it hard to put into words or find one to thank you with for being with Manding Medical Centre. It shows that we have common desire to help others.

Where there is unity of purpose there surely will be hope and chance to bring relief to others. Today embellishes the magnanimity of your hearts. The Gambia remains eternally grateful.

Who amongst us, except me, would have believed that what was once condemned as a white Elephant of a dream destined to doom or the least a catastrophic failure is now proudly flying the flagship of hope and medical service to the region while rewarding generations to come.

Friends in America and Europe use to ask, "Why are you hung up on a dream and the Gambia. Many of your peers have gone for the greener pasture and have secured comfortable lives for themselves and their families. Here you are in utter destitute state with little or no one in Gambia caring". I patiently, replied that where my umbilical cord is buried is where my body rests eternally. It is my feeling that just as each of us does have different ways of reaching and helping our homelands returning to serve the Gambia was my patriotic duty no other attraction can prevent me fulfilling.

The provision of medical aid and service to the villager was not only a responsibility but for a charitable trust. My soul, head and heart, to paraphrase, are buried into the Gambian sand. Long lives Gambia!

Yes, my critics were on the mark but failed to dissuade me for Manding Medical Centre was better and of bigger reward to the people than their scare mongering of it being a dream. Yes, I rather suffer the status of a temporal second-class human than yield my worth for a worthless end.

Our countries need whatever skill or training we accrue from our travels overseas. To deprive them tantamount to a sacrilegious wasted life.

Yes, there were times when I could not get a second-class stamp to put on an envelope without begging for it.

Further more; I slept in many rough places, including the cold and dangerous streets for a night at times more. Buoying me in this pit fall was knowledge that I was doing some thing right and needed by my villagers or the Gambia at large.

The enduring of those dark and lean days is worth the means of it all. An old man once told me, "If you wish to find the true way, right action will lead you to it directly". We all took the right action for my critics showed me the other side of the coin and so what need to be done to achieve my goal.
How great my foot solders were in making certain Manding Medical serves the villager for the Gambia. Today makes me close to thought that the villager has of me and I am with them in their reflection of me.

Abdoulie Ceesay, MP:the train station, Germany 2018

Chapter 47
An Ode to myFamily

Family is nor oddment but one's dearest flesh and blood. This ode goes to my kith and kin of the Njawara Ceesay kunda dynasty.
First praises be to the Almighty God for letting us descend to this Garden of Eden through Sisawo Ceesay and his brother Abdulie (Baba Salah) Ceesay. Both were devoted, loving parents who taught us to seek knowledge, faith and be responsible participants in our communities wherever we may find ourselves.
A million thanks goes to our mothers who stood by these men and helped them steer us in the right direction for a better tomorrow.
Binta Ceesay, born 1937, is now the oldest matriarch of the family and our gratitude and appreciation goes to her for enduring all of us through decades. She has always been a buffer and like our parents a very straightforward person who does not take sides when it comes to dealing with us her younger siblings. Bravo to Binta Ceesay for being an envied bright example to the family.
Dodou Ceesay, born 1942, is the oldest male child in the family. He having spent three quarters of his life within the Fula tribe tends to perceive life in that light. He is my brother of the same father and mother.

He is a very quite and shrewd intelegent fellow and well versed in the Quran. He too is moral support to all of us despite our philosophical divergences.

I, Dr.Alhasan Ceesay, MD; I am a medical doctor and next oldest in the family in this Njawara Ceesay Kunda clan and there is enough about me in my books that can fill the back of a stamp.

I just believed in reaching out to touch others and bring help, hope and relief to their lives. Hence one of the reasons why I became a medical doctor and proprietor of a village self-help health NGO, Manding Medical Centre at Njawara village, North Bank Region, the Gambia, West Africa.

Omar Ceesay, the gentleman of the family, is next oldest and a headmaster at one of the Primary Schools in the Kombo enclave.

The guy is so nice and gentle that I used to tease him as Baba Sallah incarnated. His attitude is carbon copy of his father Abdulie Baba Sallah Ceesay. The mannerism, laughing, and humaneness are akin to none other than Babab Sallah Ceesay. He is not the arbitrator but the easygoing fellow of the Njawara Ceesay Kunda dynasty.

Ismaila Sisay, the genes of his mother persist in him. He is a nice fellow but of a no nonsense type among the clan. Thank God he is not violent but does not let anyone push him around. He is very kind and forth in line when it comes to affairs of the clan. He is also a headmaster in the Kombo enclave.

He like his father Baba Sallah Ceesay is skilful entrepreneur and at times too competitive. He is retired and runs his private school.

Our fifth in line male child of the Njawara Ceesay Kunda clan is none other than Ebou Ceesay who is a technocrat and very gifted electronics. He once manned the Gambia's earth satellite for years before becoming Director of Operation at Gamtel House in Banjul, capital of the Gambia, West Africa.

If there be any financial endowment or call luck in the family, it went to this fellow. We all praise him for help he quietly gives to the members of the clan at various times for various reasons.

Ousman Ceesay, nick named "OS" is the youngest living male child of the clan. He too is faring well but another carbon copy of the old man Baba Sallah Ceesay. He is easy going but not laidback fellow. He is a hard worker but not cut throat competitor.

No, no I am not forgetting our sisters.

Jainaba Ceesay is next older lady following matriarch Binta Ceesay. Jainaba is one girl that epidermises and archetype of her mother, Diko Jallow. We have had our moments but still remain good friends and team members of the clan.

Fatou Isata Ceesay is our last sister on Sisawo Ceesay's linage. She is warm at heart and very easy to relate to, even though the Fula syndrome shrouds her. She participates fully in all activities of the Njawara Ceesay Kunda clan.

Mariam Ceesay is Hulay Ndongo's elder daughter for Baba Sallah Ceesay. Mariam is an easygoing girl. She has amiable attitude and personifies the old man Baba Sallah.

She too is contributor to the clan. Last but not the least is Hawa Ceesay, the youngest girl of Hulay Ndogo. She is very intelligent and smooth operator. She has an exemplary character but fierce defender of her tuff.

She too contributes to day-to-day function of the Njawara Ceesay Kunda Clan. All said and done there is no way I will exchange any of the above for another kin.

All the linage are very kind, team like most of the time, and share lot of good qualities and examples to help propel the next generation of the Ceesay family at Njawara.

We are not financially rich but have faith, abundant love, care, and participatory zeal than most in the village. Bravo to Njawara Ceesay Kunda. May God grant us longevity and prosperity with peace in this life.

Dr. Blais Tambo receiving his British
Citizenship from Mayor of Manchester 2015

Chapter 48
Odes to President Nelson Mandela And African Patriaches

Who but a patriot like President Nelson Mandela, the Madiba, can engender such unique international respect and admiration? Here is a simple man, teacher by profession, who strongly believed that God's children can exist in harmony in non-racial communities.

In his vein and for having spoken out for the natives of South Africa, he suffered twenty-seven years of incarceration in the most inhuman conditions of Robin Island in South Africa.

Some of us would have succumbed to the weight and indignities imprisonment brings to one and strikes a deal to be free. This chance he turned down several times unless the ugly serpentine head of racial segregation yields to human rights and full citizenry participation of every South African in the running of the affairs of his country.

He echoed the voices and feelings of decent people worldwide, and his refusal to pay lip service to his stand earned him much respect and admiration, which galvanized an avalanche of international protest and sanctions that almost crippled South Africa.

The same should be applied to all countries under military or dictatorship rule. What is good for the Gander is supposedly very good for the Goose.

Democracy and human rights should have the same meaning worldwide and not cloaked with current double standard international interpretation couched under terms like the developing and developed countries guided by queasy rules.

South Africa crumbled under pressure and finally did the right thing but unthinkable at the time. The world in great awe stood still to watched a miracle unfold before it on that historic Sunday of February 11,Th 1990, marking the release of humble and simple teacher Nelson Mandela.

The world joined throngs of millions upon millions of South Africans to cheer and to let go a big shy of relief. For Nelson Mandela, it was the beginning of life all over and continuance of his commitment to human rights and the equality of God's children, for lack of better phraseology, the races of mankind.

The Madiba, Nelson Mandela saw human beings to be like him and not indignant varying hues as black-white, brown or tribalism injected in the minds of the weak and selfish societies.

No wonder he worn resounding victory by landslide during the first multiracial election ever held in South African history. He set up an accommodating government and asked the people to reconcile and together forge a new future for South Africa. There evolved a democratic and peaceful transition to a multiracial South African governing body.

Will other African rulers follow his brilliant examples?

That would be the day hell would turn into paradise and the Earth will stand still to salute mankind for finally making some sense in the way they govern. The colonialist did their best to mesh up and left Africa but their replacements out surpassed colonialism by some of the most heinous physical and economic mayhem we see inflicted upon innocent people by outcast regimes that forcefully took over the governing of the peasants.

Today, in Britain, President Nelson Mandela and supporters celebrate the end of seven progressive and peaceful democratic years with a flawless transition of a democratically elected government under the stewardship of President Tambo Mbeki. Today, there are only two former presidents of our time (President Jimmy Carter and Nelson Mandela) who travel the glob to bring help and relief to others. Most former African presidents either died in office as an aftermath of a bloody coup d'etat or seek voluntary exile to some supper power state to choke on their spoils their stole from poor subjects they purportedly have been ruling democratically.

With the exile of the dictator president the United Nations and so-called supper powers gleefully praise themselves for having solved that country's nightmare.

For us Africans in the third world countries the replacement of heartless and corrupt politician by an undemocratic government rule of blood thirsty, merciless military juntas or rebels is more of adding an insult to injury than relief or kind and humane consideration of the people. President Nelson Mandela is an enigma for all decent politicians to immolate, especially fledgling African governments. Nelson Mandela rekindles hope, joy and relief to our beleaguered hearts.

Allow me to digress to some stalwarts who began the race to self-rule in Africa. Which generation of the forties can forget the grand contribution of the Pan African Movement and its struggles to topple colonialism and its empire mentality?

African got sick and tired of colonial masters' policy of divide and rule with no development of the ruled at sight. Hence, Abdul Nasser's refusal to allow a foreign power to control the Suez Canal led aspiring politicians in sub-Saharan Africa to galvanize the people and ask for independence.

The seeds of the Pan African Movement in the bodies of Kwamin Nkrumah, Modibo Keita, Saikou Ture, Jombo Kenyata, Odinga Odinga, Ndambandi Sitoli, Julius Nyere, Patrice Lumba,Tafawa Balewa, Leopold Sidat senghore, Milton Magai, and Dawada/David Kairaba Jawara just to name a few became bees in the colonial bonnet.

Nkrumah led the communist path and lost the support entrusted him by Ghana and se went Modibo Keita of Mali. This should have woken the world to the fact that although Africa gave its back to colonialism she was in no way replacing it with communism.

Trigger happy inept military men fatally brought down Tafawa Balewa setting Nigeria into a helter-skelter path of ruin. The dust from that has just started settling. Being Africa's most populous and one of the large countries Nigeria should set leadership examples and disallow further military rule.

Hence even though not of West Africa we cannot forget the likes of Patrice Lumumba of Congo who stood against the Belgian rule only to be brutally vanquished by Mabutou and his colonial proctors. Nor can we not salute our great man of Tanzania, former president Julius Nyerere.

He too lost the support of Tanzania because he went communist. Dawda Jawara was brought down by his complete reliance on the city machinery and tsars, which resulted in the founding father and farmers feeling betrayed and completely neglected and left hopeless in redressing their grievances and need by the Jawara regime.

Hence, no one came to its defense when the solders moved onto overthrow his regime. Gambian do not like military rule. We believe solders belong to their barracks and can be relied upon to defend the country and not turn over night half-baked political administrators or presidents.

To us juntas are pots calling the kettle black. Neither is the choice of the people, nor will we ever be free or progress under such stagnant situations.

Good leaders and good governance are rare, few and far apart. Who would be so heartless as not to recognize and sympathize with pain, humiliation and cruel rend the Jews met at the death gas chambers in Germany or the Palestinian youth meeting wanton, brutal and premature death for seeking the right to a piece of land to call home and dignity?

Oh my Lord why do thou watch men inflicts such cruel ends to each other? Please rain peace into their hearts for them to be human again. Violence only breeds violence. I wish there was a way to take the Olive leaf for them to make peace for themselves and for the shake of new generations of Jews and Arabs to come.

It is wrong to use religion as a cloak to kill the innocent We have seen amputation and wanton mutilations of people, women and children by rebels and yet so-called governments go to round table negotiation with leaders of such heinous devils and perpetrators of pain and suffering.

What can amputee child ever do with the stump of man's evil and wicked deeds left to remind him or her of mindless dark lowly creature of greed ravaging raving Africa?

Let us live and let others to live this life freely as God would allow them on earth. Did eons ago slave trade and today's go get rich quick Materialism left us disinterested and desensitized to the feeling and acceptance of our fellow human beings?

Has history of the world wars not taught us war has only losers and that carnage and spilling of blood is nothing but an indication of our weakness to confront the truth?

There are no victors after a war for both sides have by then lost someone dear to a family e.g. a father, businessman, husband, an uncle, a son or a friend, needless to say thousands if not millions of innocent women, the elderly and children die in the aftermath because of governments cowardly fearing to face the peace looking at it straight in the eye and stop both sides warring.

The truth is that no one wants to die, that is why we run to seek help as soon as something goes wrong with our health. We all in varying degrees feel hung pains and do need basic things like shelter and love or to be loved.

Why then do we kill each other like rats for situations we can settle amicably if we allow truth to be our only yardstick? If this is civilization then I rather be with the Neanderthals. A wise man once said, "When you come to the last page, close the book." Hence let us close the war-mongering book and rally for peace and coexistence in this unique planet of ours.

Oh, Mahatma Gandhi, Martin Luther King, Nelson Mandel and Jimmy Carter will you wake us so that we take courage to face the challenges that lies ahead not with nukes but hard work and erasing of ignorance and injustice from the surface of earth.

Life is very short and we need bury our swords and nuclear arsenals and hold onto each other dearly for our children's sake and ours. This is what the Mandelas and long ago heroes preached to us even though we continue to give deaf ears in the name of nationality and unfounded mythical power status. Does it have to be star wars or Armageddon to bring us to the simple reasonable realization we could benefit not only our generation but also future generations if work together as civilized human beings?

It is my believe that it is obligatory on us to leave better and inspiring foot prints for coming generation to follow and build upon. Let me bet if Martian were to land on earth and were to follow one of two directions i.e. one marked with blood and the other wheat and flowers they would all follow the later peaceful trail to happiness.

Hence, let us congregate for the sake of peace, progress and prosperity while shedding our hound like attitudes of wanton debasement of life. We in the villages use to wonder why the worlds supper powers are so bent on giving charity from its hard-earn taxpayer's money as grants to inhuman governments.

We do not believe these donations to be of serious intent as donor should by now know that 99% of monies and good sent to these pilfers end up in private saving accounts in equally corrupt international banking services else where.

Stop sending aid in support of bad leaders and see in we will crumble. The thieves who have been misusing your generosity in the name of Africa or the third world will be on their knees asking for your handouts but not the farmer who never had help from such gestures of yours.

Do not let anyone convince you that we need dictators, rebels, or military juntas to govern us. We have been governing ourselves well before colonialism took root in our countries and are more capable now than ever.

Just keep your guns, dirty paws and forget the double standard interpretation of democracy and human rights for the third world countries and see if Africa and places like her will not shine better than the so-called developed world.

It is my fervent wish that the world powers will now cease supplying money and good to heinous governments and directed their resources I creating environmentally friendly jobs for their own and in helping to educate and train the masses of the third world to allow a generation of enterprising people who can pass the baton of progress to others.

We beg and pray that no one trades or supplies weapons or facilitating it production or anything facilitating fertile grounds for rebel movements worldwide. Help us build schools and universities along with the determined nature of the African to get reed of poverty to allow our people leap by lightening speed into the third millennium.

I hope the supper powers will heed to appeal like this and stop dolling money to murders and pilfers in the name of the helpless masses that indeed, remained helpless because your aid never reaches them.

Please wake up to these facts if you care about doing something worthwhile for the third world. Do not stain human decency by negotiating with human butchers like rebels and heads of military juntas. They are bandits and know no better than destruction of life and property.

The world yearns for character like nelson Mandela, simple, gentle and accessible to all. I believe, even in his final hour, he will be dancing to thank God for giving him the taste of life and the privilege to serve his fellow men.

So I speak for endless millions of peace lovers when I say thank you Madiba, Mr. President Mandela for bringing the sunny side of life and hope to us all. We will strive to work as one civilized human race under peaceful democratic rule.

Chapter 49
I Rest My Case

Paul in a letter to Timothy 2 said, "I have fought a good fight, I have finished my course, and I have kept the faith." I hand this work for publication for you to be judge of the ravages of the years and how my life was that of extreme ups and downs.

In reality, I am very grateful to God even though my life met with various misfortunes, the most unbearable being the delay in my becoming a physician.

My life as witnessed in these pages was an assembly of trials and tribulation emanating from roadblocks placed on my path by inhuman laws and unfortunate dark circumstances.

Life has taught me to submit to divine decrees, whatever they may be from God. I feel on the whole overly rewarded and delivered even though I had no family here in England nor was I as lucky as others who can feel and experience the warmth of their wives and children on daily basis.

I succumbed to it as the way things were going to be for me and lived with this state of affairs while in Manchester, England.

I experienced various turns of fate, enough for ten eliphant loads, while on the little moat of the silver sea called England. With my travels I was able to see Europe, the Americas and have learnt a great deal from it as well as experienced numerous unforeseen adventures thrown on my path.

My life in England was pain; fear of deportation, hunger, extreme poverty due to joblessness, solitude and missing my wife and children I loved dearly. I had a huge sense of duty in relation to the villagers and was not ready to fail them because of personal comfort or pleasures.

Consequently Manding Medical Centre and benefits to be accrued from it became my most if not the only occupation and direction in life. Here is Manding Medical Centre if managed well it will do justice to rural health service for the next generation of Gambians to build upon.

The medical center is now a recognized charity in both the United Kingdom and America. I am committed to serve the villagers so that life of the children and young people would be better than mine when I was young.

I hope Manding Medical Centre becomes a model testimony of the boy from Njawara village who doggedly struggled to become a doctor and despite various twists of life is able to provide medical aid and service to villagers in rural Gambia.

May be this will strengthen some other fellow to strive to do better than I did to bring health and happiness to the region.

I hope my adventure persuades youngsters that man is capable of a lot more than he thinks he is capable of. Our footprints must be inspirational to give heart to new coming Gambian generations.

Twenty years ago none would dream of thinking me becoming an author or to challenge powers as I did in this little frame and life of mine. I met a beautiful Maraka girl while I was in Monrovia, Liberia, West Africa; Fatou Koma is daughter of Elhaj Ansuman Koma and Jalian Ture of Kindia, Guinea Conakry. Her positive attitudes towards me lead our meeting on weekends at Cousin Sainabou Jobe's home. We started going out together and very soon I had the courage to ask her hand in marriage.

There was no bone of contention with regards for my love for her. She was the darling of my heart at first sight and I was not going to let a fly land on her from that day onwards.

We had a simple wedding because her father did not quite approve of me because of fear for his uneducated but very pretty daughter being dump at one stage of the marriage for another educated city girl. I, in the long run, allied his fears and he ended up being one of my best friends and confidants I had up to the day he went to his maker.

Fatou Koma-Ceesay and I are blessed with three beautiful daughters; princesses Famatanding Ceesay, Binta Ceesay and Roheyata Ceesay. All of who, unlike me, had their schooling start at the age of five.

The elder girl is aspiring to become a doctor and had been admitted to start her premed courses at Alpena Community College in Alpena, Michigan, USA. Together Fatou Koma-Ceesay, the children and I went through all the tragedy of hunger, poverty and other sad experiences my sojourn in the quest of the Golden flees for the villager brought to us.

Fatou Koma-Ceesay initially hated Manding Medical Centre for she felt it consumed me and took me away from her and the children. The call got me entangled in a web of unfortunate circumstances and laws.

The marriage had at one point almost spiraled to its end as wife' move became questionable. Nonetheless she remained a good mother and wife who took care of the girls in my absence. My mother in-law was battered by confusion and as to why Fatou stuck it out with me under such immense hardship. Love is stronger glue!

We loved each other and so we were able to stand by the other in good or bad times and my trip to England was the worse ever in our connubial life. It caused great turbulences in the marriage but I stuck with it for love's shake and the children who I love dearly.

Today, we are back together as family under the same roof while planning and supporting future of our darling girls. God bless Fatou Koma-Ceesay's heart and be reassured of endless love I have for her. For now Dalliance said it best for me when he said, "Say of me what you will and the morrow will judge you, and your words shall be a witness before its judgment and a testimony before it justice.

I came to say a word and I shall utter it. Should death take me ere I give voice; the morrow shall utter it. That which alone I do today shall be proclaimed before the people in days to come."

I wrote with the hope the life enshrined herein will serve not only as an inspiration to the despondent but a lesson never to allow this sort of experience it passed through this planet.

I wrote in the hope that life enshrined in my books will serve not only as an inspiration to the despondent and downtrodden but a lesson never to allow this sort of experience it passed through this planet.

I wrote because I felt that my life has something worth revealing to the world to engender tolerance and understanding between people and their governments. I risked revealing today for all of us to learn from it and move to a better and rewarding future. Among the forces of life is one that stands a certain lofty peak a few is endowed with or able to explore its heights.

Ambition urges us to leave the lower surface of earth where the ordinary people live and ascend to heights that pierce the heavens. This mission has led to numerous Erie paths but for me this Pell-mell towards a better medical service for the neglected villager was a worthwhile adventure.

  I am profoundly grateful and indebted to my wife Fatou Koma-Ceesay and our daughters, princesses Famatanding Ceesay, Binta Ceesay and Roheyata Ceesay for enduring all the pains that we went through in thick and thin times during my sojourn to America and England.

  Also my deepest gratitude goes to Cousin Yata Sey-Corr for helping keep my family hopeful. God bless her heart eternally. I forgive my own brothers and sisters who refused to cater for my family in my absence. Hello, hats off to Sey Kunda!

Chapter 50
My Endearing Life and fate

For a while in my native innocence all I had was erudition and wit, which always misfired.Everything I touched came to nothing but failure, whatever I tried to achieve came crashing down on my head.
At any given moment some mishap befalls me and nothing surprised me any more.
I took my current plight with stride and smiled as fate taunts me. I remain poor but my in extinguishable strong will enabled me face life squarely and took me through these dark days.
The twist of fate abated but my age had advanced beyond retrieval.
The above apocalyptic life is indeed trying moments for my family and I. The only passion I have, aside passionate love for my wife and children, is providing medical service to villagers through Manding Medical Centre.
My dream spawns better future health service for future generations. I never set to write a best seller but to inform and share ideas. Also I enjoyed reading it knowing it would enlighten as well entertain than found in bookstores.
It is hoped in writing another will not experience hardship I endured before being able to provide much needed medical service/aid to Gambian villagers.

Browse: www.friendsofmandinggambimed.btck.co.uk , or www.publishkunsa.com to learn more or just contact alhasanceesay@hotmail.com
To view or purchase my books enter: amazon.com then search Dr. Alhasan Ceesay/books to view or purchase my books in support of Manding Medical Centre at Njawara, Lower Badibou, North Bank, the Gambia, West Africa.

Dr. Joyce Inyang, (RIP), a good friend. Miss you!

Chapter 51
About the Author

I was born in 1946 at Njawara Village, Lower Badibou District in the North Bank of the Gambia. I am a scion of a Mandinka and Fulani tribe and am one of five siblings.

I had my education at Kinte Kunda, then Armitage High School, ending up as a registered nurse at the Royal Victoria Hospital, Banjul, before embarking to the USA on my medical degree quest.

I graduated from the American University School of Medicine in Montserrat, West Indies, in 1992 and returned to the Gambia to start setting up a self-help village health NGO Manding Medical Centre.

The Gambia Government and the Badibou local authority registered NGO Manding Medical Centre in 1993.

The centre has treated and provided medicines to more than 9000 patients free of charge. I am married to Fatou Koma-Ceesay and we are blessed with three beautiful girls, Famatanding Ceesay, Binta Ceesay and Roheyata Ceesay.

Unlike me, all of them started school early without the roadblocks I had to cross in my early years. I am currently a medical officer at the Royal Victoria Hospital but on study leave.

It is my hope that this work will inspire others and bring much needy help to providing medical service to rural Gambia.

Ms. Binta Ceesay (daughter) Brusubi, Gambia

My elder daughter Famatanding Ceesay, Brusubi, Gambia 2014

Mission
Our objective is to improve the healthcare delivery to villagers, educating youths on STD and Drugs and quality of life for the people in rural Gambia.
The Manding Medical Centre strives to accomplish this goal through primary health care and disease prevention, the promotion of health policy, health research and increased access to health care education for the people in the Gambia.

Have your manuscript become a book by submitting it for possible publication to acquisitions publishes Kunsa. Com Please contact us to expose your work globally.

PUBLISH KUNSA.COM

GAMBIA HAS DECIDED TO BE FREE: PRESIDENT ADAMA BARO WHEELNG YAHYA JAMMEH TO EXILE IN GUINEA EQUITORIAL JANUARY 2017

www.ingramcontent.com/pod-product-compliance
Lightning Source LLC
Chambersburg PA
CBHW051032160426
43193CB00010B/911